# Mentoring Developing Leaders

Andrew Peters PhD FAIM

# Mentoring Developing Leaders

Andrew Peters PhD FAIM

MENTORING DEVELOPING LEADERS – 1st Edition 2017
Incorporating: Supervised Experienced-Based Learning – Mentor's Manual 2001
Maximizing People for Ministry published in 2002
*Overcoming Cynicism & Pessimism* – Leadership Dynamics Part One – Iona
Chronicles Vol 4 No 1 – January 2010
Enhancing Ministry Development – Iona chronicles Vol 7 No 1 – April 2014

© Andrew Peters 2017

Published by A.E. & L.A. Peters Outreach Enterprises
PO Box 225, Mansfield LPO. QLD Australia 4122
Website: www.outreachenterprises.com.au

Scripture quotations from the following version:

Unless noted Bible quotations are from the Revised Standard Version.

National Library of Australia Cataloguing-in-Publication entry
Creator: Peters, Andrew E.,  author, illustrator.
Title: Mentoring Developing Leaders / written and illustrated by Andrew E. Peters.
ISBN: 978-0-9750081-6-4     (paperback)
Subjects: Mentoring.
Leadership.
Mentoring in Education.
Mentoring in the professions.
Dewey Number:  268 Christian Education

### *Illustrations:*

Andrew Peters

### *Published by:*

A.E. & L.A. Peters Outreach Enterprises,
Mansfield Qld 4122
www.outreachenterprises.com.au

# CONTENTS

# CONTENTS

# Section One
# Introduction

# Chapter One

# Ministry Development in a time of harvest

Jesus said to His disciples, "The harvest is plentiful, but the laborers are few; pray therefore to the Lord of the harvest to send out laborers into his harvest". This fundamental call to ministry arises out of Jesus' *compassion*. Jesus' ministry involved teaching and preaching the gospel of the kingdom in both cities and villages, as well as healing those who were sick. Matthew notes that when Jesus saw the crowds, he had compassion for them "because they were harassed and helpless, like sheep without a shepherd" (Matthew 9:35-38). Jesus' ministry was cutting-edge amongst the cities and villages of Galilee and its surrounding districts. Mathew emphasizes this by noting that Jesus did this in *all* the cities and villages; and healed *every* disease and infirmity. What motivated Jesus' compassion was the need that he found everywhere He went - people who were harassed and helpless, with no one to care for them, that is, like sheep without a shepherd.

The cause of Jesus' compassion – people who were like sheep without a shepherd – was the condition of the people of God that Jesus encountered. It also described an eschatological event of God in the midst of that need. The word eschatological usually refers to last things or end times - specifically to history's consummation and the events directly associated with the second coming of Jesus Christ. However, I use it here to refer to the fulfillment of the promise that God made to His people through the prophets Isaiah and Jeremiah. That is, that God Himself would care for His people who were like sheep without faithful shepherds.[1] The promise they proclaimed was that God Himself would shepherd His people. They described the people of God as sheep who had suffered at the hands of uncaring shepherds. These were Leaders who had no understanding, who no longer sought God's purpose and wisdom and who had turned each to his own gain.

This lack of care had brought desolation, despair, and destruction to the people of God and resulted in them being scattered and lost (Isaiah 56:11-12).[2] God promised to care for His people by sending shepherds who would care for them, feed them, and give them knowledge so that they might be fruitful, and multiply (Isaiah 40:10-11; Jeremiah 3:15; 23:3-4). However, it was through the prophet Ezekiel that God declared that He *Himself*

---

[1] J.B. Green, Scot McKnight, and I. Howard Marshall, "Dictionary of Jesus and the Gospels," (Accessed: Intervarsity Press, 1997). Characteristic of the Gospels is the note of eschatological fulfillment and the focus of eschatological hope in the person of Jesus.

[2] Isaiah 56:11-12; Jeremiah 10:21; 23:1-4; 50:6-7; Jeremiah 12:10-11. Many shepherds have destroyed my vineyard, they have trampled down my portion, they have made my pleasant portion a desolate wilderness. They have made it a desolation; desolate, it mourns to me. The whole land is made desolate, but no man lays it to heart.

would come to shepherd His people (Ezekiel 34:1-31). He charged the shepherds with having failed to feed and nurture His people:

> The weak you have not strengthened, the sick you have not healed, the crippled you have not bound up, the strayed you have not brought back, the lost you have not sought, and with force and harshness you have ruled them. So they were scattered, because there was no shepherd; and they became food for all the wild beasts. My sheep were scattered, they wandered over all the mountains and on every high hill; my sheep were scattered over all the face of the earth, with none to search or seek for them (Ezekiel 34:4-6).

God then declares that He himself will seek out his people – He will be the shepherd of His sheep. He will seek the lost, rescue them, feed them, and bring them back. He will bind up the cripple, strengthen the weak and bring justice. He will bless and prosper them so that they will be fruitful. Ezekiel writes,

> For thus says the Lord GOD: Behold, I, I myself will search for my sheep, and will seek them out. As a shepherd seeks out his flock when some of his sheep have been scattered abroad, so will I seek out my sheep; and I will rescue them from all places where they have been scattered on a day of clouds and thick darkness. And I will bring them out from the peoples, and gather them from the countries, and will bring them into their own land; and I will feed them on the mountains of Israel, by the fountains, and in all the inhabited places of the country. I will feed them with good pasture, and upon the mountain heights of Israel shall be their pasture; there they shall lie down in good grazing land, and on fat pasture they shall feed on the mountains of Israel. I myself will be the shepherd of my sheep, and I will make them lie down, says the Lord GOD. I will seek the lost, and I will bring back the strayed, and I will bind up the crippled, and I will strengthen the weak, and the fat and the strong I will watch over; I will feed them in justice (Ezekiel 34:11-16; 25-31).

Jesus stands as the eschatological fulfillment of that promise. His compassion is God's compassion for His people. Jesus' teaching, preaching and healing was indicative of the power of God at work to gather His people – to feed, strengthen and make them whole that they once again might prosper and be fruitful. Jesus carried out this ministry of shepherding. Jesus' reference, noted above, to sheep without a shepherd not only recalls the words of the prophets but also proclaims the fulfillment of those words.

However, the ministry of Jesus was the *beginning* not the end of God's action to shepherd His people. When Jesus instructs the disciples to pray to the Lord of the harvest for laborers, He brings His disciples and all those who turn to follow Him to join in the ingathering of His people. Jesus begins a ministry that His Church has carried out for over two thousand years. In calling for such prayer, Jesus notes two things:

1/ there is a harvest to be gathered, and

2/ we are personally needed in that harvest.

This theme of harvest arises again as part of Jesus' encounter with the Samaritan woman at the well in John 4. Jesus had convinced the woman that He was indeed the Messiah who was to come. She then left Him to run back to her village to tell them of this encounter. Right at that point, the disciples arrive back from buying food and provisions. They wondered why He had been speaking to the woman. They prepared the meal and called Jesus to eat. He responded by saying:

> "I have food to eat of which you do not know." So the disciples said to one another, "Has any one brought him food?" Jesus said to them, "My food is to do the will of him who sent me, and to accomplish his work. Do you not say, 'There are yet four months, then comes the harvest'? I tell you, lift up your eyes, and see how the fields are already white for harvest. He who reaps receives wages, and gathers fruit for eternal life, so that sower and reaper may rejoice together. For here the saying holds true, 'One sows and another reaps.' I sent you to reap that for which you did not labor; others have labored, and you have entered into their labor (John 4:31-38).

Jesus makes it clear that the harvest is ready now. It needs reaping. Jesus makes this statement just as the Samaritan villagers were coming across the fields to Jesus, because they had believed the woman's testimony about Him.

Although the harvest was ready, the disciples were not. They were distracted and busy with their everyday needs, not realizing that a spiritual harvest was ready for reaping and gathering into the kingdom of God. Jesus challenged them to lift up their eyes to see that the harvest was ready now. It was natural for the disciples to think that the harvest was still some time off. Not only was the natural harvest still four months away, but the spiritual harvest also seemed far away, after all they had just begun to learn from Jesus. However, the spiritual harvest is not the same as the natural; it was ready for reaping. At this point Jesus unfolds an insight into the spiritual harvest that distinguishes it from the natural harvest. Those who were to reap were not those who had sown. He calls his disciples to reap a harvest that they had not sown and to enter into the labor of others.

This call to the harvest calls us beyond ourselves and our own resources. It is a combined effort for a people who find their unity in Jesus Christ. There are seeds that we sow today for which we may never ever see the harvest, but unless we sow them, our brethren in Christ will not be able to reap the harvest of those seeds in the future. Likewise, when we enter into a harvest of seeds that we have not sown, we need to appreciate those who came before us and sowed seeds which have ripened over time and reached their harvest point in our time and place. The disciples of Jesus took up this call and after the coming of the Holy Spirit at Pentecost began a Church that has some 2 billion adherents at some level or other today. Jesus makes the same call to prayer today, to pray that the Lord of the harvest will send laborers into the harvest.

We live in a day that is both old and new. Our call to the harvest is a continuation of the outworking of that call to the disciples two millennium ago - one that the Church has carried on down through the ages. However, we also live in a new day, in a new paradigm, and the dynamics of witness and harvesting have changed with the years. It is indeed a time to pray for laborers, but it also a time to equip those laborers so they may be effective to reap a harvest that has eternal fruit. This book aims to equip those involved in ministry development and formation to help prepare men and women of God for the harvest. As such, much of the developmental work we do is with those who are already in the throes of the harvest and require 'on-the-job-training'. This is not only because it is an effective way to train people, but because the harvest is now, the harvest is on.

## Ministry Development

Ministry Development highlights the ongoing need to equip and train the people of God for ministry. Ministry Development of the whole people of God operates on the understanding that God created each and every one of us for a purpose. God did not create you and then thought He better find something for you to do. God created you for a purpose. Ministry Development aims to help people find and maximize that God given purpose, using the skills and abilities that God has given to them. It aims to place people in the arena of ministry God has called them to and help them to be effective in that particular ministry. Ministry development applies to all God's laborers – ordained ministers, priests, pastors and deacons, as well as the laity of the church.[3] The principles and processes outlined in this book have been fruitful in equipping the laity for ministry; preparing men and women for ordained leadership as pastors, evangelists and missionaries; and for those who are ordained pastors, priests or ministers to continue to develop and grow in their ministry.

**Personal Experience in Ministry Development:**

**Country Victoria:** my own experience of the development of both ordained and lay ministries, which extends over twenty years, began with the development of lay leadership of ministry as parish priest in the Anglican country parish of Ballan/Bungaree (just east of Ballarat in Victoria). It was there that I developed a training program called Pastoral Care Workshops and saw some 23 new lay leaders, not only take up significant areas of ministry, but were effective in leading those ministries. They also managed to engage the entire congregation of the Ballan Church and some members of the other congregations in ministry (the Parish consisted of 5 churches in different country locations over an area of 1200 sq. kilometres).

---

[3] The term *laity* refers to the distinction between those who are *ordained* to the offices of bishops, priests and deacons (or *authorised* as pastors) and the *unordained* or *unauthorised* (laity) in the church who do not hold those offices. In the past this was also linked to those who did ministry – the ordained or authorised – and those who were excluded from ministry – the unordained or unauthorised (laity). See the Excursus at the end of this chapter for further explanation.

**Melbourne: Southern Cross Bible College and Richmond AOG** - later I was to take up the position of Head of the Faculty of Ministry Formation at Southern Cross Bible College (part of Richmond AOG in Melbourne) where I pioneered the mentoring course that forms the basis of this book (Section 3 Mentoring Course – chapters 9 – 17). A consistent response from the Bible College students who first did the course was that it was the first time anyone had asked them what they thought they needed to learn in regard to their ministries. Using the same Pastoral Care Workshop material I also trained 70 new lay shepherds of Richmond AOG in a significant new stage in the ministry of that church. The Senior Pastor of Richmond AOG later noted that the effect of that training would ripple through the life of their church for decades to come.

**Brisbane: Garden City Christian Church** – in 1999 I took up a two-fold ministry with Garden City Christian Church (GCCC) in Brisbane as:

1/ **Ministry Development Pastor** of the Church, which included the ongoing ministry development of over 20 pastors and the training of some 300 lay leaders. It also included the training of the new lay shepherds for the church with the use of the Pastoral Care Workshop material noted above. I also engaged and trained a Ministry Development Team whose role was to engage the laity of the church in ministry. Part of that training is included in this book (Section 2 – Enhancing Ministry Development – chapters 4-8). One of the Members of that team assisted me in writing a Gift Discovery Course for the church. GCCC had tried two major Gift Discovery courses before my coming to the church that had failed, the first in its implementation, and the second before it was completed. The new Gift Discovery Course was tested by the executive pastors of the church, with some minor amendments and then used with some 150 pastors and leaders with good results. A version of that course (without the GCCC particulars) is included in this book ( Section 4 - Section Four – Maximizing People for Ministry – chapters 18-23).

2/ **Principal of Garden City College of Ministries,** which included being Head of Faculty for Ministry Formation. The same mentoring program noted above was part of all the students training and related to their on-the-job training in field placements with churches and other Christian ministry organisations. This program ensured that the students had field positions that gave them a real opportunity to do ministry, as well as to have learning goals that they aimed to achieve in the midst of those field positions.

**Brisbane: St Jude the Apostle Anglican Church Everton Park** – since 2003 I have trained and developed lay leaders and team members in the Pastoral Care Workshops, Leadership Programs and the Gift Discovery Course – Maximising People or Ministry. Those lay leaders have carried the governance, building, pastoral, counselling, welcoming, evangelism and training ministries of our church whilst we built a new church complex on our site in Flockton Street, Everton Park.

## Ministry of the Laity

In regard to the laity it is important to understand that ministry development is not simply a matter of mobilizing the laity for ministry, nor is it providing additional help for the minister or pastor as he or she carries out his or her pastoral duties. It is about mobilizing and engaging the laity in *their* ministries, to which they have been called by God and equipped by His Spirit. They are not there just to assist the ordained ministers in their ministry, but to be fruitful in their ministries. The role of the minister or pastor has changed from the doing of ministry to the management and leadership of well-equipped and organised lay ministry teams. This does not remove the minister or pastor from the heat of ministry, but calls us to broaden the parameters of ministry and truly open the doors for the laity to minister. This will also require the redefinition of ministry from that which has been previously limited to the pastoral tasks of the minister, priest or pastor.

Ministry plays a critical part in the life of the church and its ability to fulfil its God-given purpose. Bruce Larson in *Letting the Laity Pastor* notes that:

### *"The basic product of the Church is people in ministry."*

Ministry belongs to the people of God, both ordained and lay members alike. When the people of God are effectively doing ministry together, it produces within the Body of Christ the following results:

- a unity of faith;
- an experiential presence and knowledge of the Son of God;
- a maturity and stability in the Body;
- an openness and honesty in personal relationships and
- a community permeated with the presence of the love of God, which is evident in the life of its members (Ephesians 4:11-16).

Paul notes that when the leadership of the church is carrying out its God given purpose of *effectively* equipping and enabling the people of God to do ministry, it will produce a church that is open in its internal nature and cohesiveness. However, in a church where ministry is operating dysfunctionally, it is doubtful that we might see much more than a glimpse of such characteristics.

## MINISTRY DEVELOPMENT COURSE

Lynette and I have recognised the pivotal nature of training and ministry development in the lives of those moving to obey God and serve in His Church. As such, we have published a number of resources to assist in this development. This manual contains three of those resources for your use:

- **Enhancing Ministry Development Course** – this aims to increase the intuitive discernment and understanding of those who are working to develop and train leaders in ministry.

8

- *Ministry Mentoring Course* – for leaders in ministry
- *Maximizing People for Ministry (Gift Discovery Course)* - it enables developing leaders to recognise and understand their own gifts and skills; the purpose of God for their lives; and the place where God initially wants them to serve.

All three of these resources are appropriate in the ministry development of ordained pastors and leaders, lay pastors and leaders, church workers, and students training for the ordained ministry.

## Discussion/Reflection Questions:

1. Discuss/reflect upon a particular person for whom you have had compassion and what you did for him or her;

2. Discuss/reflect on a situation of need you have been in that has given you insight into how you could care for someone in a similar situation;

3. Discuss/reflect upon an aspect of your life where someone has sown the seed, but another has reaped the harvest;

4. Discuss/reflect on at least one area of ministry you know you have.

5. Discuss/reflect upon where you feel weak and in need of training;

6. Discuss/reflect upon who does the ministry in the church you belong to;

7. Discuss/reflect upon the 5 results of effective ministry noted above; and

8. Discuss/reflect upon an important ingredient needed to step out into developing and training people in ministry.

# Excursus – Differentiation between Ordained and Lay Ministries[4]

The term *laity* refers to the distinction between those who are *ordained* to the office of bishops, priests and deacons and the *unordained* (laity) in the church. In the past this was also linked to those who did ministry – the ordained – and those who were excluded from ministry – the unordained. This distinction did not exist in the early church, where both those who held the office of bishop, priest or deacon shared ministry with those who did not hold such offices. The New Testament reveals a very broad and diverse understanding of those who did ministry in the church. However, From the time of Constantine, there developed a more pronounced differentiation between the *kleros*, the ordained clergy, and *laikos*, the unordained laity, which saw the laity marginalised to the role of passive observers of the church's worship.

By the time of Boniface VIII (1294 A.D.), not only was the laity pushed to the periphery of the church, but also the church itself became identified solely with the hierarchy of bishops, priests and deacons and other related offices. A layperson was seen as "a passive article of pure receptivity. He (or she) has nothing to do *in* the church (except contribute financially), for he has no ecclesiastical function, nor ministry or charism".[5] The Reformation was the turning point in the understanding of the layperson's role in the church and their ontological nature as the people of God and the priesthood of all believers. Even though that understanding did not re-establish the ministry of the laity. What the Reformation did, however, was to give the laity a new understanding of their equal standing before God, along with the clergy, through baptism, faith and participation in the priesthood of all believers.[6]

Over the last fifty years we have seen a movement to a new paradigm which I argue is a paradigm of diversity in my book *The Emerging Paradigm of Diversity: Its Effect on the Church and Its Leadership.* The movement to a paradigm of diversity brings with it a modification of the distinctions between the clergy and the laity that enables a more inclusive understanding of ministry to occur. It notes that both the ministry of the clergy and laity derive from the same source, the high priesthood of Jesus Christ and the call of

---

[4] For a fuller discussion of the historical distinction between the role of the ordained offices in the church and the unordained and how this has changed with the emergence of a new paradigm of diversity see in Andrew Peters, *The Emerging Paradigm of Diversity: Its Effect on the Church and Its Leadership* (Mansfield, Qld: A.E & L.A. Peters Outreach Enterprises, 2013).

[5] Peters.234ff Fahlbusch and others, eds., 227, 228. *Laikos* (of/from the people) and *kleros* (lot, allotment, inheritance). Thomas Hoebel, *Laity and Participation*, ed. James Francis, Religions and Discourse (Oxford: Peter Lang, 2006), 50. Evdokimov, 229. Papesh, 37. Fahlbusch and others, eds., 228. Origen proposed that the chief "ministry of the laity" (the first appearance of this phrase) is to provide clerics with the material resources necessary for their upkeep.

[6] Collins, *Are All Christian Ministers?* , 24-26. The Second Helvetci Confession of the Calvinists in 1566 had "no wish that the commonness of one condition, namely priesthood, should provide occasion to erode the exclusiveness of the other prerogative, namely ministry". Deryck Lovegrove, ed., *The Rise of the Laity in Evangelical Protestantism* (London: Routledge, 2002), 24. *Fah*lbusch and others, eds., 229. Hoebel, 43.

the *Laos,* the people of God.[7] There is only one ministry of the church, which belongs to both the clergy and laity, because the whole church is the *Laos.*[8] This new understanding comes with a new obligation on all participants, the laity and the clergy. It is a participation that occurs at every level of the life of the church and its mission to the world. This participation in ministry does not infer a blurring of the functions of clergy and laity, but opens up the dimensions of both to a greater involvement and effectiveness, one that is inseparable and interdependent.

Its aim is not to diminish the role of the clergy but to enhance it, for the ministry of the clergy is not able to achieve its full effectiveness without the ministry of the laity. At the same time, the effectiveness of the ministry of the laity is dependent on the leadership of the clergy.[9] In Ephesians 4:11ff Paul notes that the ministry of the five-fold leadership team of apostle, prophet, evangelism, pastor and teacher, aims not only to develop the spiritual maturity of the people of God (the saints) through their *perfection*, but also to bring them into the fullness of ministry through *equipping* them.[10] This passage also gives substantial support to the emerging paradigm's reorientation of clerical ministry, from the doing of ministry to the coordination and development of ministry through others – the laity. Although the ordained ministry always retains a sacramental dimension, and shows a competence in ministry, the matrix of its activity moves from the activity of ministry to the leadership of ministry. Just as managers are critical for business, so also is the leadership of the clergy for the effective development of the ministry of the laity and the use of the diversity of their gifts, skills and abilities for the purposes of God in a new paradigm.[11]

---

[7] Neill and Weber (eds) 32. Geoffrey Wainwright, *Lessie Newbigin: A Theological Life* (Oxford: Oxford Press, 2000), 158. Newbigin noted: "A minister does not cease to be a layman when he is ordained. The ministry is not a separate body from the whole people of God (Greek *Laos*)".

[8] James Cook, ed., *The Church Speaks: Papers of the Commission on Theology Reformed Church in America 1959-1984`*, The Historical Series of the Reformed Church in America, vol. 15 (Grand Rapids, Michigan: Wm B. Eerdmans Publishing Co, 1985), 124. Nicholas Ferencz, *American Orthodoxy and Parish Congregationalism* (New Jersey: Georgias Press, 2006), 65-66; Neill and Weber (eds) 10.

[9] Hoebel, 75, 78, 83, 84. Robert Schwartz, *Servant Leaders of the People of God* (New York: Paulist Press, 1989), 160-161. Board of Mission and Unity of the General Synod of England, *The Priesthood of the Ordained Ministry* (London: Church House Publishing, 1986), 99. For the ordained priesthood's "ministry may be called priestly in that it is their vocation to help the whole people to realise their priestly character".

[10] Collins, *Are All Christian Ministers?* , 21. Collins notes two varied groups of translation of *katartismos*: (1) *perfecting* and *consummation* which suggests that the saints are brought to the peak of their existence or performance as Christians; and (2) *edifying* and *gathering together*, which bring in the idea of preparing the saints for some task. Colin Brown, ed., *The New International Dictionary of New Testament Theology*, 4 vols., vol. 3 (Devon: The Paternoster Press, 1986), 350. Brown notes that the word itself suggests a process of preparation that has a more functional, rather than qualitative meaning. E. W. Bullinger, *A Critical Lexicon and Concordance* (London: Samuel Bagster and Sons Limited, 1971), 580. Bullinger defines it as, "...the act of making fully ready, the act of perfectly equipping and fully preparing."

[11] Greg Ogden, *Unfinished Business: Returning the Ministry to the People of God* (Grand Rapids, Michigan: Zondervan, 2003), 28. Anthony Robinson, *Transforming Congregational Culture* (Grand Rapids, Michigan: Wm B. Eerdmans Publishing Co, 2003), 124.

# Chapter Two

# Mobilising the Laity for Ministry

## MISUNDERSTANDING LAY MINISTRY

The mobilization and engaging of the laity for their ministries can be one of the most exciting, enhancing and worthwhile things a pastor or priest can do. Alternately, its impact can make "Nightmare on Elm Street" seem like a kindergarten party. On the one hand, equipping and engaging the laity in ministry can produce a cohesive team of clergy and laity interactive and inter-dependent upon one another in an effective outworking of ministry in a local church. In this type of church the clerical leadership is seen as essential for the outworking and development of the lay ministry in the church. Lynette and my initial development of lay ministry in a country parish resulted in such a team [I outline some of the aspects of that church in this chapter]. On the other hand, it can produce a divisive team of autonomous lay leaders working independently of the clerical leadership and resisting any direction, correction or guidance from that leadership. The outworking of such as process can result in an implosion within the life of that church. Lynette and my subsequent attempt to develop lay leadership within a city church resulted in such an outworking (I outline some of the aspects of that church in Chapter Three).

There is another aspect of the development of lay ministry that lies somewhere between the exciting and nightmare that is common but somewhat unnoticed because of the mundaneness within which it lives. This occurs where neither the clergy or laity are very focused on the development and engagement of lay ministry at all. Often the clergy are in control mode and the laity are content for that to happen as long as it does not get too extreme. It is often the movement from this mode that poses the threat of whether you will end up with a cohesive team of clergy and laity working together or where the nightmare on Elm Street becomes very real. Staying in that mundane mode, however, results in the eventual death of that local church (or close enough to it). That is it struggles to keep its head above water, pay the bills and keep everyone happy. Peter Corney notes three different modes of operations that a local church can fall into:

## *MISSION MODE*:

- has vision, goals; is growth orientated
- has outreach plans and strategies
- is orientated to new members
- has a strong sense of being a community
- is actively involved in practical, compassionate service to its community
- is growing in depth, training and mobilization of laity

- teaches stewardship; has budgets that are a challenge to growth and faith
- is youth orientated
- has relevant, vibrant worship
- has strong, clear leadership
- embraces creative change

## MAINTENANCE MODE:

- has static or declining numbers
- is not outward looking
- is concerned with pastoral maintenance rather than growth
- has little or no active planned evangelism
- is not making new Christians (biological and transfer growth only)
- has no visions or goals
- has low level of lay involvement
- has little training of adults
- has small number or non-existent youth work
- has maintenance budgeting only
- avoids change

## SURVIVAL - DEATH MODE

- maintenance mode is exaggerated
- has declining numbers
- has rising age level
- is struggling to meet minister's stipend
- is pre-occupied with dollars and has constant dollar crisis
- has very little, if any, community outreach
- is centered around a few families
- has tiny or non-existent Sunday School and Youth work
- has no growth goals
- may have real determination to live which leads to action and growth plans
- reluctantly accepts negative change.[12]

One of the significant differences between a church that is in mission mode, compared to one in maintenance or survival mode, is the level of engagement of lay people in ministry. The health and growth of a church, according to Paul in Ephesians 4, is dependent on the development of the lay members of the church in ministry by those who have the gifts of apostle, prophet, evangelist, pastor and teacher.

The often mixed results, especially negative ones, from endeavors of clergy to equip and engage the laity ministry, including in lay leadership, can occur for a number of reasons. They can arise out of:

---

[12] Peter Corney, *The Local Church and Mission: A Congregational Workbook* (Canberra: Acorn Press, 1989), 11-14.

- the pain suffered by both clergy and laity when things do not go well, often resulting in an us/them situation;

- a traditional understanding of the nature of ministry and who are "ministers" in the Church;

- a confusion instigated by church pundits, who in their attempt to deal with the dysfunctional nature of "clericalism," only manage to instigate an even more dysfunctional "anticlericalism" or "layism";

- a misunderstanding of lay leadership and its relationship to ordained ministry.[13]

But more than anything else such negative results can arise out of a misunderstanding of the nature of the paradigm or foundational changes that has impacted the planet over the last fifty or so years. Lynette's and my own awareness of these changes occurred in 1994 just as I returned from a three-month sick leave after two major operations.

**Ballan Church in 1994** - During that sick leave my wife Lynette and I spent some time praying and reflecting on our sense of bankruptcy in ministry development – certainly in the mobilisation of the laity for ministry and leadership. We had spent some eight years trying to develop lay leadership in ministry, only to have each leader withdraw from the ministry after a few weeks and the ministry area itself collapse. During that time of prayer we told God that we did not know how to do something that we always thought we did – to link lay people to ministry and leadership. We asked for His inspiration and direction. Just as I came back to work my PA encouraged me to attend a conference on church growth in Melbourne, with speakers from AOG churches in Sydney and Perth, including Brian Houston. This was in the early days of the growth of Hillsong church in Sydney which at that point had approximately 3,000 members. The Perth church had 1,500 members – just a few more than we had attending our five country churches on the east side of Ballarat in Victoria.

Brian Houston's opening statement noted that he had not come to teach us any church growth principles. That staggered me, because I had just travelled over 100km to learn principles on how to grow our churches. Rather, he said that he had come to teach us about our hearts. That is exactly what he did and it changed the life our church. The night after the conference we held our first Vestry (Board) meeting since my return from sick leave at one of our main centres at Ballan. Something shifted deeply that night during our meeting that we identified sometime later as the heart of our church changing. Within eight months of that meeting we added 23 new lay leaders to ministry in our church. Each leader was effective in their leadership, and not one of those areas of ministry collapsed. Within twelve months they had connected every member of the Ballan church to ministry. At that point in time we didn't realise the unprecedented nature of that achievement.

---

[13] Moreover, one thing that has emerged in this process is the invention of an idea and phrase called the "ministry of the laity," which represents a change in consciousness. A term that Mead notes had not been in existence before the late 1930s. Loren Mead, *The Once and Future Church* (New York: Alban Institute Publications, 1991), 24, 25, 115..

When I returned from the conference I showed Lynette a Hillsong music video and her response was that we were in the Ark. I noted that if we were in the Ark then where was everyone else, because we were the most contemporary church in our Diocese and according to the Bishop had established the only two music bands in the Diocese. It was at that point we realised that the world around us was changing dramatically and our church was being left behind. It was time to change and that we did. We decided to add Hillsong music to our church music at Ballan. The trouble was that our entire band was classically trained and none of them had experience playing rock music, especially our 85 year old organist. I connected with the son of one of our ex-members, who played guitar in a rock band. I asked him to come in and train the band, which he did and they really got a hold of Hillsong music - at times playing so well that I could not differentiate between the music on the CD and them.

For the wider Church, the misunderstanding of the nature of the paradigm or foundational change that had occurred led to an attempt to endure, rather than to change with it. This confusion caused and continues to cause much of the frustration and pain that both clergy and lay people have experienced in what it means for people to be in ministry. It is not that the Church hasn't made changes, but the changes have rarely been of the right type and texture.[14] Although much of the change that has occurred in the Church has appeared disruptive, it has really been continuous change. This included proposals by church pundits such as Loren Mead that the leaders and theologians of the future will be the laity.[15] This severely missed the point, as it simply proposed to change the power base without changing the nature and use of that power itself. Charles Handy notes that continuous change is comfortable change and that we are often "too comfortable with continuity to realise that continuous change at some point becomes discontinuous and demands a change in behaviour."[16] The difference between continuous change and discontinuous change is that continuous change simply reiterates what has gone on before, sometimes in a different guise - whereas discontinuous change takes us somewhere else altogether.

## THE IMPACT OF DISCONTINUOUS CHANGE ON THE EMERGENCE OF LAY MINISTRY

The intensity of the changes that have occurred over the last fifty years cannot be underestimated, nor the impact that it has had on both the Church and the world in which we live. Peter Drucker in *The New Realties* notes that its magnitude has encompassed the entire world and the way it operates. It has called forth a total revision of the way organisations and people work, and has effectively impacted everyone. He notes that this included groups such as unions, governments, revolutionaries, the military and any

---

[14] Loren Mead, *Transforming Congregations for the Future* (New York: Alban Institute Publications, 1994), 23. Mead sounds a warning bell in 1994 when he wrote, "The situation the churches are in is much worse than we have been led to think by leaders whistling in the dark, telling us the troubles have "bottomed out" or that "we are turning around."

[15] Mead, *The Once and Future Church*, 59.

[16] Charles Handy, *The Age of Unreason* (London: Business Books Ltd, 1989), 3,19.

Charisma style leadership.[17] This equally applies to non-profit organisations such as the Church, since these changes affect all organisations because of the foundational nature of the change. It is in the midst of these catastrophic or discontinuous changes that the Church has been confronted with the emergence of *lay ministry* in its many forms and dimensions. How it deals with the nurturing of this emergence will determine the effectiveness it will have in fulfilling the purposes of God in a rapidly changing environment. The way forward calls us to move through the adversities of the times to establish ordained and lay ministry that is complimentary, collegial, interactive and inter-dependent. If the basic product of the church is *"people in ministry"* then it is incumbent upon us to ensure that both our ordained and lay people reach their full potential in serving God and using the gifts He has given to them.

The level of change that has impacted our planet is so great that it has changed the very foundations upon which we operate and communicate in all levels of our society. This includes the Church. Even when the Church is in the world, but not of the world, it still operates and communicates upon the same foundations as that of the world. The perception of this change in foundations has been picked up by significant business, as well as, church writers. They note that this catastrophic or discontinuous nature of change brought with it a sense of the *crumbling of the foundations.*[18] Frances Schaeffer, a Christian theologian and philosopher, gave early warning of this crumbling in the mid-1970s with a proposed loss of the *status quo* by the church.[19] At the same time business guru Peter Drucker noted that change had become catastrophic or discontinuous in nature. He saw it as a movement from slow incremental evolutionary change to fast, traumatic, revolutionary change. He notes its point of ascendancy occurring with the global oil crisis, in what he terms the 1973 divide.[20]

It is, however, the theologian Paul Tillich who drew a broader picture of the disturbance of the foundations than Schaeffer when he noted that science's greatest triumph "was the power it gave to man [sic] to annihilate himself and his world".[21] For Tillich, the shaking of the foundations is historic in the sense that:

---

[17] Peter Drucker, *The New Realities*, 1st ed. (London: Manderin Paperbacks, 1990), 38. Drucker notes that it has impacted: labour unions (p. 185); social 'interest' groups such as farmers and labour (p. 21); any "isms" focused on 'salvation by society" (p. 10); the *mystique of the revolution*'s ability to impact society (p. 13); military capacity and potency (p. 41); government economic & social programmes (p. 65); government privatization (p. 55); 'Charisma' style leadership (pp 102-103).

[18] Peters, 160 ,163.

[19] Peters, 21.; Francis Schaeffer, *The Church at the End of the Twentieth Century* (London: Hodder and Stoughton, 1995), 97, 98, 101.

[20] Peter Drucker, *The Age of Discontinuity, Guidelines to Our Changing Society* (New Brunswick: Transaction Publishers, 1992; reprint, 2003), xiii. He sees this paradigmatic movement as a change from European to World history.

[21] Paul Tillich, *The Shaking of the Foundations* (Harmondsworth: Penguin, 1962), 15.

[Whenever humanity] has rested complacently on his cultural creativity or on his technical progress, or his political institutions or on his religious systems, he has been thrown into disintegration and chaos; all the foundations of his personal, natural and cultural life have been shaken. As long as there has been human history, this is what has happened; in our period it has happened on a larger scale than ever before. Man's claim to be like God has been rejected once more; not one foundation of the life of our civilization has remained unshaken. [22]

Tillich proposed that this current paradigm change has shaken all the foundations of the life of our civilization. Whereas Schaeffer noted that this paradigm-change will bring about a disturbance to the church's *status quo*, Tillich proposes that it now calls into question all *status quo*. [23]

To clearly understand the structural and other changes the church needs to make we need to know the nature of the foundations that have just crumbled, as well as the nature of the new foundations that have replaced it. This is a significant point, because it releases the Church from some of the negative perceptions that have been proposed about itself and its future. Rather than the current change in foundations being demonic or anti-Christian, it shows signs of divine activity. If we take Tillich's point, the shaking of the foundations is a call back to the One who not only shook the foundations themselves but also laid them in the first place. Faith therefore calls the community of faith to look beyond the disintegration of the current foundations to see the hope of a new beginning upon an entirely different foundation. The Psalmist asks the question: "if the foundations are destroyed, what can the righteous do" (Psalm 11:3 NASV)? In such a time, influence and effectiveness go to those who ride the changes and engage the principles and processes of the new foundations that are being established and subsequently upon which the church can build. [24]

It is not only important to know what this change in foundations means, but also to know what it doesn't mean. It is important to understand what changes will assist the Church in its mission and what changes would only serve to damage the Church's ability to address the situation and leave it impotent against the forces that rage outside its doors. In the early 1960s a scientific philosopher, Thomas Kuhn, produced the first edition of his book *The Structure of Scientific Revolution*. In it he picked up the term *paradigm*, which traditionally described the nature of models or patterns. He used it to describe gestalt or revolutionary change in scientific understanding or procedures. His book gave a language

---

[22] Tillich, 16.

[23] Peters, 163.

[24] Peters, 163. Tillich, 18-20. Tillich says, "He is the foundation on which all foundations are laid; and this foundation cannot be shaken. There is something immovable, unchangeable, unshakeable, eternal, which becomes manifest in our passing and in the crumbling of our world".

to a world-wide concern about the nature of the catastrophic or discontinuous change that had impacted the planet affecting, as Drucker noted above, every organization. It became common language across every discipline including business and theology.

### Discussion/Reflection Questions:

1. Discuss/reflect on the positive and negative aspects of lay ministry that you have encountered.

2. Discuss/reflect on why the discontinuous change we have experienced has seen the emergence of lay ministry.

## CLARITY ON PARADIGM AND CHANGE IN FOUNDATIONS

Kuhn's understanding of the term paradigm became blurred in the ongoing discussion and dialogue. Whereas he saw it as a revolutionary process affecting the foundations of scientific endeavours, it became commonly focused on organizations *changing the models* they used in their businesses or organisations. As a result, organisations were encouraged to use different and better models in more diverse ways. I first picked up the term in a Doctor of Ministry course on leadership in 1999. I recognised that since 1982 we had been working on changing the foundations of the churches we led, allowing the old to crumble and establishing new ways for those churches to operate and communicate. Now I was beginning to discover a terminology to describe and reflect on what changing the foundations really meant. By the time I began work on my doctoral thesis in 2003 the term *paradigm* had become over-used and for some obsolete. I remember in 2001 hearing Archbishop Hollingsworth promise that he would stop using the term – a term that in Anglican and Uniting Churches in Australia had been made popular by church writers such as Loren Mead.

So the first task of my thesis was to determine not only what the term itself meant, but more seriously what the world-wide (and inter-disciplinary) discussion and dialogue was trying to identify and describe with the use of the term. The most common use of the term in that dialogue was the implementation of more diverse models of doing things, which followed the traditional meaning of the term. However, that was not the meaning that Kuhn himself had taken, nor was it really the nature of the entity that had changed.[25] What had changed were the very foundations upon which the world operated upon. I thus re-defined the term as follows:

> A paradigm is the *foundation* upon which all entities rest and operates, as well as the *benchmark* or *standard* that assesses their effectiveness.[26]

---

[25] Peters, 39-40.; Thomas Kuhn, *The Structure of Scientific Revolutions* (Chicago: University of Chicago Press, 1970), 23.

[26] Entities refer primarily to organisations and groups, but can also relate to individuals.

So at the very heart of all the discussion and dialogue was our attempt to grapple with the fact that the very foundations upon which every organisation operated and communicated had changed. The old foundations had crumbled and had been replaced by entirely new foundations. Mead called the past foundations the *Christendom paradigm,* and in his book *The Once and Future Church* gave us some good insights into the nature of these old foundations or paradigm. He also highlighted the impact of significant change that instigated the emergence of an entirely different paradigm, even though he was not able to identify its nature.[27]

Mead demonstrated that this Christendom Paradigm, which had reigned for over 1,500 years (from the time of Constantine in 313 A.D. to the mid-1950s), functioned from a base of "one answer, one way."[28] It meant that in every field of activity there was only one answer to any problem and one right way of doing something. The Christendom-paradigm produced an operational process that saw that there was only one right way of doing anything, with only one outworking of a particular truth or picture of truth. There were of course, divergent views on what that *right* way might be, but each view saw its own beliefs as being the *only right* ones.

> A colleague gave an example of this concept when he referred to his dad, who adamantly believed that there was only one right way to hammer a nail. With the invention of the nail gun, however, we no longer need a hammer at all. This is an example of a fundamental or foundational change.

This perspective not only brought about a strong uniformity to those beliefs, but also strong coercion to adopt those beliefs. Although the Catholic Church reigned for much of that time, when its control was disturbed by the Reformation, and subsequently the Enlightenment, each and every one of them continued to operate in the same way and according to the hierarchical principles that were central to the paradigm. For each of them, their way was the only true way.[29]

It is Peter Drucker, in *The New Realities,* that opens up our understanding of the new foundations that have now been laid, which focuses upon "diverse answers, many ways."[30] Drucker proposes that one of the key aspects of the current paradigm-change is a movement away from *one answer, one way* to that of *diverse answers, many ways.* He

---

[27] Mead, *The Once and Future Church*, 13-14.

[28] Mead, *The Once and Future Church*, 17.

[29] *Peters, 169-170.*; W.T. Jones, *Kant to Wittgenstein and Sartre* (New York: Harcourt, Braxe & World, Inc, 1969), 3. 18th century Enlightenment excluded from nature and reason the unpredictable, miraculous and intervention by supernatural forces from outside the closed system of nature. They envisaged God who, having created an orderly universe, left it strictly alone.

[30] Drucker, *The New Realities*, 11-12, 17. Drucker notes that, "This has become evident in the realm of social needs and problems, which if they can be solved at all, always have several solutions – and none is quite right."

notes that this has become evident in the realm of social needs and problems, which if they can be solved at all, always have several solutions – and none is quite right. The solution or rather *solutions* will need to be addressed on a much broader and diverse base.[31] That is, the new foundations, or realities in Drucker's terms, produce a much broader and diverse approach to operational and communicative factors for all organisations or groups. The Christendom-paradigm, with its emphasis on *one answer, one way*, held a certain understanding of reality that saw the interaction of unity and diversity in the form of uniformity to a particular meta-narrative or world view, along with a coercion to that meta-narrative or world view. In this process, diversity became subordinate to uniformity or sameness.

> **Meta-narrative** in this sense means "an over-arching account or interpretation of events and circumstances that provides a pattern or structure for people's beliefs and gives meaning to their experiences'".[32]

The emerging foundational paradigm based on diversity, with its emphasis on *diverse answers, many ways*, suggests that the interaction between unity and diversity will operate on an entirely different level. In this process, unity cannot be coerced at the expense of diversity. The Christendom-paradigm and the emerging paradigm of diversity present entirely different perceptions of reality and engagement with that reality. As such, leadership in either paradigm operates on distinctly different foundations and engages different, even opposing, leadership dynamics.[33]

The Christendom paradigm operated from a controlling hierarchical leadership base, along with an enforcement and coercion of unity seen as uniformity or sameness. Whereas, the emerging paradigm, establishing a very different foundation, has brought with it an operational, management and communicative structure that revolves around a polycentric understanding of church life, non-authoritarian leadership (though it may retain a more flexible hierarchical structure) and a diversity-relatedness understanding of unity.[34] That is, diversity is not to be interpreted as individualism, nor is it an excuse for us to act independently from others. It retains a high level of relatedness to others, whilst unique and diverse approaches and perceptions are encouraged to be used. By polycentric we mean that it does not have one dominant or central way of doing things. Polycentric

---

[31] Peters, 181. Drucker, *The New Realities*, 11-12. Reinhart Koselleck, *Critique and Crisis: Enlightenment and the Pathogenesis of Modern Society* (Cambridge, Massachusetts: The MIT Press, 1988), 5.

[32] https://en.oxforddictionaries.com/definition/metanarrative © 2017 Oxford University Press

[33] Peters, 383-384.

[34] Metz, "New Paradigm: Political Theology," 364-365. Johann Baptist Metz, "Unity and Diversity," in *Faith and Future*, ed. Johann Baptist Metz and Jürgen Moltmann(New York: Orbis Books, 1995), 57. Hans Küng, *Global Responsibility: In Search of a New World Ethic*, trans., John Bowden (London: SCM Press, 1991), 4.

businesses and organisations take into account, rather than ignore or override, the obvious differences that occur amongst people and groups when working through the style or model of structural organisation they use with such people or groups. [35]

What emerges through this is a new understanding of the value of the human person in his or her relationship to the effective working of the organisation's operational and communicative structures.[36] Such values become more innate within the human person the more settled the emerging paradigm becomes. The emerging paradigm of diversity also calls for a redefinition of the matrix of the church's ministry that re-engages the laity in the ministry and mission of the church. This affects the place and activity of the ordained leadership of the church - from the *doing* of ministry to the *coordination, development* and *leadership* of ministry.[37]

### *Discussion/Reflection Questions:*

3. Discuss/reflect on what a change in the foundations upon which the church operates might mean for those who do ministry and how such ministry is carried out.

4. Discuss/reflect on how coercion affects the life of a church and its people.

5. Discuss/reflect on how diversity can be respected and its use encouraged within a church.

## A CHANGE IN HOW WE UNDERSTAND PEOPLE

Whereas earlier societies saw people as expendable, the new paradigm compels us towards seeing people as assets that require maintenance, love and investment, rather than costs the organization has to endure.[38] This emergence of what Drucker calls the *knowledge-worker* is far more than a social change; it is a change in the human condition. They have not only set new values and norms for our society, but also have changed the way in which businesses are managed.[39] Drucker notes,

> The wise organization realizes, too, that intelligent individuals can only be governed by consent and not by command, that obedience cannot be demanded and that a

---

[35] The polycentric orientation operates under the premise that countries around the world have so many differences in cultural and economic mores that striving to translate practices from one country to another may be fruitless. Therefore, when a company assumes a polycentric orientation, it adapts its products, marketing and support functions for each country it operates in.
http://yourbusiness.azcentral.com/polycentric-orientation-27300.html

[36] This can be seen in what Drucker calls the emergence of the *knowledge worker* and the change in place of minorities in Western cultures. Drucker, *The New Realities*, 214,215. Handy, 132.

[37] Peters, 211-212.

[38] Drucker, *The New Realities*, 88.

[39] Handy, 20. Peter Drucker, *Managing in a Time of Great Change* (Oxford: Butterworth-Heinemann, 1995), 203. Drucker, *The New Realities*, 169.

collegiate culture of colleagues and a shared understanding is the only way to make things happen.[40]

Although this can be frustrating to implement, it calls forth a change in mindset for managers, who Charles Handy encourages to understand that, "the authority you need is not based on being able to do the job better yourself, but on your ability to help others do the job better, by developing their skills."[41] This emphasis on developing the human person, which lies at the heart of the new paradigm, calls forth a new understanding of management.

Peter Drucker notes that the impact of the current paradigm change has not so much diminished the role of the manager but enhanced it. He writes,

> Management explains why, for the first time in human history, we can employ large numbers of knowledgeable, skilled people in productive work. Until quite recently, no one knew how to put people with different skills and knowledge together to achieve common goals.[42]

Not only has the manager's role been enhanced by these changes, but also that role has become an essential ingredient to the effective use of resources for the growth and effectiveness of business organisations. These are businesses that are trying to come to grips with the same paradigm change that confronts the Church. Drucker notes, "Equally it is management, and management alone, that makes effective all this knowledge and these knowledgeable people."[43] But hasn't management always done that?

Management has led and organised employees in the past, but the difference now relates to the emergence of a new type of person. These are people who are better educated, informed and expecting more from both their job and their employer than has been the case before. This has been a tough, but necessary, call for managers in business organisations, as well as, not-for-profit or volunteer intensive organisations. It also seems to be an even tougher call for ordained leaders in the church, because of its focus on ministry and serving the purposes of God. Although complete correlation of business principles across to the precinct of the church can be fraught with difficulties and misunderstanding, some correlation is essential, especially when we are dealing the same change in foundations that the rest of the world is attempting to master. We also need to note that the culture of servanthood in the church is not simply volunteering – as one our lay leaders noted – it is always something more – because it is about ministry and servanthood.

---

[40] Handy, 113. Handy quotes Drucker in this reference.
[41] Handy, 132.
[42] Drucker, *The New Realities*, 214.
[43] Drucker, *The New Realities*, 215.

### Discussion/Reflection Questions:

6. Discuss/reflect on whether people are different today than they have been in the past.

7. Discuss/reflect on how you expect to be treated by your leader or boss.

## RESTORATION OF THE MINISTRY OF THE LAITY

The mobilisation of the laity for ministry does not call forth a devaluing, minimizing or marginalizing of the ordained priesthood or ministry. It does, however, call for a change in the *matrix* of the church's ministry. Whereas the church in the Christendom paradigm developed a strong sense of ordained ministry, to the detriment of lay ministry, the emerging paradigm of diversity once again engages the laity in the ministry of the church. It does this by a reorientation of the ministry of the clergy, which is seen in a movement from simply the *doing* of ministry to the *coordination, development* and *leadership* of ministry. It thus calls forth a new understanding of the relationship between the ordained ministry and the priesthood of all believers, and the ordained ministry and the ministry of Christians as a whole. One does not exclude the other, nor is one better than the other. The move to a foundational paradigm focused on diversity brings with it a modification of the distinctions between the clergy and the laity that were held in the past. It enables a more inclusive understanding of ministry to occur. It notes that both the ministry of the clergy and laity derive from the same source, the high priesthood of Jesus Christ and the call of the *Laos,* the people of God.[44] There is only one ministry of the church, which belongs to both the clergy and laity, because the whole church is the *Laos*.[45]

As noted in the Excursus above, one of the outworking's of the Reformation was to re-establish the concept of the *priesthood of all believers*, that saw all Christians become, through baptism, not only a part of God's family, the people of God, but also members of a new priesthood through Jesus Christ. This was also acknowledged by the Catholic Church through Vatican II that saw both the laity and clergy having a real ontological sharing in the eternal priesthood of Jesus.[46]

---

[44] S. Neill and H. Weber (eds) *The Layman in Christian History* (London: SCM Press, 1963), 158. Newbigin noted: "A minister does not cease to be a layman when he is ordained. The ministry is not a separate body from the whole people of God (Greek *Laos*)".

[45] James Cook, ed. *The Church Speaks: Papers of the Commission on Theology Reformed Church in America 1959-1984`,* The Historical Series of the Reformed Church in America, vol. 15 (Grand Rapids, Michigan: Wm B. Eerdmans Publishing Co, 1985), 124. Nicholas Ferencz, *American Orthodoxy and Parish Congregationalism* (New Jersey: Georgias Press, 2006). Neill and Weber (eds) 10.

[46] Theo Clemens and Wim Janse, eds., *The Pastor Bonus: The British-Dutch Colloquium at Utrecht, 18-21 September 2002* (Leiden: Brill, 2004), 459-460. Micahel Papesh, *Clerical Culture: Contradiction and Transformation* (Collegeville, Minnesota: Liturgical Press, 2004), 45.

Membership of this royal priesthood is noted by Peter and John:

> Coming to Him *as to* a living stone, rejected indeed by men, but chosen by God *and* precious, you also, as living stones, are being built up a spiritual house, a holy priesthood, to offer up spiritual sacrifices acceptable to God through Jesus Christ (1 Peter 2:4-5 NKJV).

> But you are a chosen generation, a royal priesthood, a holy nation, His own special people, that you may proclaim the praises of Him who called you out of darkness into His marvelous light; who once were not a people but are now the people of God, who had not obtained mercy but now have obtained mercy (1 Peter 2:9-10 NKJV)

> To Him who loved us and washed us from our sins in His own blood, and has made us kings and priests to His God and Father, to Him be glory and dominion forever and ever. Amen (Revelation 1:6 NKJV).

Both clergy and laity share a sacerdotal (priestly) understanding of priesthood, not in regard to the "sacrifice of the mass" in Catholic theology, but in regard to the offering of spiritual sacrifices to God through Jesus Christ. This sacerdotal nature of the laity and clergy goes beyond offering praise to God, to also proclaiming the call to all humanity to join that priesthood and offer spiritual sacrifices to God. Paul undergirds this when he refers to his ministry as "ministering as a priest the gospel of God" (Romans 15:16 NASB).

Although the ministers of the Reformation worked to re-establish the concept of the priesthood of all believers, they did not aim to displace the ministry of the clergy by opening its ranks to include the laity – a priesthood of all believers did not include the ministry of all believers. The hierarchical nature of the Christendom-paradigm kept that responsibility in the hands of the leadership of the church.[47] The Christendom-paradigm was confident in the belief that the knowledge, will and purpose of God must be taught by those authorised, gifted, and anointed by God to interpret such things – i.e. the ordained ministry - and teach them to those who are not authorised. The new foundational paradigm of diversity calls us to extend the understanding, nature and implementation of ministry to the laity. As noted above, this affects the place and activity of the clerical leadership of the church - from the *doing* of ministry to the *coordination, development* and *leadership* of ministry.

### Discussion/Reflection Questions:

8.  Discuss/reflect on how ordained ministers might *coordinate, develop* and *lead the lay* ministry of your church.

---

[47] Neill and Weber (eds) 139.  J.N. Collins, *Are All Christian Ministers?* (Newtown, N.S.W.: E.J. Dwyer, David Lovell, 1992), 25. Second Helvetci Confession of the Calvinists in 1566 had "no wish that the commonness of one condition, namely priesthood, should provide occasion to erode the exclusiveness of the other prerogative, namely ministry."

## PURPOSE AND FUNCTION OF THE ORDAINED MINISTRY

It is important not to marginalise the ordained ministry, as proposed by Mead and others, because the ordained ministry fulfils three functions that are crucial not only to the liberation of the laity, but also to a mobilization of the laity to fulfil its purpose in God. Those functions are:

1.  to highlight and symbolize the very nature and character that God expects from His Royal Priesthood, the people of God;

2.  to equip and enable the people of God to fulfil their priesthood in the world; and

3.  to lead the people of God in their mission to the world.

The ordained leadership of the Church forms an essential ingredient that will draw together and liberate the incredible latent power of the ministry of the laity in our midst - a latent power that, if Bill Hybels is right, only finds its expression in one percent of churches across the world.[48]

**1.    Symbol of Nature and Character:** the ordained ministry is to highlight and symbolise the very nature and character what God expects from His Royal Priesthood, the people of God. The ordained ministry must exemplify what God expects of his priests and ministers so that the people of God have a glimpse of what they are meant to be, then through Jesus Christ move to attain that nature and character.

**2.    Equipping the saints or people of God:** secondly, the ordained ministry is called to equip and enable the people of God to fulfil their priesthood in the world. Without a proper understanding of ministry and an ongoing equipping, enabling and support of laity for ministry in the world, very few, if any, could last very long out there in the world, which can be at times be a volatile environment.[49]

The traditional approach to the ministry of the laity failed to understand that ministry is meant to produce something. Ministry to the laity was meant to produce ministry by the laity. It was meant to produce action. But when action is philosophically prohibited, even subtly, then atrophy occurs. That is, lay ministry wastes away due to a lack of use. The ordained ministry is called to equip and enable the laity so that they can confidently take up their ministry of priesthood to both God and the world. Stevens and Collins define

---

[48] B. Hybels, *"Pastors Elective Tuesday 1,* (Hillsong Teaching, Castle Hill, 1996) Tape.

[49] My own Rector rarely did anything specifically to train and equip me to do ministry in the world. But if at any point that ministry was stumbled, and there were times when it was badly stumbled, he was there to pick me up, dust me down and send me out again. He managed to look after me so well that my ministry in the world was to see hundreds of people come to know Jesus Christ in their lives.

leadership as, *"Christian leadership is the God-given ability to influence others so that believers will trust and respond to the Head of the church for themselves, in order to accomplish the Lord's purposes for God's people in the world."*[50]

In Ephesians 4 Paul gives us an understanding of the nature of leadership and its role in the Church. A misunderstanding of the nature of that leadership has led to confusion in the church about the call of the laity to ministry.

- **Place of the Comma:** The interpretation of what Paul wrote in Ephesians 4 took three different forms, due to the addition of a comma that is not evident in the original Greek text. In the original Greek text there is no comma after *tov hagiov (the saints).*

  > And He gave some as apostles, and some as prophets, and some as evangelists, and some as pastors and teachers, [12] **for the equipping of the saints for the work of service** (*ministry*), to the building up of the body of Christ (Ephesians 4:11-12).

  However, over the last four hundred years some English translations have included a comma after *saints*. The inclusion of the comma resulted two proposals:

  1) **A Ministry orientated Ordained Leadership:** writers such as J.N. Collins contend that ministry is right-fully and solely the domain of the ordained ministry. That is, it is the role of the Apostle, Prophet, Evangelist, Pastor and Teacher is to do ministry, not the people. Their ministry is to:

     - Equip or perfect the saints;
     - Do the work ministry (service);
     - Build up the body of Christ.[51]

  2) **A Laity allowed to do ministry:** Others contend that it does not matter whether Paul intended his use of *diakonia (ministry or service)* in v.12 to refer to ministry of the five ascension gifts or to the ministry of the saints. Kevin Giles suggests that both translations are possible, but neither really excludes the ministry of all believers, since verse 7 "speaks of the grace (to minister) given to each Christian, and verse 16, which speaks of 'each part working properly [to] promote bodily growth'."[52] However, there is a huge difference between being allowed to do ministry by the ordained leadership, and being equipped, encouraged and challenged to do it by an ordained leadership who sees that such equipping is a specific part of its role.

The comma does not exist in any of the original Greek manuscripts. Thus the five leadership gifts of apostle, prophet, evangelist, pastor and teacher have a specific

---

[50] R.P. Stevens and P. Collins, *The Equipping Pastor* (New York: Alban Institute Press, 1993), 109.
[51] Collins, 119.
[52] Kevin Giles, *What on Earth Is the Church* (Nth Blackburn, Victoria: Dove, Harper Collins, 1995), 141.

function in the church to equip the people of God (saints) for ministry (service). This means that there is a third possibility:

3) **A Ministry orientated Laity:** This takes the position that the specific call upon the five gifts that Jesus gave of Apostle, Prophet, Evangelist, Pastor and Teacher is not only to do ministry, but also to equip God's people so that they too can do ministry (service).

- **katartismos (equipping/perfecting): This equipping role is also indicated by the use of** *katartismos* (English trans: equipping, perfecting, consummation, edifying, gather together) in Ephesians 4:12:

> And He gave some as apostles, and some as prophets, and some as evangelists, and some as pastors and teachers, [12] for the **equipping [Greek: *katartismos*]** of the saints for the work of service, to the building up of the body of Christ (Ephesians 4:11-12).

John Collins notes two varied groups of translation of *katartismos*. They are:

(1) *perfecting* **and** *consummation* which suggests that the saints, or people of God, are brought to the peak of their existence or performance as Christians; and

(2) *edifying* **and** *gathering together*, which brings in the idea of preparing the saints, or people of God, for some task.[53]

The first group, he suggests intends to exclude the possibility of the general body of Christians being involved in the work of ministry.[54] However, both groups of translation infer preparation for some activity or task: for what is the end product of a fully *kataptismon* saint? What does "the peak of their experience or performance as Christians" actually mean? What is a Christian who has reached a place of maturity "to the measure of the stature of the fullness of Christ" meant to do (verse 13)? The word itself suggests that it involves a process of preparation that has a more functional, rather than qualitative meaning.[55] Bullinger also defines *katartismos* as, "the act of making fully ready, the act of perfectly equipping and fully preparing."[56] To prepare a saint, or person of God, for maturity and perfection and then to suppress any substantial outworking of that maturity in ministry can only serve to produce an atrophy of the worst kind. The ordained ministry needs to once again acknowledge that it is there to serve primarily

---

[53] Collins, 21.

[54] Collins, 21. Having done this survey on Bibles going back as far as the 16th Century he further notes that amongst more modern versions the only ones supporting the first idea are Roman Catholic, which he believes intends to exclude the possibility of the general body of Christians being involved in the work of ministry.

[55] Colin Brown, ed. *The New International Dictionary of New Testament Theology*, 4 vols., vol. 3 (Devon: The Paternoster Press, 1986), 350.

[56] E. W. Bullinger, *A Critical Lexicon and Concordance to the English and Greek New Testamen* (London: Samuel Bagster and Sons Limited, 1971), 580.

God's interests[57] and God's interests are to see His people equipped for ministry, to take up and fulfil their priesthood, which is to "declare the wonderful deeds of him who called you out of darkness into his marvelous light."[58]

- **Ministry or Servanthood:** the term *ministry* or *service/servant* comes from the Greek *daikon-* word group. It is used to describe a type of ministry or the nature or essence of ministry (or both). In some contexts it refers to the office of ministry such as "deacon", which in the Anglican Church is the first of the three-fold orders of Deacon-Priest-Bishop (1 Timothy 3:8-12). In other contexts it refers to the nature or essence of ministry which is focused upon an understanding of the call of God in our lives, which may have a variety of outworkings and encompasses all of God's people. Jesus used it in regard to Himself when he said, "the son of Man did not come to be served but to serve;" and at the Last Supper when He washed the disciples feet. Paul uses it to refer to his calling as an apostle in both the preaching of the gospel, and as an appointment to a divine office for the church.[59] Paul also uses the same word to describe Timothy's ministry as an evangelist,[60] as well as to refer to the combined ministry of his own team.[61]

**Two distinct groups of people:** in Ephesians 4:11-16 Paul identifies two distinct groups of people called to do ministry:

- The first are those gifted with leadership skills and abilities that are called forth to equip, prepare or perfect the saints, or people of God, so that they might do ministry. These are the apostles, prophets, evangelists, pastors and teachers.

- The second group is the saints or people of God who are called to do ministry (service) and to build up the Body of Christ.

**The signs of the effectiveness of the ministry (service) by the saints or people of God:** Paul notes that when the leadership of the church is carrying out its God given purpose of effectively equipping and enabling the people of God to do ministry (service), it will produce a church that is open in its internal nature and cohesiveness.[62] He notes that such a church will have:

---

57 Stevens and Collins, 110.

58 1 Peter 2:9.

59 Ephesians 3:7; Colossians 1:23, 24-25.

60 1 Timothy 4:6.

61 1 Corinthians 3:5; 2 Corinthians 3:6; 6:3-4.

62 Peters, 270-271. Systems theory sees an organisation as a *system* or *whole*. It addresses the interrelationships between the different parts, elements or subsystems of that system and its relationship to its external environment. Open systems grow and maintain themselves through a continuous interaction of energy with their environment. They remain differentiated from their environment because of their ability to constitute and maintain permeable boundaries that regulate that difference. This interaction with the environment does not threaten the church's identity and differentiation, because of the establishment of its self-producing boundaries. The interaction and resonance with its external environment stimulates the

- a unity of faith;

- an experiential presence and knowledge of the Son of God;

- a maturity and stability in the Body;

- an openness and honesty in personal relationships; and

- a community permeated with the presence of the love of God, which is evident in the life of its members (see Ephesians 4:11-16).

However, in a church where ministry is operating dysfunctionally, it is doubtful that much more than a glimpse of such characteristics might be seen. Such a situation requires a change in the heart and mind of the ordained ministry, so that they move from seeing their role as simply doing ministry, to that of leading and equipping ministry. But it also requires a change in the heart and mind of the people of God, who need to recognize that Jesus Christ has placed these leaders in His Church, and given them the necessary gifts and authority for the people of God to be truly equipped for all that God has for them to do.

> The importance of developing and equipping lay people for ministry was made clear to us in 1994 and 1995. During my stint in hospital noted above, I came out of my second major operation with a totally sizzled brain. I couldn't read quietly or even watch TV. I felt like I was climbing the walls. The Anglican Chaplain came in and gave me communion. Afterwards I told him how I was feeling. He said he never heard of that before and promptly walked out. Later that night I saw a Catholic Priest pass my room and called the nurse, asking her to have the priest come and see me. He came in and I explained what I was going through. He suggested we pray about it. He put his arm around my shoulder and prayed. The heightened feelings decreased and my mind became stable and I was at peace, no longer climbing the walls [we later recognised that I was allergic to the morphine anesthetic!!!).

> Some three months later I was in hospital again for a repeat operation, with another three months of sick leave. I was unsettled about the effect this would have on our five country churches. The Anglican chaplain came in and gave me communion. I told him I needed to talk about some things that were concerning me. He said he had to go and promptly walked out. At least I wasn't climbing the walls this time round. As I lay there that night I said to the Lord – is this really what we do to people? Are we so busy that we do not hear the voice crying out for help at a critical time? It wasn't that he didn't stay to chat generally, but didn't stay when I said I needed help. Through that time of prayer I decided that we were in a difficult situation as pastors and priests. People did slip through the cracks because of that.

---

church's self-transformation. Although the environment instigates the change, the church not only makes the change but also determines the character of that change. It is by focusing upon the interaction of self-differentiation, interrelatedness and interdependence that clerical leadership is able to develop and deepen the internal and external responsiveness of their local churches.

I decided to do something with our own lay leaders so that we might work to address that problem. We started a program called Pastoral Care Workshops that went for over twelve weeks. Eighteen of our lay leaders went through that program with me. It was a really important time of growth for them, and as I noted above all of them were effective in their ministry leadership. We also took them through a Gift Discovery Course and discovered that all 23 of our new leaders had the right gifts and abilities for the areas they were leading. Since then I have conducted Pastoral Care Workshops to train lay shepherds in two of the largest churches in Melbourne and Brisbane. I took 70 lay shepherds through the program at Richmond AOG. We also conducted the program at Garden City Christian Church in Brisbane, where I was the Ministry Development Pastor of the Church (now Hillsong Church Brisbane) and Principal of their College. We have now taken our lay leaders at St Jude the Apostle Anglican Church in Everton Park in Brisbane through the program a couple of times. Whilst at Garden City Christian Church we also wrote a Gift Discovery Course, a version of which is included in this manual called *Maximising People for Ministry*.

An important note to finish, some six months later I was in hospital again for a checkup – no operation this time. A different Anglican Chaplain came in to give me communion. At that point in time we were having some difficulty with our new bishop about confirmation. After communion I told the chaplain that I needed to talk about some things that were bothering us. He said that unfortunately he needed to go (could you believe that), but then noted that he could come back the next day and chat. He came back, listened to my concerns and then went and discussed the matter with the new bishop and turned the situation around completely.

This is the Church's hour, it is our time, and it is the day in which true ordained "leadership" comes into its own. It is the time for the whole people of God, both ordained and lay members to move out in mission to the world around them.

3.    **Leading the Mission:** The ordained ministry is called to lead the people of God in its mission to the world. One thing that is clear about the new paradigm or foundations is that it calls forth a new understanding of mission. Whereas, in the past mission was something you did overseas, it was not necessarily something that was done at home. For instance, the basic English concept of church held that all members of the community within a certain parish area were seen to be members of the church, at least conceptually. All members of that community would have seen themselves as members of the church, even if they did not attend its services.[63] Within the foundational changes that have occurred; the front door of the church has now become the crossing point into missionary territory for both the clergy and laity.[64]    The world outside the church has become the new

---

[63] Mead, *The Once and Future Church*, 13-16.

[64] Mead, *The Once and Future Church*, 53. Mead argues that the front door of the church was now the mission frontier for the laity, but I argue in my book *The Emerging Paradigm of Diversity* that the clergy must also see that as the frontier for at least part of their ministry, least of all for equipping the laity for their ministry in the world – the new mission field.

missionary frontier and field. These changes challenge both the clergy and laity to go well beyond their previous comfort zones into a totally new existence or consciousness. We need to change our perceptions or mindsets in order to envisage the opportunity that exists for the church in a world that has a total different openness to the church and its message than has existed in past decades.

However, a change in consciousness does not infer a change in location. It is not that the laity are now moving out into a world in which they have not ventured before ( although this might be the case for the clergy). But the perception of their role in that world has now changed, for they are becoming aware that "they" too have a mission to the world. Because of this there is a need for our churches to move from being havens of refuge to being dynamic centers for transformative mission in society.[65] To do this we need an ordained leadership that will not only equip the laity for mission, but also lead them in doing that mission. Thus the focus of leadership for the missionary pastor will be in the world, not the church."[66] In this regard Mead was a bit premature when he suggested that the new paradigm required a change in leadership from the clergy to the laity. Since leadership is primarily the interaction between the leader, the followers and the situation, leaders can learn different styles of leadership to apply to differing situations.[67]

If the new paradigm change confronts the Church with a change of situation, in which new perceptions have been formed, then what is really required is a change in the way we do ministry and leadership, rather than a change in leadership personnel itself. But whichever way we look at it the clergy can no longer see their role as simply as that of doing ministry. They are being called forth more than ever before to lead the people of God in ministry, for the authority they have been given is no longer "based on being able to do the job better yourself but on your ability to help others to do the job better, by developing their skills".[68] It is not an issue of clergy doing ministry better, but learning how to equip others in doing the ministry better, the others here are clearly the people of God, the majority of them being lay people - to work with them in a collegial atmosphere of respect and trust.

## CONCLUSION

'Oscar Feuch said, "The priesthood of all believers can be lost in a single generation." And with the loss of every-member ministry goes every-member mission.'[69] Because of the

---

[65] Stevens and Collins, 126.

[66] K Callahan, *Effective Church Leadership* (San Francisco: Harper and Row, 1990), 1.

[67] P Hersey, K Blanchard, and D Johnson, *Management of Organizational Behavior* (Upper Saddle River, NJ: Prentice Hall, 1996), 91. Hersey, Blanchard, and Johnson, 117. "The primary reason why there is no one best way of leadership is that leadership is basically situational, or contingent."

[68] Handy, 132.

[69] Stevens and Collins, 139.

intensity of the paradigm change that has occurred, this generation cannot afford to lose the priesthood of all believers, nor the every-member ministry that comes with it. This is the Church's hour, it is our time, it is the day in which true ordained "leadership" comes into its own. It is the time for the whole people of God, both ordained and lay alike, to rise up in an intensity of ministry and mission that will ride the wave of this paradigm and use it to fulfil the purposes of God. The "prime ministers" of the church are neither the laity or the clergy, but the whole people of God, both ordained and lay alike.[70] The spheres of their activity are both the church and the world. The intensity of their activity in either sphere is more dependent upon their individual gifts rather than their status or the office they hold in the church. "The whole Church is the *laos*, the people of God,"[71] and as such "ministry" belongs to us all. Truly, the basic product of the Church is *people in ministry*.

### *Discussion/Reflection Questions:*

9. Discuss/reflect on how the ordained leaders in your church reflect the nature and character that God wants His people in your church to take up and do.

10. Discuss/reflect on how the lay people in your church are being equipped to do ministry.

11. Discuss/reflect on how the mission of your church is going and how impacting are the ordained and lay members of your church are in engaging those outside the church.

---

[70] Anne Rowthorn, *The Liberation of the Laity* (Connecticut: Morehouse-Barlow, 1986), 22. This challenges Rowthorn's claim that "The laity are the prime ministers of the Church. They are the normative Christians, the means through whom Christ enters the world and participates in every aspect of human activity."
[71] Neill and Weber (eds) 10.

# Chapter Three

# Overcoming Cynicism & Pessimism

## INTRODUCTION

Before we move further into the nature of mentoring developing leaders, it is important to understand why and how the development of the ministry of laity can go really wrong by looking at the impact of cynicism and pessimism. Noting of course that ordained ministers can also sink into the depths of cynicism and pessimism.

Some years ago the Lord gave me a vision of a burnt-out forest where all the trees had been completely demolished by a fierce fire. There were only thin sticks still standing. Suddenly these sticks began to move and they represented men and women who had gone through the fire and were completely covered in ash. The Lord told me that a *fire* had ravaged His church that had not come from Him. The figures I saw moving were men and women of God who had gone through the fire and survived, blackened though they might be. These men and women were going to rise up and lead His Church into the future. The fire that had ravaged His Church was *cynicism*. Sometime before this vision we had been through such a ravaging fire in one of our churches. A group of lay leaders in the church initially began highlighting my weaknesses and criticised my leadership because of those weaknesses. However, when that did not seem to daunt me they began on my strengths; attributing impure motives to all that I did. I felt stripped raw from the ongoing criticism and murmuring.

> For instance, Lynette and I had a practice in previous parishes that we would put on a dinner at the end of each year for our Parish Council members and their spouses. This was meant to be a non-business social night as our thanks for the time they had put in over the year. During dinner we did notice that things seemed a bit tense. After dinner, over coffee, they asked what did we want? We asked what did they mean. They told us that we must have had some ulterior motive in inviting them to dinner and wanted to know what we wanted. No explanation we gave them convinced them that there was no other reason for the dinner apart from our thanks. Things did not get better from then on.

During that period I remember attending an evening service at an Assemblies of God church we visited. I had asked God to give me a word as I was feeling pretty low. During the service the visiting evangelist was preaching a gentle message on God's healing power. In the middle of the message he stopped and did a complete detour from the message he was preaching. He asked the congregation what was the name of the man in the Old Testament who had three sons; and the names of his sons. We informed him that he was talking about Noah and his sons Ham, Shem and Japheth. He then compared the difference between the actions of Ham who exposed his father's nakedness and his two brothers who covered up that nakedness. He told us that not only should we support our leaders in their strengths, but to also cover up their weaknesses (these weaknesses do not refer to immorality). To expose our leader's weaknesses was similar to Ham's action of exposing his fathers' nakedness.[72]

I felt God lifting my spirit up as he spoke those words, even though they totally messed up the flow of his message on healing. Upholding a leader's strengths and covering up his or her weaknesses is totally opposite to the ravaging effect of cynicism upon the church's life and leadership. Cynicism often arises in people's hearts when they suffer from leadership malnutrition. The effect of such malnutrition is to ill-equip a leader or team member for the difficulties that ministry or leadership brings and the failures that often occur. This can lead to the development of cynicism and pessimism in a leader or team member's life and ministry.

## LEADERSHIP MALNUTRITION:

Leadership malnutrition occurs when a person has not had enough training for the work that he or she is expected to do. It is not that there is no training, but it is not enough to equip them for the difficulties they will face in ministry in the church and the world. This includes training our leaders in the wrong dynamics for the work we expect them to do. In addition to the lack of training there also occurs a lack of support for them as they attempt to do that ministry. There may also be no real process to discern their actual skills, gifts and abilities and they are often appointed to areas of ministry and leadership that they are not equipped or gifted to do. Or they are appointed too early to leadership positions that they are not mature enough to handle.

Paul notes that we should not appoint a new Christian to a leadership position too early lest they be lifted up in pride and fall into the trap by the devil.[73] As leaders we are often pressured by circumstances to promote people far too early in their development of maturity and they often do not survive the outcomes. Yet if we wait and develop them then they bear fruit for their efforts. In one church we had in country Victoria I had felt in prayer that one of our young men should be our children's ministry leader. The problem was that he and his wife were not happy with our new contemporary music and disagreed with what we trying to do with the children's ministry. There was no way that I could appoint him to that position whilst he had trouble with our music and children's ministry. We decided to love and nurture them for some time.

---

[72] Genesis 9: 19-23.
[73] 1 Timothy 3: 6.

Then one evening at a Parish Council meeting,[74] which consisted of representatives from our five churches, an older man from one of our traditional churches commented that they didn't like the new music we had at our main contemporary church. As this just came from left field, without any instigation, there was complete silence in the room. Then this voice rang out and noted "We don't like the music you have at your church either." I turned to see who had spoken, and was surprised to discover that it was the young man who had previously disagreed with our contemporary music. Now he was defending it. Something had changed. He not only liked our music, but when I spoke to him at his home later, he really began to see what we were trying to do with our children's ministry. Under his leadership the new family and children's ministry called the *Simpson Street Family* became one of the best areas of ministry we had in our church.

Malnutrition in leaders also arises because they have had little or no debriefing during difficult times and they found no place to share the problems and difficulties they incurred. Such leaders are also given no real direction for their area of leadership or ministry and do not receive a clear definition of the boundaries of their ministry and leadership. This occurs when the leader, who delegated them to their position, abandons them; makes no time for them; and secures no ongoing direct links with them.[75] This, coupled with an ongoing lack of appreciation and encouragement, means that when they meet with obstacles and problems in achieving any real growth in their area of ministry they have nowhere to go to resolve those problems. It is from such processes or lack of processes that the seeds of cynicism and pessimism are sown in the hearts of budding leaders.

## LEADERSHIP CONDITION

Cynicism is sceptical of, and sneers at, goodness – it interprets it as naivety. Cynicism is given to tearing off the veil from human weakness – finding the weaknesses of leaders and attempting to strip them of their authority, often by the use of innuendos and murmuring. Pessimism is the belief that the evil in life outweighs the good. It is the tendency to expect the worst outcomes. Leaders affected by pessimism have a disposition to finding the gloomiest possible view. "What is the worst case scenario?" they proclaim, pretending that they are simply being realistic or pragmatic. They tend to believe that Murphy's Law rather than Maxwell's Law applies in all circumstances.

---

[74] The Parish of Ballan/Bunagaree had both a Parish Council that looked after matters relating to the Parish and its responsibilities over the six churches in the parish; and two Vestries that care for the specific requirements of the church at Ballan and the church at Bungaree. The other six churches being too small to require a Vestry to look after its needs.

[75] Hersey, Blanchard, and Johnson, 206. They note the following ineffective leadership dynamics have a negative effect on developing new leaders: abandoning, dumping, avoiding and withdrawing.

Murphy's Law notes that:

> Nothing is as easy as it looks; everything takes longer than you expect; and if anything can go wrong, it will and at the worst possible moment.

Maxwell's Law notes that:

> Nothing is as hard as it looks; everything is more rewarding than you expect; and if anything can go right, it will and at the best possible moment.[76]

Adopting a negative framework is not being realistic, because it only sees the lack in any situation, instead of the abundance of resources that can enable a group to take the next step towards achieving their goals or vision. Cynicism and pessimism produce attitudes of defeatism, despair, hopelessness and despondency in these leaders.

## THE UNDERLYING SHEATH

Cynicism and pessimism produce in these leaders an invisible underlying sheath over their minds and hearts. This is an impervious barrier over their souls that prevent them from:

- Growing in maturity (1 Corinthians 3:1-3; Hebrews 5:11-14); and

- Allowing the true purifying work of God's refining fire to have real effect in their souls (Malachi 3:1-4; 1 Corinthians 3:10-23).

They even pray for God's fire believing it to be some type of magical essence that transforms them without there being a change in their attitudes or behaviour. This is because they misunderstand the nature of that fire. God's refining fire comes in the form of trials and tribulations that test our faith, heart and attitudes to see whether we reflect a pure trust and faith in God. It tests our obedience to His will and purpose no matter what the circumstances might be. When we sing or pray for fire we are *asking* God to send trouble our way.

These leaders can develop a resistance to hearing wise counsel and teaching from the leaders over them in the Lord. The outworking of cynicism and pessimism in their lives develops an autonomous attitude of heart and closes them off from sound direction and instruction from those leaders.[77] This underlying sheath of cynicism and pessimism produces:

- Defensive behaviour;

- An unteachable spirit;

---

[76] John Maxwell, *The Winning Attitude*.
[77] Hebrews 13: 7, 17.

- Unbelief;

- Stubbornness;

- An underlying murmuring and grumbling;

- Disloyalty;

- Mistrust – doubting other people's motives; and

- A depreciation of other people's skills and abilities.

## AN ANXIETY VIRUS

Peter Steinke describes such leaders as anxiety viruses operating in the life of the church. He notes that

> In a human community, murmurers function much in the same ways as a virus does in a human body. A host cell (person, group) tolerates the virus's invasive behaviour. It offers the virus free room and board. [78]

He describes it as an intracellular parasite whose single purpose is the replicate itself. The characteristics of this virus are:

- Cannot say "no" to itself;

- Has no boundary, respects no boundaries;

- Cannot regulate itself, goes where it doesn't belong;

- Has no ability to learn from its experience;

- Cannot sacrifice for the sake of others; and

- Is an intracellular parasite with no life of its own.[79]

In an organisation, group or church the effect of this virus upon the life of that group is to produce negative, self-defeating attitudes and actions that include the proliferation of:

- Secrets (gossiping, whispering);

- Accusations (blaming, fault-finding);

- Lies (deceiving); and

- Triangulation (shifting burdens elsewhere).[80]

---

[78] Peter Steinke, *Healthy Congregations, a System Approach* (New York: Alban Institute, 1996), 56.
[79] Steinke, 56.
[80] Steinke, 57. "The presence of secrets or triangles is not themselves the disease. Rather, secrets and triangles

There are a number of biblical passages that describe the influence and effect of cynicism and pessimism on the community of faith. Paul and Jude often referred to the early church as being infected by elements that would destroy its unity, peace and effectiveness:

- "Grumblers, malcontents, loudmouthed boasters" (Jude 16);
- People who "bite and devour one another." (Galatians 5:15);
- Groups unbending in their contentiousness (1 Corinthians 1:10-17).

Paul warns against "godless chatter", "a man who is factious", and "quarreling, jealousy, anger, selfishness, slander, gossip, conceit, and disorder". Murmurings against the Lord and His servant Moses cost a generation of the Israelites their inheritance and destiny.[81] Despising the Lord's provision in hard and difficult situations, and a desire for the fleshpots of Egypt, cost them their destiny.[82] Luke and John use the word *goggizo* (to grumble, murmur, speak complainingly against someone, and speak secretly or in a whisper) on several occasions:

- The Jews, Pharisees and scribes murmuring against Jesus (Luke 15:2; John 6:41);
- Hellenists murmured against the Hebrews over the distribution of food to the widows (Acts 6:1);
- The disciples murmuring against what Jesus had said (John 6:61).[83]

## OVERCOMING CYNICISM & PESSIMISM

Any leader who is going to be effective in his or her ministry needs to identify cynicism and pessimism as enemies that will rob him or her of that effectiveness. To overcome the corroding activity of cynicism and pessimism in their souls they need to:

- Recognise its presence in his or her soul;
- Repent of disbelief and its outworking (this is because cynicism involves a failure to believe in God's power and that He will do what He said He would do);
- Ask God's forgiveness;
- Stand against it in the name of Jesus, rebuking the enemy and commanding him to yield the ground he has taken in his or her life;
- Build new hope in their lives – the hope that does not disappoint (Romans 5:1-5).

The stance against cynicism and pessimism needs to be an ongoing aspect in a leader's life and the team he or she leads. We need to challenge one another to move beyond the

---

enable the disease process. The disease requires a combination of the secrecy and the host cells (people who permit secrets to exist)."
[81] Exodus 16: 7; Numbers 14: 27.
[82] Exodus 17: 7; Numbers 21: 5.
[83] Steinke, 55.

unbelief of such corrosive influences in our life, fighting the battle of faith to achieve the vision and goals that have been laid before us.[84]

## Discussion/Reflection Questions:

1. Discuss/reflect upon a particular person or church you know that has been impacted by cynicism and/or pessimism. What has been its effect upon them?

2. Discuss/reflect upon how a lack of leadership development and support has affected the effectiveness of your ministry?

3. Discuss/reflect upon how we might dilute or minimalise the impact of a person with cynicism or pessimism in our community's life and activity.

4. Discuss/reflect upon the elements of a underlying sheaf and how they contribute to a lack of maturity and righteousness.

5. Discuss/reflect upon a situation where you have seen the anxiety virus in action and how it affected the life and vitality of the people or community in that situation.

6. Discuss/reflect upon whether it is possible to totally eradicate cynicism and pessimism from our lives. Use 2 Corinthians 10:3-6 and 1 John 1:8-10 to work through this question.

---

[84] For further reading see: *Realising Hope* by Andrew Peters.

# Section Two
# Enhancing Ministry Development

# Chapter Four

# Introduction – Intuitive Ministry

The effectiveness of those working to develop and train those in ministry requires them to have a fundamental intuitive understanding of the nature of people and how they act and react to different situations. Intuitive training aims to assist us in sensing where people are, knowing what God is wanting to do in their lives, and how we can best impart that understanding to them. Such intuitive interpretation depends more upon us than them. In order to pick up signals or indicators from them we need to be in a framework where we can receive, recognise and correctly interpret those signals or indicators. We need to look at who we are, that is, to know ourselves and to be comfortable enough to be ourselves. This will enable them to be relaxed and to be themselves with us. The ability to help them relax comes more from knowing who we are, not from who they are.

In his book *The Power of the Other*, Dr. Henry Cloud notes that our ability to go to the next level of development of our skills and abilities involves the input of others. Our development involves the interaction of our brain, relational connections and minds.[85] But it is not just any type of relational connectedness. He writes:

> If the relationships are positive, attuned, emphatic, caring, supportive, and challenging, then they cause positive development in the brain and increase performance capacities. If they are not quality connections, they either cause *nothing* to happen when something *should* be happening, or *bad* things to be built into us when they *shouldn't* be – "bugs," such as an over reactive brain, distrust, squirrelly thinking, an inability to focus and attend, impassivity, controlling behaviour, sensitivity to failure, and other liabilities. [86]

Each person is always in one of *four* places of connection with others. Of these four places of connectedness only one of them will help the person thrive. For us then, as we look to develop others in their ministry lives, need to ensure that we are people of connectedness that can help them thrive. These four places (or corners) of connectedness are:

1. **Disconnected, No Connection** – people in this corner are usually highly independent people who are disconnected from their own needs and are usually not able to produce strong relational cultures in their business or church.

2. **The Bad Connection** – people in this corner tend to have connection to people in their lives that always make them feel really bad about themselves or not good enough. The dynamics imposed upon them include: high expectations,

---

[85] Henry Cloud, *The Power of the Other* (Harper Business: New York, 2016), 13-15.
[86] Cloud, 18.

perfectionism, unreasonable demands, a critical spirit, withholding of praise, shame, guilt, put downs, silence. This type of connectedness pushes the person into an ongoing defensive mode where they are continually trying to catch up. It produces anxiety, fear, guilt, shame, and feelings of badness or inferiority. It tends to annihilate high performance through self-doubt and self-depreciation.

3. **The Pseudo-Good Connection** – people in this corner tend to have connection to people in their lives who produce flattery of them that generates positive feelings, but does not help them to grapple with reality in their business or ministry lives. Although this flattery tends to produce positive feelings, they are more addicted to hearing good news, rather than good feedback that enables them to address the difficulties and troubles in their business or ministry lives in a timely fashion.

4. **True Connection** – people in this corner tend to have connection to people in their lives who encourage them to be their whole, real and authentic selves. This corner involves caring, honesty and results – caring enough about someone to not be hurtful in how we say it, the honesty to say it to them directly, and a focus on behavior change and better results.[87]

Some of the *developing leaders* we seek to develop will come from the disconnected area where they are extremely independent in their lives and ministries. It will take time for them to begin to see their need for our input and assistance in developing a healthy ministry life. The other three areas relate to the type of person we might be and how we will influence their lives. If we are going to enable them to grow, then we need to be using dynamics related to the fourth place or corner of connectedness. Where we are, as ministry developers, affects the type and quality of assistance that we give to *developing leaders*.

Cloud notes the four types of feedback that come from the different corners of connectedness:

> Corner One is getting no feedback at all. Corner Two is getting it without caring and probably without accuracy, as the other person always has a standard that is somehow unhelpful or unreachable. In Corner Three, anything but feel-good backslapping or flattery is off-limits. Only Corner Four provides both caring and reality in the form of useable, actionable information. When we get that, it helps build self-control and the realization that we can do better. We are in control of outcomes.[88]

To give good, positive, realistic and helpful feedback to *developing leaders* we need to be operating out of Corner Four connectedness. It means that our investment in the process

---

[87] Cloud, 34-39, 39-44,44-55,51-68, 116-117.
[88] Cloud, 117.

doesn't come from our own agenda, but from a desire to care for them and wanting them to succeed. It involves providing support, growth, respect and accountability. It means supporting them whilst letting them have control over themselves, which builds limitless potential - the recipe for greatness.[89] Their development and growth through this process is dependent on how much we understand and know ourselves and can produce a relationship that is caring, honest and able to produce results – to help them thrive. To do that we need to understand the power of freedom, acceptance, hearing and wisdom in our own lives and how to subsequently develop that power in them.

### *Discussion/Reflection Questions:*

1. Discuss/reflect on the four places or points of connectedness and people you have known who reflect those places.

2. Discuss/reflect on people who have made you feel small and how you tried to compensate for that.

3. Discuss/reflect on how you might develop true connection in your own life and apply it to developing leaders you will be mentoring.

---

[89] Cloud, 55, 95, 99.

# Chapter Five

# The Power of Freedom

Freedom plays an important role in ministry development. By freedom, we do not mean freedom from boundaries or authority, but freedom to be the person or persons God made us to be. Our ability to allow people to be free to be themselves will determine the effectiveness of the development of their ministry potential. Our ability to allow others to be free will depend dramatically upon the level of freedom operating within our own lives. If we are not free to be ourselves, free to be the person or persons God made us to be, then we will find great difficulty in allowing others to be free to be the person or persons God made them to be.

Few of us have a completely clear picture of God's call on our lives or an understanding of the full extent of our destiny. That being the case, we need to tread very carefully when we think that we can determine those very things in another's person's life and ministry. The prophet Samuel managed to work his way through seven of David's brothers before he really learnt to see things the way God sees them.[90] Despite that episode, even David's brothers could not understand the role that David was to play in leading Israel.[91] For we find David's eldest brother rebuking him when he came up to the battleground to deliver supplies. David in natural terms was the least qualified of his family to lead Israel, yet from God's perspective he was the most qualified to lead. Ministry Development is about enabling others to discover and fulfil God's purpose for their lives, not to determine what that destiny or purpose should be. We are not aiming to mould people into a preconceived understanding of ministry or purpose, but to enable them to take up the unique ministry call God has placed upon their lives. This requires the development of a flexibility of approach and an ability to think outside the box, in order to begin to see people as God sees them, and not to see people from our preconceived boxes of what they should be. This chapter, and the next, will thus look at the nature of the freedom that Christ has brought into our lives and how we develop that freedom within us.

## THE BARRIERS TO FREEDOM

Many of the impediments or hindrances to freedom revolve around our potential to be bound, enslaved, manipulated and controlled.[92] The forces that seek to bring such control

---

[90] 1 Samuel 16:1-13.

[91] 1 Samuel 17:28.

[92] We are susceptible to slavery and often prefer it over above an opportunity to be truly free. Paul notes this in Galatians 5:1 where he challenges the Galatians not to accept the yoke of slavery again. Jesus challenges the Jews who refused to receive the freedom he came to give them and withdrew into the security of their tradition, which was by then bankrupt in its ability to salvage them (John 3:16ff; 8).

include sin, death, the devil (including his demonic hordes), and people. Linked with each of these is the power of fear, which robs us of the love and blessing of God (Luke 1:74; 1 John 4:17-19). One of the prime themes of freedom in the New Testament revolves around the power of sin in bringing us into slavery, which is then followed by the power of the law that establishes and reinforces the punishment that sin brings.

***The Power of Sin:***

Paul argues that sin has come about due to the trespass of one man, Adam, and through his trespass sin and death has flowed down to all mankind.

> But the free gift is not like the trespass. For if many died through one man's trespass, much more have the grace of God and the free gift in the grace of that one man Jesus Christ abounded for many. And the free gift is not like the effect of that one man's sin. For the judgment following one trespass brought condemnation, but the free gift following many trespasses brings justification. If, because of one man's trespass, death reigned through that one man, much more will those who receive the abundance of grace and the free gift of righteousness reign in life through the one man Jesus Christ (Romans 6:15-17).

Death was a result of the trespass of Adam and its power was inflicted upon all who followed Adam, whether consciously or not. There are only two notable exceptions to this: Enoch whom God took, for he was not (Genesis 5:18-24); and Elijah who exited in a fiery chariot (2 kings 2:1-15). Although they eluded death, sin still stalked their lives as Elijah's foray with Jezebel highlights (1 Kings 19:1-18).

Paul notes that in Christ a "new state"[93] has been attained, which moves us from death to life, from sin to righteousness. Paul underlines this again when he writes, "Therefore, if anyone is in Christ, he is a new creation; the old has passed away, behold, the new has come" (2 Corinthians 5:17).[94] This movement from death to life, from sin to righteousness, occurs through God's free gift to us in Christ. It is important to understand that this movement, from death to life, and from sin to righteous, comes about through an unearned, undeserved, unwarranted free gift from God that comes entirely out of His graciousness, not anything we have done or could do. This movement in "state" occurs purely out of God's graciousness and love towards us and our reception of that love. The result of this "new state" empowers us to defeat sin's power and influence in our lives, to

---

[93] J.W. Wenham, *Elements of New Testament Greek* (Cambridge: Cambridge University Press, 1965), 65. A state of being is reflect by the Greek perfect tense, which represents a "present state resulting from a past action."

[94] Or "the old things passed away, behold they have become new." "Passed away" is seen as an action having occurred in a point in time, here is the past, however, "become new" is in the perfect tense and refers to a movement to a "state of being", that is, of "becoming new." That is, the state remains no matter what occurs around it.

nullify sin's punishment, and to drive away the fear that stalks us. The nature of our focus has changed, from doing the works of unrighteousness to being slaves of righteousness. We have changed our allegiance from sin to righteousness, from self to God:

> But thanks be to God, that you who were once slaves of sin have become obedient from the heart to the standard of teaching to which you were committed, and, having been set free from sin, have become slaves of righteousness. I am speaking in human terms, because of your natural limitations. For just as you once yielded your members to impurity and to greater and greater iniquity, so now yield your members to righteousness for sanctification. When you were slaves of sin, you were free in regard to righteousness. But then what return did you get from the things of which you are now ashamed? The end of those things is death. But now that you have been set free from sin and have become slaves of God, the return you get is sanctification and its end, eternal life. For the wages of sin is death, but the free gift of God is eternal life in Christ Jesus our Lord (Romans 6:17-23).

It is important to understand Paul's stance here, for it is fundamental to our exercising power over sin and its dominion. We receive this new life purely as a free gift from God. The reception of the free gift brings about a change of state in us and that change of state forms the base from which we defeat sin on a daily basis.

> So you also must consider yourselves dead to sin and alive to God in Christ Jesus. Let not sin therefore reign in your mortal bodies, to make you obey their passions. Do not yield your members to sin as instruments of wickedness, but yield yourselves to God as men who have been brought from death to life, and your members to God as instruments of righteousness (Romans 6:11-13).

Sin as a power has been broken in our lives by faith in Jesus Christ. We then need to implement that victory over sin, on a daily basis; by the newfound freedom we have been given. However, the movement to righteousness is not motivated nor activated by a self-help program or even a pick-myself-up-by-my-bootstraps-and-try-to-imitate-Jesus kind of righteousness. Paul does not call us to yield ourselves to righteousness for sanctification, without knowing that it is the underlying grace and power of God that both enables and sustains our ability to do so.

### The Power of the Law:

Though both Jew and Gentile understand the power of sin and its impact upon our lives, even Christians do not fully understand the power of the Law and its ability to hold us in bondage and slavery. In Galatians Paul hopes to put to death the Law and its commands once and for all. Paul's issue is not the goodness of the Law but its inability to produce life. He notes:

> Is the law then against the promises of God? Certainly not; for if a law had been given which could make alive, then righteousness would indeed be by the law (Galatians 3:21) .

But the law cannot give life, and it never did. At the best the Law can only contain sin, not eradicate it. Paul indicates that it held a purely custodian role until Christ came (Galatians 3:24). Yet so many Christians turn from grace to law, where having been saved by faith they now live by obedience to the law and its demands. They do not understand that by making such a turn they have cut themselves off from Jesus and the freedom He has given to them. Paul emphasises this when he states, "You are severed from Christ, you who would be justified by the law; you have fallen away from grace" (Galatians 5:4).

The fundamental issue revolves around what justifies us before God. Paul notes, "I do not nullify the grace of God; for if justification were through the law, then Christ died for no purpose" (Galatians 2:21). It is a matter of what needs to happen for us to get right with God, which lies at the heart of our condition and bondage to sin and subsequently to the Law. Paul goes on, "man is not justified by works of the law but through faith in Jesus Christ, even we have believed in Christ Jesus, in order to be justified by faith in Christ, and not by works of the law, because by works of the law shall no one be justified" (Galatians 2:16).

Yet the Law is not neutral in this whole episode, for its power to condemn is immense and its demand for retribution beyond anything we could survive. As Paul notes,

> For all who rely on works of the law are under a curse; for it is written, "Cursed be everyone who does not abide by all things written in the book of the law, and do them" (Galatians 3:10).

Linked with the law's inability to give life, is our inability to meet all its demands. We are truly then lost and forlorn, "having no hope and without God in the world." (Ephesians 2:12). But God does not leave us destitute and without hope for "Christ redeemed us from the curse of the law, having become a curse for us -- for it is written, "Cursed be every one who hangs on a tree" (Galatians 3:13). The whole issue for Paul is not what we do, but what Christ has already done for us that matters. The whole issue of character then revolves around the contest between me-in-me, instead of Christ-in-me.

## A STATE OF FREEDOM:

What we have looked at so far has set the scene for our understanding the true nature of freedom that Christ has bestowed upon us. Paul's focus so far has been on what we have been delivered from: sin, which clings so closely from within, and the Law, which condemns so fiercely from without. But what are we being delivered into? We have already seen that in Christ we move into a new state of existence. Now Paul exemplifies it further when he proclaims, "For freedom Christ has set us free; stand fast therefore, and do not submit again to a yoke of slavery." (Galatians 5:1). Freedom here has shifted even further, so no longer is it simply that we have moved from being slaves to sin to being slaves of righteousness, now freedom is given in order that we might be free indeed! That is, we might move to a place or state of freedom, where we are now free to be free. We are free again to make original decisions and choices, without anything or anyone manipulating what those choices should be.

So extensive is this freedom that Christ has given to us, that Paul is moved to warn us of its misuse when he writes, "For you were called to freedom, brethren; only do not use your freedom as an opportunity for the flesh, but through love be servants of one another." (Galatians 5:13).[95]   He is also moved to warn us against moving away from this freedom and the impact such a movement will have upon our relationship with God through Jesus Christ. Not only is this freedom gained for us by Jesus Christ, as John notes: "So if the Son makes you free, you will be free indeed"; but His word works to sustain its activity in our lives: "and you will know the truth, and the truth will make you free"" (John 8:32-36).

Returning once again to where we began, freedom revolves around our propensity to become bound, enslaved, manipulated and controlled. Even a call to freedom can come as a manipulation by those proclaiming freedom for their own ends. Peter highlights this when he writes, "They promise them freedom, but they themselves are slaves of corruption; for whatever overcomes a man, to that he is enslaved" (2 Peter 2:19). To be free indeed encompasses allowing Jesus to work in our lives, releasing us from the shackles of sin, death, fear, manipulation and the law.

## Discussion/Reflection Questions:

1. Discuss/reflect  upon what is the important thing we need to understand about freedom;

2. Discuss/reflect  upon what forces lead us to be enslaved and controlled;

3. Discuss/reflect upon what power robs us of the love and blessing of God;

### The Power of Sin

4. Discuss/reflect upon what movement occurs in our 'new state' in Christ;

5. Discuss/reflect upon if someone gives you a gift, would you expect to have to pay for it?

6. Discuss/reflect upon what our 'new state' in Christ empower us to do; and

7. Discuss/reflect upon what we need to do to implement it on a daily basis?

---

[95] Peter also notes this as well when he writes, "Live as free men, yet without using your freedom as a pretext for evil; but live as servants of God" (1 Peter 2:16).

### The Power of the Law

8. Discuss/reflect upon what is it the law cannot give us;

9. Discuss/reflect upon what impact turning to the law has on us. Note at least 3 things;

10. Memorise one of the following verses and meditate on it this week. Galatians 5: 1, Galatians 5: 13, John 8:32-36.

### Impact on Ministry Development

11. Discuss/reflect upon how our lack of freedom in Christ might impact our development of others?

12. Discuss/reflect upon how this freedom challenges the perspective from which we approach the person being developed?

13. Discuss/reflect upon how this freedom challenges the way in which we see them attain and develop character, righteousness and their walk with God?

# Chapter Six

# The Power of Acceptance

The need of acceptance is strong in all of us. It is often much stronger than our need for love. The power of acceptance impacts our relationship with others as well as our relationship with God. It also affects our ability to help others develop in ministry. Our ability to give and receive acceptance will affect the freedom we have to let others be the persons God created them to be. We need the ability to make people relax and feel comfortable in our presence. Without a high level of acceptance in our own lives, this will be impossible to achieve. Inevitably, we will impart our own unease and uncomfortableness to them. If we dislike or hate ourselves, then we will unintentionally pass those feelings onto those whom we are ministering. We need to cultivate a high level of personal worth through understanding and receiving God's love and acceptance of us. This includes our acceptance and love of ourselves.

## SELF-ACCEPTANCE – GOD'S PRIORITY

True acceptance of ourselves comes from our love relationship with God through Jesus Christ. He first loved and accepted us that we might love and accept Him. We are commanded to love God and love our neighbours as ourselves. As Jesus said,

> You shall love the Lord your God with all your heart, and with all your soul, and with all your mind, and with all your strength. The second is this, you shall love your neighbour as yourself (Mark 12:30-31).

Our first priority is to love God with everything we have: our mind, emotions, spirit, soul and strength. We bring to God both our talents and strengths, along with our weaknesses and failures. From Him we receive acceptance and love, acceptance of who we are, not what we have done, for "God showed his love for us in that while we were yet sinners Christ died for us." (Romans 5:8). It is an awesome thing to understand that God actually likes us! No matter who we are; where we come from; or what we have done God actually likes us! He does not like our sin and rebellion, but He does like and love us. Our love for God is not only our first priority, but is essential if we are going to be able to fulfil God's second priority, to love our neighbours as ourselves.

Our ability to love others, however, can be restricted by our own attitudes and inadequacies. One of these inadequacies is our lack of true self-worth or self-acceptance. If we hate or dislike ourselves then we are going to have difficulty in loving and accepting others. This is because we can only love others to the extent that we love and accept ourselves. It is what we are inside, either love or hatred that flows out to other people. Jesus said:

> The good man out of the good treasure of his heart produces good, and the evil man out of his evil treasure produces evil; for out of the abundance of the heart his mouth speaks (Luke 6:45).[96]

This loving 'yourself' is not vanity or pride. Rather, it is truly accepting ourselves for who we really are in the eyes of God. It is the acceptance of the persons God created us to be in this world.[97] God made us to love and be loved. Jesus paid the price for us to come to a place of both knowing and experiencing what it means to be loved and to love, both for ourselves and others. For freedom Christ set us, free to be the people God created us to be (Galatians 5:1-2).

## PLAYING HAVOC WITH THE CONSCIENCE

Our conscience plays havoc with our understanding of ourselves. When we reject conscience and its call, we lose touch with the person God called us to be. When we act against conscience, we not only act against God and others, but we also act against our true self. Dietrich Bonhoeffer notes:

> Man is aware of a disunion between himself and God and between himself and other men. If a man goes against his conscience then he is also in disunion with himself.[98]

Although, on one hand, we cannot separate this disunion with God from going against the conscience; what Bonhoeffer highlights is the impact upon our internal harmony of deliberately disregarding the voice of our conscience and acting against its guidance.

### *Who we are* gets lost in *what we do*

Thus to go against conscience is to divide oneself off from oneself, a rejection of our true identity and a rejection of ourselves.[99] John Macquarie notes that "If conscience directs us to authentic self-hood, then to go deliberately against it would seem to be equivalent to deciding to destroy oneself.[100] Yet is something that we all tend to do.

---

[96] Jesus questions the Jewish tradition that fastidiously cleanses the external aspects of the body and sacramental utensils, but leaves the heart untouched. It is the heart's response or reaction to external events that highlights who we are, not the external events themselves (see Mark 7:20).

[97] G.R. Collins, *Christian Counselling* (Berkhamstead, Herts: Word Publishing, 1980), 349. Some Christians, "equate self-love with an attitude of superiority, stubborn self-will or self-centred pride.... Self-love means to see ourselves as worthwhile creatures, valued and loved by God, gifted members of the body of Christ (if we are Christians), and bearers of the divine image. We can love ourselves because God loves us, and we do not deny the abilities and opportunities which God has given. This biblical view of self-love must become the basis of self-esteem.

[98] Dietrich Bonhoeffer, *Ethics* (London: Collins, 1964), 148-149.

[99] A major step forward towards acceptance of self occurs when our consciences are cleansed by the blood of the lamb (Letter to the Hebrews 9:14; 10:22).

[100] John Macquarie, *Three Issues in Ethics* (London: SCM Press Ltd, 1970), 112.

When we turn away from our true identity, a void is created in our psyche that desperately needs to be filled. We thus become susceptible to the standards and pressures of the world around us, and its call to live up to its standard of behaviour and success. The world offers us a substitute identity that covers every area of our lives including:

- SOCIAL
- CULTURAL
- EDUCATION
- FINANCIAL
- RELIGIOUS
- PHYSICAL
- SEXUAL
- APPEARANCE
- APPEARANCE

Thus, a successful person in terms of Mr. or Ms. Universe is someone who is attractive, rich, extroverted, has high intelligence, and who is fantastic at sport. Unfortunately, very few of us, if any, match up to the standard set by the world. When we look at the standard we are striving to imitate, and then at ourselves, we see an enormous gap between what we think we should be and what we really are. As a result we develop a high level of self-rejection and inferiority that can lead to an ever deepening spiral down into fear, insecurity, and introversion. We question ourselves, our background, and our own personal worth, rather than questioning the standard that has been set for us by the world.

Paul confronts our susceptibility to accepting and trying to live by the standard set by the world when he says, "Do not be conformed to this world but be transformed by the renewal of your mind, that you may prove what is the will of God, what is good and acceptable and perfect." (Romans 12:2). Our conditioning by the world, and even sometimes the church, affects the way we see people, what we expect of them, and the boxes in which we place them. Our acceptance of ourself, and our valuation of ourselves according to God's perspective, gives us the ability the break open the categories or boxes in which we place ourselves and other people. It subsequently helps us to release them to be the unique ministry persons God has called them to be. Second, they will also have preconceived ideas of what ministry is about and what certain roles are acceptable in the church. The stereotyping of ministry roles may in fact be preventing them from taking up the call God has placed upon their lives. Such stereotyping may also be impacting the opportunities or lack of opportunities they have to do ministry, because they do not fit our preconceived ideas of what a ministry person should be. Who would have thought that that scrawny kid David would have the ability to lead the nation into possessing the land God had promised to Abraham.

## IMPACT OF SELF-REJECTION

A number of aspects of self-rejection affect our ability to effectively minister to others and to develop their ministry potential. We will approach each of these aspects from the point of view as to how it influences our effectiveness as ministry developers if we have these aspects of self-rejection in our lives. We must always take into account that the people we are ministering to will also need to overcome self-rejection in their lives to be effective in ministry. These aspects include:

### Lack of faith and trust in God

When we reject ourselves then we also reject God as our creator. This is a subtle aspect of self-rejection and often goes undetected. It results in an unconscious bitterness towards God. Its outward symptoms are a lack of faith and trust in God, His love, care and provision. We unconsciously blame God for our lot in life: for the parents, family, opportunities and hardships we have had to bear. When we have rejected God's creating hand in what He has already done in our lives, we find it hard to trust Him with our future, because we are afraid that it will be as bad as our past.

As ministry developers however, such unconscious bitterness within us will impact the faith we need to impart encouragement to others. It will cloud our judgement and colour our counsel. It may also produce jealousy and envy, especially if God opens areas of ministry for them to do, when we feel God has not supported us or given us the opportunities we desire.

The remedy for this bitterness towards God is:

1. Forgive God for our what we feel that He has done or not done for us in the past. Even though the Bible tells us that God can do no wrong or evil, our underlying perception or feelings are that in some way or other He has wronged us. So we need to forgive Him.

2. Ask God's forgiveness for our bitterness towards Him.

3. Thank God for who we are and the way He made us.

4. Put ourselves back on the potter's wheel and allow God to mold our lives in the present so we can be all that He intended for us to be.

> And *there is* no one who calls on Your name, who stirs himself up to take hold of You; for You have hidden Your face from us, and have consumed us because of our iniquities. [8] But now, O LORD, You *are* our Father; we *are* the clay, and You our potter; and all we *are* the work of Your hand. [9] Do not be furious, O LORD, nor remember iniquity forever; indeed, please look—we all *are* Your people (Isaiah 64:7-9)!

### Inability to love others

Our attempts to show love to our neighbours and friends and our endeavours to help them often fail miserably. The desire to love them may be there, but the ability to do so effectively is lacking. This aspect of self-rejection tends to produce a dominance and abruptness within us that nullifies the good that we try to do. We tend to be inflexible and judgmental and thus impose our standards and ideas upon others. As ministry developers, this severely restricts our ability to minister to others, because we cannot see past the blinkers we have on. Jesus said,

> Why do you see the speck that is in your brother's eye, but do not notice the log that is in your own eye? Or how can you say to your brother, 'Brother, let me take out the speck that is in your eye,' when you yourself do not see the log that is in your own eye? You hypocrite, first take the log out of your own eye, and then you will see clearly to take out the speck that is in your brother's eye (Luke 6:41-42).

Remember, that we are asking people to allow us to *delve* into their lives to assist them in discovering what God has given to them and the purpose he has for their lives. This is not a fault-finding exercise, but a discovery adventure to identify their strengths and abilities and then to find opportunity for them to use their skills in building the kingdom of God. Our attitude should be that we would need magnifying glasses to even begin to find a speck of dust in their lives.

### Over attention to clothes and appearance

Self-rejection produces an over-dependence and focus upon external appearances. We might try to compensate for the inadequacies we perceive in our appearance by the type of clothes we wear and our general appearance. This can, on the one hand, result in an over-attention to appearance, especially in the area of clothes, make-up, hair, etc. Or, on the other hand, it can express itself in a complete disregard these things altogether. Such focus on outward appearance will affect us, as ministry developers, in our ability to discern God's call in a person's life, especially if they do not match our preconceived notions of what we believe is required for that ministry.

## Criticism of others

Criticism of others about their actions, appearance and abilities may stem from a rejection of self. Self-rejection in this area tries to compensate for our negative feelings about ourselves by criticising those whom we think are inferior to us or superior to us. Our criticism however arises from our own feelings of inadequacy rather than any inadequacies in the other person. A highly critical spirit will cause people to withdraw from us into their internal places of security. It will intensify their wariness of sharing anything with us that are of any importance. This proves counter-productive to us as ministry developers, for much of the effectiveness in what we are doing relies heavily on people being open to share with us.

## Inability to concentrate

When we reject ourselves we might find great difficulty in concentrating on our work or study because we are continually concerned about what others think of us. If we are continually worried about what others think, it will be extremely difficult to stay focused on any one thing for too long a period. As ministry developers this aspect of self-rejection can hinder the accurateness of our interpretation of a person's abilities, skills and gifting, as well as how they might effectively be used in the body of Christ. Our internal distraction will affect our ability to read the subtle messages people send to us about areas where they hurt or are not very confident.

## Rejection of Authority

When we reject God as our Creator and Lord, it can often result in a floating bitterness that shows itself in rejection of the authority of our parents, ministers and other people in our lives. If we, as ministry developers, have a floating bitterness and rebellion towards authority it will result in a distortion of the way in which ministry can be developed in the church. This is because the susceptibility to encourage autonomous leaders and maverick ministries in extremely high. The long term result is to destroy the effective work of God in the Church.

## Wishful Comparison with others

When we reject ourselves we tend to have an ongoing wish to be like others, who we think look better or have better circumstances and opportunities in their life. There is a deep desire to have the qualities and looks of other people that we might too be accepted and liked as they are accepted. We then tend to minimize the importance of our own unique skills and abilities and the call God has placed upon our lives. As ministry developers, we can severely underestimate the importance of what we are doing and not probe closely enough into their lives. We inadvertently leave important aspects of their development in abeyance because we have not seen the importance of those particular gifts and abilities or the importance of that particular contribution to the life of the church.

## Perfectionism

If we always strive to be perfect we may really be attempting to gain approval for ourselves, in compensation for our self-rejection, by trying to cover every base and to be correct in every way. The sad thing is that our perfectionism tends to put people off rather than getting their approval. It can also be seeking self-glory rather than giving God the glory. This aspect of self-rejection can affect us as ministry developers on a couple of levels. Firstly, we will be too interested in impressing the other person to be seriously concerned about where they are and what they need. We will often talk too much and listen too little. Secondly, we might carry too high an expectation for them to fulfil, and possibly daunt them even further in their attempt to find God's purpose and destiny for their lives.

## Inferiority

When we compare ourselves to other people and seek to live up to other people's expectations of us we develop inferiority. This inferiority can manifest itself in three ways:

1. **Superiority** - if we have this attitude we will tend to restrict our comparison with others to those over whom we think we excel. It usually means we have not accepted our own weaknesses.

2. **Sophistication** – if we have this attitude we will tend to select our associations to build up our own image and yet never let anyone get really close to us.

3. **Shyness or lack of self-confidence** - if we have this attitude we will be so preoccupied with our own deficiencies that we will avoid people for fear of drawing further attention to those inadequacies and deficiencies and thus being rejected.

Inferiority will always impact our effectiveness as ministry developers; no matter in which form it comes. Superiority and sophistication will tend to demean those we minister to and will undermine the confidence they need to place in us. Shyness or a lack of self-confidence will cause us to hold back insights and counsel that they might need to develop what God has given to them. We will be too busy debating with ourselves about what they think, and too focused on their opinion of us, to be objective enough to give them sensible and godly counsel.

## GOD'S PERCEPTION OF US

To understand God's perception of us we need to see the difference between our heart's desire to serve him and life's impact on our ability to do so. Genesis chapter three records the story of the *Fall* of men and women from a state of grace and peace with God, and from their original state of dignity and innocence. Adam and Eve represented humanity in relationship to God. They represented us at "the temptation" that came by the Devil, which instigated them to disobey God's command and to exalt themselves above God. Having sinned against God, by disobeying His word, they fell into a state of rebellion and enmity with God. The word "state" used here is indicative of a way of "being" that is as deep a part of our personality that can possibly be (Genesis 2 & 3). This spiritual condition of rebellion and arrogance has been imparted to all members of the human race (Romans 3:23; 5:12, 19). Through sin and disobedience men and women were separated from the presence of God and have thus been spiritually dead and lost. For "All" have sinned and fallen short of the glory of God (Psalm 14:1-3; Isaiah 53:6; Romans 3:23; 1 John 1:8-10).

This produced in us an estrangement from God;[101] a bondage to self or selfishness;[102] a disharmony with other people;[103] and spiritual death.[104] Through sin the image and likeness of God in us has been distorted and damaged. It also brought us under the wrath of God. God's wrath is described throughout the New Testament as resting on those who continue in ungodliness and wickedness (Romans 1:18); those who take for granted God's kindness (Romans 2:5ff); those who are factious and do not obey the truth (Romans 2:8); those who continue in fornication, impurity, passion, evil desire, and covetousness, which is idolatry (Colossians 3:5-6); those who hinder the proclamation of the Gospel (1 Thessalonians 2:16); those who continually disobey God's commands (Hebrews 4:1ff) ); and it is stored up for the sons of disobedience (Ephesians 5:6). That wrath is stored up and waiting for God's time.[105] So where is the good news? God did not leave us in that condition, but through Jesus Christ has provided a way for us to escape His wrath and enjoy the blessing and benefits of being members of His family. "For God has not destined us for wrath, but to obtain salvation through our Lord Jesus Christ" (1 Thessalonians 5:9 see also                    1 Thessalonians 1:10). God sees through His wrath to what He made us to be and towards whom we can become through the sacrifice of His Son.

### Made in God's Image

We are important enough to God for Him to stamp His own image upon us. We are important to Him because we are made in His image and likeness, with His nature and characteristics. This image in us has been marred and distorted by sin, but this has been restored and renewed in us through our Lord Jesus Christ.[106]

---

[101] Genesis 3:10; Isaiah 59:1-2; Romans 8:7-8.
[102] James 1:14; Galatians 5:19-24.
[103] Genesis 4:8; Colossians 3:5-9.
[104] Genesis 2:17; 3:24; Romans 6:23; 8:6; Ephesians 2:1; James 1:15.
[105] John 3:36; Revelation 6:16;14:10,19; 15:1,7; 16:119, 19:15.
[106] Genesis 1:26ff; Hebrews 1:3; Col 3:10;,12-14; Ephesians 4:22-24; Romans 12:1-3.

### A Unique Design

We are made in God's unique design, even the parts of our body are according to His plan. God has made us the way we are because He has a purpose that He wants to accomplish through each one of us. Even in our mother's womb God was at work creating and moulding us to be who we are. God did not create us and then thought He should find something for us to do. God had a purpose and created us to fulfil it.

> For You formed my inward parts; You wove me in my mother's womb. [14] I will give thanks to You, for I am fearfully and wonderfully made; Wonderful are Your works, And my soul knows it very well. [15] My frame was not hidden from You, When I was made in secret, And skillfully wrought in the depths of the earth; [16] Your eyes have seen my unformed substance; And in Your book were all written The days that were ordained for me, When as yet there was not one of them (Psalm 139:13-16).

### Our Appearance

Although our body is not to be despised, what God really desires to do is develop the inward qualities in our lives that will enable us to show the love of God to others. God is more concerned with what is in a person's heart, than what he or she looks like.

> For the Lord sees not as man sees; man looks on the outward appearance, but the Lord looks on the heart (1 Samuel 16:7).

### God is Still at Work

God is not finished making us yet - when we accept ourselves, and submit ourselves to obey Him, then He is able to mould our lives to be what He always wanted us to be.

> For we are His workmanship, created in Christ Jesus for good works, which God prepared beforehand, that we should walk in them (Ephesians 2:10).

> And I am sure that he who began a good work in you will bring it to completion at the day of Jesus Christ (Philippians 1:6).

God has a universal ideal that He wants to develop in each of our lives. This ideal is the character and nature of our Lord Jesus Christ. His purpose is that we might be developed and conformed in His image.

> We know that in everything God works for good with those who love him, who are called according to His purpose. For those whom he foreknew he also predestined to be conformed to the image of his Son (Romans 8:28-29).

> My little children, with whom I am again in travail until Christ be formed in you" (Galatians 4:19).

Our happiness and achievement is based on our ability to develop this inward ideal in our lives. [107]

---

[107] Galatians 5:22ff; Matthew 5:1-12; 5-7.

## THE PURPOSE OF SELF-ACCEPTANCE

### Acceptance of God as Creator

When we accept ourselves, our appearance, family, abilities and opportunities in life and thank God for the way He made us, then we are free to love Him without fear. We can like David thank God for His wonderful works, those works being ourselves. As he says,

> For thou didst form my inward parts, thou didst knit me together in my mother's womb. I praise thee, for thou art fearful and wonderful. Wonderful are thy works (Psalm 139:13-14).

In this Psalm the wonderful works of God that David was referring to was himself. It is noted that David's kingship arose out of God seeing his heart not his outward appearance.

### Free to seek true values

When we accept ourselves then we are free to seek true values in life. We now desire to please God and live in the light of His opinion of our appearance, family, abilities and opportunities in life. We are no longer bound by trying to gain acceptance by seeking to live up to the values and standards that others place upon our appearance, family, abilities and opportunities in life.[108]

### Sane estimate of ourselves

When we accept ourselves then we are able to see our true identity and also to be ourselves without the fronts and barriers we put up towards other people. We are able to see ourselves as we really are with all our weaknesses and strengths. It enables us to have humility before God and other people. Pride can quite often be a result of rejection of self and thus a substituting something else for the real person. Paul and Peter said:

> Don't think you are better than you really are. Be honest in your evaluation of yourselves, measuring yourselves by the faith God has given us (Romans 12:3 NLT).

> Clothe yourselves; all of you, with humility toward one another, for God opposes the proud but gives grace to the humble (1 Peter 5:5-6).

### See clearly God's purposes for our lives

When we accept ourselves then we are able to see more clearly God's purpose for our lives. Our ambitions and motives are no longer initiated or instigated by an acceptance from other people, and we are thus better equipped to seek out God's purpose for our

---

[108] Romans 12:2: "Do not be conformed to this world but be transformed by the renewal of your mind, that you may prove what is the will of God, what is good and acceptable and perfect."

lives and to fulfil that purpose. We can be confident that God's plan for our lives is a plan for good and not evil, to give us a hope and a good future as He said through Jeremiah:

> For I know the plans I have for you, says the Lord, plans for welfare and not for evil, to give you a future and hope (Jeremiah 29:11).

### We can recognise our strengths and note our weaknesses

Our acceptance of ourselves enables us to recognise both our weaknesses and our strengths. We can thus come to God thanking Him for our strengths and talents and like Paul asking Him to be strong in our weaknesses. Paul relates God's replies to his constant prayer for healing:

> 'My grace is sufficient for you; my power is made perfect in weakness.' I will all the more gladly boast of my weaknesses, that the power of Christ might rest upon me. For the sake of Christ, then, I am content with weakness, insults, hardships, persecutions, and calamities; for when I am weak I am strong (2 Corinthians 12:9f).

### We are able to cope

When we accept ourselves we are able to gain more confidence in ourselves and in God. This enables us to realise that the trials that we go through are there to draw us nearer to God and to create in us the nature of our Lord Jesus Christ, rather than being there because there is something radically wrong with our personality or appearance (2 Corinthians 1:8; Philippians 4:11-13).

### It enables us to love our neighbours

It allows God to develop the qualities of compassion and mercy in our lives, so that we might have empathy with those in need. It releases us from the pitfalls of pitying people and using manipulative love that tends more to boost our own egos and meet our own needs.

> For he gives us comfort in our trials so that we in turn may be able to give the same sort of strong sympathy to others in theirs (2 Corinthians 1:3-8).

## BASIC STEPS TO SELF-ACCEPTANCE

God deals firstly with the restoration of our conscience and the deep disunion that has occurred with ourselves within us. He then works to transform our lives so that we begin to reflect the nature and qualities of our Lord Jesus Christ.

### God Restores the Conscience

The conscience is restored when we come to God confessing our sin and rebellion and turning away from the things that have separated us from God, from others and from ourselves. The blood of Jesus cleanses our conscience and restores its guiding powers.

> But if we walk in the light as he is in the light, we have fellowship with one another, and the blood of Jesus his Son cleanses us from all sin. If we say we have no sin, we deceive ourselves, and the truth is not in us. If we confess our sins, he is faithful and just, and will forgive our sins and cleanse us from all unrighteousness (1 John 1:6-9).

> Therefore, brethren, since we have confidence to enter the sanctuary by the blood of Jesus, by the new and living way which he opened for us through the curtain, that is, through his flesh, and since we have a great high priest over the house of God, let us draw near with a true heart in full assurance of faith, with our hearts sprinkled clean from an evil conscience and our bodies washed with pure water (Hebrews 10:19-22).

### *Steps to Self-Acceptance*

- Acknowledge to God your bitterness towards Him for the way He made you.
- Forgive God for the perceived wrong you feel he has done to you and ask God's forgiveness for your bitterness.
- Thank God for the areas of your life that you have rejected, i.e. parents, family, friends, abilities, appearance, opportunities in life.....
- Aim to love God and your neighbour as yourself.

### *Discussion/Reflection Questions*

1. Discuss/reflect upon why self-acceptance is important in ministry?
2. Discuss/reflect upon what happens when we turn away from our true identity;
3. Discuss/reflect upon what impact the stereotyping of ministry roles have;
4. Discuss/reflect upon which of the 9 aspects of self-rejection do you think impact you most;
5. List some of the outcomes of when we accept ourselves. Discuss/reflect upon which one resonates with you most?
6. Discuss/reflect upon what are the 4 steps to self-acceptance.

# Chapter Seven

# The Power of Listening

The power of listening involves listening to three different sources of information. It involves listening to God, listening to yourself and listening to others. To help a person develop his or her ministry you need to become competent in listening to all three of those sources. We often miss the intuitive signals that any person or situation sends out, because though we listen to others and we listen to God, we often fail to listen to ourselves. If a person is simply a body with a bunch of chemicals running around inside, then what we pick up from the five senses of sight, touch, hearing, taste and smell would be more than enough to inform us about what we need. However, once we add a soul and spirit to the equation then we must realise that communication does not simply occur on the physical level alone.[109] How we feel and how we sense our spirit responding to a person or situation will tell us much more than the physical senses could possibly do. The signals that our soul and spirit pick up go towards the intuitive understanding of the people and situations we encounter.

Certainly some people are more intuitive than others. The intuitive process however, may simply involve their ability to read external and internal data rapidly and understand the *key issues* that arise from that data. What they do instinctively and instantly can be learned if we begin to focus upon the external signals our environment is sending out, and the internal responses they elicit. However, even those who have a high level of intuition improve that process by an ongoing reflection upon and analysis of the situations and people they encounter. It is not that others do not hear or see the key issues involved, they simply do not listen for them. Therefore, when they come, they do not recognise their importance or the underlying activity they reveal. Recognition is more than simply hearing what has been said; but assessing what has been said and understanding the importance of the issue or issues involved. For those who listen the key issue involved often stands out as abnormal or inconsistent with everything else that has been said.

## LISTENING TO GOD

In the time of Isaiah God challenged His people about their inability to hear Him and understand His ways and purposes. He said to them, "For my thoughts are not your thoughts, neither are your ways my ways, says the LORD. For as the heavens are higher

---

[109] Though we might see the demise of the spirit with the emergence of modernism, and the subsequent demise of the soul with the emergence of post-modernism, the biblical record indicates the nature of a tri-partite person, even though some would not want to split the soul and spirit.

than the earth, so are my ways higher than your ways and my thoughts than your thoughts" (Isaiah 55:8-9). This passage has been read as meaning that God's thoughts and ways are beyond our understanding or ability to understand. They are in a different realm, one to which we cannot attain. God's issue here, however, is that Israel is unable to read His thoughts or know his ways because of the wickedness of their ways and the unrighteousness of their thoughts. He says, ""Seek the LORD while he may be found, call upon him while he is near, let the wicked forsake his way, and the unrighteous man his thoughts; let him return to the LORD, that he may have mercy on him, and to our God, for he will abundantly pardon" (Isaiah 55:6-7). If they will forsake their ways and thoughts and turn back to God then His thoughts will become their thoughts and His ways will become their ways.[110] When we take time to listen to God, to hear His thoughts and to understand His ways, then indeed His ways become our ways and His thoughts become our thoughts.

Having turned away from the wickedness of our ways and the unrighteousness of our thoughts, the movement from our ways to God's ways and our thoughts to God's thoughts involves seeking His counsel at every opportunity. We need to continually seek Him so that we can understand what He understands and know what He knows. David writes, "I bless the LORD who gives me counsel; in the night also my heart instructs me. I keep the LORD always before me; because he is at my right hand, I shall not be moved. Therefore my heart is glad, and my soul rejoices; my body also dwells secure" (Psalm 16:7-9). Notice how David mixes his listening to God to his listening to his own heart, to listening to himself. Whilst he listens to God's counsel, he allows his own heart to instruct him. Our effectiveness grows when we develop our understanding of God, as well as an understanding of ourselves. We grow when we listen to the heartbeat of God, as well as our own heartbeat.

God speaks with a small still voice, yet what He says speaks volumes louder than any other voice in the universe. When God confronted Elijah on the mountain top we are told:

> And behold, the LORD passed by, and a great and strong wind rent the mountains, and broke in pieces the rocks before the LORD, but the LORD was not in the wind; and after the wind an earthquake, but the LORD was not in the earthquake; and after the earthquake a fire, but the LORD was not in the fire; and after the fire a still small voice (I Kings 19:11-12).

In our listening to God, we need to push our way through the ruckus going on around us until we hear the still small voice of God speaking to us. With experience we grow sensitive

---

[110] John Oswalt, *The Book of Isaiah: Chapters 40-66*, ed. R.K. Harrison and Robert Hubbard. Jr., The New International Commentary on the Old Testament (Grand Rapids, Michigan: William B. Eerdmans Publishing Company, 1998), 444. He notes, A person's *ways* are one's patterns of behavior, and those must be changed if one is ever to live with the God of the Bible.

to God's voice, as well as the other voices that speak into our lives. Our ability to listen to God and hear His voice is dependent upon how much we want to walk in His ways and not our own. God reveals His heartbreak over His people's inability to do this: "But my people did not listen to my voice; Israel would have none of me. So I gave them over to their stubborn hearts, to follow their own counsels. O that my people would listen to me, that Israel would walk in my ways (Psalm 81:11-13)!

## LISTENING TO OURSELVES

This initially feels like the most unlikely form of listening we should do, but is probably the most important. We are not simply a sieve through which the word and life of God flows to others. We simply do not operate that way. God speaks His word through us to others, not by bypassing our mind and personality, but by using them. We become more effective as we let God work in us, rather than simply working through us. Listening to ourselves, however, does not mean we should be asking ourselves our own opinion about each and everything. It is, rather, a matter of sensing within us a knowing about things that are going on about us. A sensing of the atmosphere, the emotional tensions, or other aspects of the person or situation we confront. It is listening to, and discerning, our sensitivity to things that may not have been verbalised, but certainly have been expressed. In other words, picking up and correctly interpreting the inner questioning or turmoil going on in someone else, despite it not having been stated by them or anyone else.

Jesus showed an ongoing sensitivity to what was going on within His own being that gave Him insight into what others were thinking or feeling. This is seen in the story of the woman with a flow of blood, who touched the hem of His garment and was instantly healed. Jesus, did not see her do this, but still sensed within himself what had happened.

> And Jesus, perceiving in himself that power had gone forth from him, immediately turned about in the crowd, and said, "Who touched my garments" (Mark 5:30)?

It is also seen in a number of situations where Jesus often understood what was going on in the hearts and minds of others. Each time this is described as, His knowing or feeling within Himself. Note that in each case, the person involved is going through some inner turmoil or questioning, the substance of which Jesus picks up from His own spirit.

> But Jesus, **knowing in himself** that his disciples murmured at it, said to them, "Do you take offense at this? ....For Jesus **knew from the first** who those were that did not believe, and who it was that would betray him (John 6:61-64).

> And immediately Jesus, **perceiving in his spirit** that they thus questioned within themselves, said to them, "Why do you question thus in your hearts? Which is easier, to say to the paralytic, 'Your sins are forgiven,' or to say, 'Rise, take up your pallet and walk' (Mark 2:8-90)?

In the following passage, the Pharisee was questioning within himself about what Jesus was doing. Jesus then proceeded to answer the question that the Pharisee was asking, despite his not having verbalised it to Jesus.

> Now when the Pharisee who had invited him saw it, **he said to himself**, "If this man were a prophet, he would have known who and what sort of woman this is who is touching him, for she is a sinner." And Jesus answering said to him, "Simon, I have something to say to you." And he answered, "What is it, Teacher?" "A certain creditor had two debtors; one owed five hundred denarii, and the other fifty. When they could not pay, he forgave them both. Now which of them will love him more (Luke 7:39-42)?

Jesus also showed an ability to read and understand men's hearts and was often reluctant to trust Himself to them.

> Now when he was in Jerusalem at the Passover feast, many believed in his name when they saw the signs which he did; but Jesus did not trust himself to them, because **he knew all men and needed no one to bear witness of man**; for he himself knew what was in man (John 2:23-25).

> One man was there, who had been ill for thirty-eight years. When Jesus saw him and **knew that he had been lying there a long time,** he said to him, "Do you want to be healed" (John 5:5-6)?

> They asked him, "Teacher, we know that you speak and teach rightly, and show no partiality, but truly teach the way of God. Is it lawful for us to give tribute to Caesar, or not?" But he **perceived their craftiness**, and said to them, "Show me a coin. Whose likeness and inscription has it?" They said, "Caesar's." He said to them, "Then render to Caesar the things that are Caesar's, and to God the things that are God's" (Luke 20:21-25).

This is not clairvoyance or physic insight, but our spirit in tune with the activity of the Holy Spirit, which results in a clarity of understanding of the key issues going on in a person's life or the situation we encounter. We can develop a sensitivity to our own spirits that can pick up and interpret the inner turmoil or questioning others are going through. This sensitivity can also assist us in hearing and noting what the key issues are in regards to person's life and situation. The development of this sensitivity also enables us to be more sensitive to the use of the gifts of the Holy Spirit in our ministry to others.

This sensitivity or intuition is not simply reading energy waves flying through the air, but observing natural indicators in our environment that speak volumes more than they are meant to. Our intuitive observations of those around us, what they say and what they do, if tuned in upon, can assist us in understanding the key issues involved in their lives. It involves listening for it.

## LISTENING TO OTHERS

Listening to the person we are assisting to develop is essential to our effectiveness in that task. Dietrich Bonhoeffer highlights this when he said:

> Many people are looking for an ear that will listen. They do not find it among Christians, because Christians are talking when they should be listening. He who no longer listens to his brother (or sister) will soon no longer be listening to God either…. One who cannot listen long and patiently will presently be talking beside the point and never really speaking to others, albeit he be not conscious of it (Dietrich Bonhoeffer).[111]

What people are really looking for is an ear that will hear, not just listen. The first step towards hearing is to listen. Our listening to others can achieve a number of things in the process of mentoring them or maximizing their ministry potential. If we want to maximize people for ministry, then we need to create a relationship with them that will enable them to accept us in that role. This does not necessarily mean a long-term relationship, for some of what we do is short-term, often with very little build-up, which involves significant investigation and guidance in their lives. Listening does a number of things:

*Listening enables us to show acceptance of the person:* we all have a basic need to be loved and accepted. We need to impart acceptance to those whom we are developing or maximizing. You must accept the person for what he or she is, not what you think he or she ought to be.

- Do not judge, criticize or condemn the person. If you project any criticism for the person, they will sense it;

- Most people will be sensitive to your feelings and opinions of them. So be positive and encouraging throughout the work you will be doing with them;

- Do not let stereotyping or preconceived assumptions dictate how you approach them; and

- Do not make assumptions and act on them before checking with reality.

*Listening enables us to express empathy:* empathy plays a critical role in counseling people, as well as playing some role in helping a person in ministry development. It is the depth of the empathy needed and the focus of that empathy, which changes from a counseling situation to a ministry development situation.

- Empathy is important in the area of ministry development, because it is important for the person you are developing to know that you understand them, their past and their possibilities in the present and future;

---

[111] Howard Clinebell, *Basic Types of Pastoral Care and Counselling* (London: SCM Press Ltd, 1984), 72.

- Empathy means "the ability to identify oneself mentally with, and so understand, a person or thing."[112] It helps people to know that we actually do understand them;

- Heinz Kohut notes that "Empathy is the accepting, confirming, and understanding [*of the*] human echo evoked by the self";[113] and

- People can get very nervous about talking about God's purpose and destiny for their lives. They fear that if they shared their true thoughts about what God has called them to, we like others might belittle either them or the call itself. When they hear the same echo expressed through the perceptions and understanding of someone else, they will have more confidence to take up God's call and fulfill their destiny.

***Listening helps overcome the barriers to hearing:*** one of the greatest barriers to listening is talking. If we are too carried away with what we have to say, or our mind is too preoccupied about what we are going to say next, then we will fail to hear the person in front of us. "We can listen a lot faster than we can speak. The disparity between these two rates can create a tension and cause a listener to lose focus."[114] We inevitably will race ahead of the person speaking and inadvertently presume we know what they are going to say next. We thus interrupt them with the answer before they have asked the question, and think we have been clever in anticipating them so well. However, because we do not listen very well, we will forget to check with them, whether what we have said really answered the question we didn't give them chance to ask. We have to deliberately remain focused and attempt to hear what they are really trying to say. Peter Drucker remarked, "The most important thing in communication is to hear what isn't being said," If you expend your extra energy by observing the other person closely and interpreting what he or she says, your listening skills will improve dramatically.[115]

***Listening helps us overcome stereotyping:*** so many problems could be simply overcome if we took time to listen carefully and understand the issues involved. "Stereotyping others can be a huge barrier to listening. It tends to make us hear what we expect rather than what another person actually says."[116] Stereotyping or placing people in boxes inevitably closes off our ability to hear what they are really saying. Even when they say something that questions the stereotype itself, we will either filter that statement out of our hearing, or reinterpret it so it makes some sort sense within the stereotype.

---

[112] The Australian Oxford Dictionary, (Herron Publications, West End, Qld, 1988), 147.
[113] Clinebell, 77.
[114] John Maxwell, *Becoming a Person of Influence* (Nashville: Thomas Nelson Publishers, 1997), 86.
[115] Maxwell, *Becoming a Person of Influence*, 86.
[116] Maxwell, *Becoming a Person of Influence*, 87.

***Determined listening will overcome our inability to hear:*** anytime a person has an axe to grind, the words of others will be drowned out by the sound of the grindstone.[117] Our attitudes and grievances can dramatically affect our ability to hear another person's need or issues. It is only as we are at peace with ourselves, and at peace with God can we truly hear the echo of another self in the voice of its owner. The more determined we are to listen to what a person really has to say; the greater is our chance of hearing them.

***Listening helps us ask the right questions:*** there will be a number of times we will have to ask questions in a ministry development situation. The more focused we have been in listening to them, the more relevant and accurate our questions will be. Our questions will reveal to the person how clearly we have heard them.

***Listening helps us to interpret their situation more accurately:*** if we have followed carefully the principles outlined above, the greater is our chance of accurately interpreting their situation. The more accurately we interpret and understand their situation, the more confidence they will have in us. They are then more likely to open up to us and share about themselves more freely. If they are going to heed our guidance and assistance in the development of their ministry potential, then they need to know we are pretty good at understanding the issues involved in their situation itself.

***Discussion/Reflection Questions:***

1. Discuss/reflect upon  the 3 different sources of information that the power of listening involves;

2. Discuss/reflect upon the intuitive process and think about whether you are naturally intuitive;

3. Discuss/reflect upon  what does the section on listening to God reveal about the passage "for my thoughts are not your thoughts, neither are your ways my ways";

4. Discuss/reflect upon a circumstance where listening to yourself gave you insight into the situation;

5. Discuss/reflect upon what is the difference between listening and hearing; and

6. Discuss/reflect upon the 7 keys to listening. Which one do you need to attend to most?

---

[117] Maxwell, *Becoming a Person of Influence*, 88.

# Chapter Eight

# The Power of Wisdom

The power of wisdom practically comes down to knowing when to keep quiet. Our ability to discern when it is time to talk or time to keep quiet will be affected by what drives us. James faces this issue head on when he writes.

> Who is wise and understanding among you? By his good life let him show his works in the meekness of wisdom. But if you have bitter jealousy and selfish ambition in your hearts, do not boast and be false to the truth. This wisdom is not such as comes down from above, but is earthly, unspiritual, devilish. For where jealousy and selfish ambition exist, there will be disorder and every vile practice. [17]But the wisdom from above is first pure, then peaceable, gentle, open to reason, full of mercy and good fruits, without uncertainty or insincerity. [18]And the harvest of righteousness is sown in peace by those who make peace (James 4:14-18).

James gives us the basis upon which to judge the wisdom that is being delivered to us through someone else. Heavenly wisdom will have certain characteristics that are primarily related to the way the wisdom is delivered, rather than its content. If the wisdom is from above then it will have these characteristics:

- It **will be pure** - the motives of the giver of the wisdom will be clean and above board. There will be no strings attached or ulterior motives involved. It will not boost his or her ego or serve their own selfish ambition, nor come out of a heart of bitter jealousy. What the wisdom itself teaches will also be pure, and not suggest or require anything that is out of the boundaries of what God has ordered;

- **It will be peaceable** - it will not bring with it condemnation or judgement, nor will it create contention or dissension;

- **It will be gentle** - it will be devoid of manipulation and will not be given in an over-bearing manner;

- **It will be open to reason** - the wisdom and its delivery will be flexible to testing. We will be able to question its authenticity and reject it if it does not meet the tests we apply. It is open to discussion;

- **It will be full of mercy** - it will not diminish me as a person, nor tear me down. It will enhance God's love and forgiveness to me and give me room to move and grow;

- **It will be full of good fruits** - the results of the wisdom will be encouraging, increase the kingdom of God and will bear fruit in our lives;

- **It will be without uncertainty** - because those who deliver the wisdom do not have any self-serving motives in delivering the wisdom, they will make sure they have really heard from God and deliver it with certainty and assuredness; and

- **It will be without insincerity** - once again the motives will dictate the sincerity with which it is given.

The important thing for us to note is that each person is given the permission to reject any word of wisdom that does not come with the above characteristics attached to it. So if we have wisdom to impart then we must take incredible care about how we deliver that wisdom and the condition of our heart in giving it.

In order to be a bearer of wisdom James challenges us to confront what drives us. What drives us distorts the wisdom we might have been given. Even if I have wisdom that has come down from heaven my method of delivery can deny the very basis of the wisdom itself. If I have a bitter or jealous heart it will distort the wisdom God wishes to share through me. If I have self-centered ambition, not just simply ambition, but selfish ambition then it will cause friction, disorder and a multitude of vile practices. What may have begun with God will become earthly, unspiritual, and devilish.

### Reproving & Teaching a Wise Person

- "Do not reprove a scoffer, or he will hate you; reprove a wise man, and he will love you" (Proverbs 9:8).

- "Give instruction to a wise man, and he will be still wiser; teach a righteous man and he will increase in learning" (Proverbs 9:9).

### Wise People Bring Healing & Life

- "There is one whose rash words are like sword thrusts, but the tongue of the wise brings healing" (Proverbs 12:18).

- "The tongue of the wise dispenses knowledge, but the mouths of fools pour out folly" (Proverbs15:2).

### A Wise Person is Persuasive

- "The mind of the wise makes his speech judicious, and adds persuasiveness to his lips" (Proverbs 16:23).

### Wisdom Brings a Heart of Discernment

- "The wise of heart is called a man of discernment, and pleasant speech increases persuasiveness" (Proverbs 16:21).

### The Wise Bring Calm to Troubled Waters

- "Scoffers set a city aflame, but wise men turn away wrath" (Proverbs 29:8).

### A Wise Man Knows how to Contain His Anger

- "A fool gives full vent to his anger, but a wise man quietly holds it back" (Proverbs 29:11).

### Fools Despise Wisdom:

- "Fools despise wisdom and instruction" (Proverbs 1:7).

- "Do you see a man who is hasty in his words? There is more hope for a fool than for him" (Proverbs 29:20).

- "Do you see a man who is wise in his own eyes? There is more hope for a fool than for him" (Proverbs 26:12).

### Fools have no Restraint:

- "A fool throws off restraint and is careless" (Proverbs 14:16).

- "He who goes about gossiping reveals secrets; therefore do not associate with one who speaks foolishly" (Proverbs 20:19).

### Do not Try to Correct a Fool:

- "A rebuke goes deeper into a man of understanding than a hundred blows into a fool" (Proverbs 17:10).

### Do not Argue with a Fool:

- "If a wise man has an argument with a fool, the fool only rages and laughs, and there is no quiet" (Proverbs 29:9).

### Discussion/Reflection Questions:

1. List the 8 attributes of wisdom;

2. Discuss/reflect upon a situation you have been in where there were strings attached and the implications that had on the situation;

3. Discuss/reflect upon how listening to ourselves (noted in the previous chapter) relates to the attributes of wisdom?

4. Choose 7 of the verses from Proverbs quoted above. Memorise and meditate on one each day of the coming week.

# Section Three

# Mentoring Course

# Chapter Nine

# Introduction to Ministry Mentoring

## MINISTRY MENTORING COURSE

For the purpose of this course the term "***developing leaders***" will be used for those receiving mentoring rather than the term *mentoree*.

The Ministry Mentoring Course is specifically aimed at developing and mentoring people in ministry. It enables us to develop a diversity of ministry in the life of the church and its outworking globally, by building and developing people's individual and unique ministry skills. As such:

- It works to develop their strengths, whilst minimizing their weaknesses;
- It works to help them reflect on themselves as persons in ministry, whilst they actually do ministry;
- It helps to move them from independence or dependence, to interdependence in ministry;
- It works to develop their unique gift-mix and its effectiveness in ministry;
- It works to help a person "improve" their ministry skills and abilities; and
- It works to help a person evaluate their own ministry activity and its effectiveness.

### Ministry Pressures in A Rapidly Changing Environment

We are all aware of immense changes that have occurred throughout the world over recent decades that have impacted on the way all organisations work and operate. We have entered into a new paradigm that has brought with it a high level of discontinuity. Discontinuity relates to the extent that decisions in a new paradigm can rely on and be guided by processes and events that occurred in the past. Traditionally the concept of time and history has viewed change as continuous and intrinsic. Lyle Schaller, for instance, notes that within the city, the seven decade period, 1890 to 1960, was a time of refining and expanding old ideas and that:

> It was reasonably safe to expect that tomorrow would be like yesterday – only bigger and better. With the exception of the airplane, there were no important new inventions that directly greatly altered the face of the American city. The changes that occurred were the changes produced by growth and by the refinement, improvement, and wider use of the basic invention that emerged during the nineteenth century.[118]

---

[118] David Limerick and Bert Cunnington, *Managing the New Organisation* (Chatswood, N.S.W.: Business & Professional Publishing, 1993), 5.

That is, the nature of the change is a continuation from that which has gone on before and builds upon the things of the past.[119] Continuous change is often slow and incremental. It is comfortable change, because it usually refers to processes of change that occur within a stable system that remains unchanged.[120]

Discontinuous change holds a certain element of catastrophic movement about it. It may have no relationship to nor builds upon anything that has happened in the past.[121] It often involves a complete break with the past and a major reconstruction of almost every element of the organization.[122] It does more than simply demand a change in behaviour, for it dislocates both individuals and organizations, so that whatever the form the change might take it will have complications greater than those encountered under continuous change. So, it is not simply being too comfortable with continuous change,[123] or lacking a willingness to move out of our comfort zone, but there is no idea what changes should be made or what benefits they may produce.This movement to discontinuous change has meant that the way we make decisions and assess the effectiveness of ministry have changed. So intense has been these changes and so strong is the sense of discontinuity that many ministers and church leaders have stepped back from effective decision-making. Rather, they have attempted to tread water in the hope that things will settle down soon and get back to normal. They stand afraid of making significant decisions because they fear that those decisions will be wrong.

The impact of discontinuous change has also meant that changes in the life and ministry of the Church have often simply changed the periphery elements of the Church's activity without bringing significant change in the way in which the Church operates. This has meant that important core values and traditional beliefs have been swamped in an attempt to be relevant, whilst the significant changes that the new paradigm has required of the church have not been made. The Church often continues to operate within the dynamics of the old paradigm, whilst pretending to be relevant to the new. We need to move the Church's ministers and leaders from the sense of dislocation or displacement they feel to become masters of discontinuous change. We need to train and develop them in decision-making processes that give them, not so much a confidence with the decisions being made, but an awareness of those decisions and their outcomes. That is, decisions

---

[119] Lyle E. Schaller, *The Change Agent*, (Nashville: Abingdon Press, 1986), 51-52.

[120] Handy, 3. Hersey, Blanchard, and Johnson, 469.

[121] Drucker, *The Age of Discontinuity, Guidelines to Our Changing Society*, xii. Though it may result in or even produce violent movement or revolutions, it is not violent or revolutionary in itself. The revolutions themselves result from discontinuities: "from the build-up of tension between a new underlying reality and the surface of established institution and customary behavior that still conform to yesterday's underlying realities."

[122] David Nadler and others, *Discontinuous Change* (San Francisco: Jossey-Bass Publishers, 1995), 22.

[123] Handy, 19.

during times of discontinuity cannot be guaranteed, but they can be monitored, revised and reversed when necessary.

The current period of discontinuous change has brought a disruption to our perception of the human person and the way in which he or she operates within a church or organisation. It has also opened up the nature of ministry to a far broader group of people, both ordained and lay. It has changed the focus of the ordained leadership of the Church and called forth the need for the equipping of the saints, or people of God, for the *work of ministry*. Ministry no longer remains the sole domain of the ordained leadership. Rather, the management and development of ministry within an environment of discontinuous change has become the new role for the ordained leadership to engage.

Ministry development involves three aspects of learning in a leader's life, whether ordained or lay:

- Formal or informal study (assists the gaining of knowledge and understanding);

- Ministry activity and work in conjunction with a ministry supervisor (which ensures accountability for the responsibilities we have as leaders); and

- Reflection with a mentor (which enables the development of leadership praxis).

Leadership praxis involves the interaction of theory or conceptual analysis; concrete action; and transforming change of the world through that action. This process will be outlined later. It involves the developing leader in a process of action, reflection and then further action refined from what has been learnt in the reflection process.[124]

*Study:* without knowledge the people of God perish.[125] Knowledge in this context refers to experiential knowledge of God and His Kingdom. That is, knowledge goes beyond theoretical propositions and understanding to a real intimate relationship with God. However, this does not exclude theoretical propositions and understanding; it simply calls it beyond rational thought and grounds it in real engagement with God. It ensures that such knowledge has its proper outworking in the lives of leaders and those they lead. However, experiential knowledge without the development of theoretical and conceptual understanding can see leaders drift away from the primary mission, vision and goals of the

---

[124] Peters, 288.

[125] Hosea 4:6 notes that: "My people are destroyed for lack of knowledge; because you have rejected knowledge, I reject you from being a priest to me. And since you have forgotten the law of your God…" This is linked with a lack of knowledge of God in Hosea 4:1 when God says: "Hear the word of the Lord, O people of Israel; for the Lord has a controversy with the inhabitants of the land. There is no faithfulness or kindness, and no knowledge of God in the land."

Church or organization in which the leader works or ministers. We are reminded that we are to love God with "all our minds" including rational thinking faculties (Matthew 22:37). We are also instructed by Paul to "Study to shew thyself approved unto God, a workman that needeth not to be ashamed, rightly dividing the word of truth" (2 Timothy 2:15 KJV). We are called to combined study and the gaining of knowledge and understanding with an experiential relationship with God through Jesus Christ. Such theoretical knowledge and understanding can be learned either through formal study, on-the-job training or a combination of both.

*Ministry Activity:* Accountability to a supervisor for our ministry activity and work is an essential ingredient for both balance and effectiveness in ministry. The supervisor of course varies according to the leader's position and level of responsibility and authority. For a Senior Pastor or Rector/Priest-in-Charge it will be accountability to a denominational leader or a small reflective committee. For others, it will be his or her ministry leader. However, at the end of the day we are all accountable to Jesus Christ for our obedience to and fulfilment of God's call on our lives and its subsequent outworking in ministry activity.

*Reflective Mentoring:* reflective work with a mentor is quite a different type of accountability. It is being accountable for the growth goals that the developing leader has set, in conjunction with the mentor, and their outworking in the life of the developing leader. It also involves accountability for the reflective process itself and making sure that the reflective tasks are carried out in an appropriate way and in a timely fashion. To do this we need to develop within our ministers and leaders a sense of leadership praxis – the interaction between action and reflection. This involves the combination of reflection and action as it relates to real ministry experience. Ministry is not simply made of theory and action but of a relationship between the two which is integrated in the minister or leader's life.[126]

This mentoring course is aimed at helping leaders grow in leadership praxis by enabling a process whereby the leader's unique gifts and abilities are addressed, developed and extended through a process of ministry experience and reflective thought. This course aims to develop and extend the diverse gifts and abilities that reside in our leaders, whilst at the same time enabling those gifts and abilities to blossom.

---

[126] Andrew Peters, *The Emerging Paradigm of Diversity: Its Effect on the Church and Its Leadership* (Mansfield, Qld: A.E. & L.A. Peters Outreach Enterprises, 2013), 242-248.

# CHAPTER TEN

## SUPERVISED EXPERIENCED-BASED LEARNING

For the purpose of this course the term *"developing leaders"* will be used for those receiving mentoring rather than the term *mentoree*.

**Supervised Experienced-Based Learning -** has three components:

> **Learning** - it is not simply a *developing leader* having some ministry experience, but learning from that ministry experience how to do ministry better.

> **Experience** - it involves the *developing leader* in the actual doing of practical ministry that relates to the type of ministry he or she will encounter as pastors, evangelists, teachers, missionaries or leaders.

> **Supervised** - the *developing leader* is accountable for the learning process he or she does. He or she is accountable to two people in this process:

> > • Ministry Supervisor

> > • Learning Mentor

**Supervised Experienced-Based Learning** provides a means by which *developing leaders* can *reflect* on their ministry development and growth whilst they are actually doing ministry. They do this with the help of an experienced *mentor* who helps them address and evaluate the learning goals that are established as a part of this programme.

**Supervised Experienced-Based Learning** provides an opportunity for *developing leaders* to develop the unique gifts, abilities and characters they have as they prepare for and do the ministry God has called them to do. It also gives the *developing leaders* input into what they believe they need to learn and where they need to grow through the set ministry goals.

**Supervised Experienced-Based Learning** operates on the understanding that God has had some input into the *developing leaders'* lives before the mentoring process begins. They are men and women of God, that God has called us to help develop, train, equip and establish in the unique ministry call He has placed upon their lives.

**Supervised Experienced-Based Learning** is optimal as part of the formation of the *developing leader*'s ministry when it is focused upon:

mixing

# Academic Excellence

with

# Ministry Experience

## ACADEMIC EXCELLENCE

People vary to the extent they enjoy and engage with academic learning. Someone can be focused on ministry practice and still do well in academic endeavours. For many though, academic endeavours are hard, uninteresting and to be endured not enjoyed. We have constantly told our students, including our own children, to enjoy their exams. This is simply a shift of attitude that encourages good mental activity, and who knows you just might enjoy yourself.

However, applying ourselves to academic excellence takes a level of humility and accountability because not only is it a means by which we can learn, but it is also a place whereby we are tested. We are tested not simply in academic techniques, but in our theology and its outworking in ministry. As such, academic excellence is never and should never be used as a means to bring conformity of thought or expression. Rather, it is a place to develop our understanding and refine our ability to present the gospel and to argue for the faith which has been entrusted into our care. A trust we should not take lightly.

My own experience of academic study has seen my theology assessed and critiqued by a broad group of lecturers and examiners. They have included Evangelical, Anglo-Catholic, Charismatic, Calvinist, Catholic and Liberal scholars. These have occurred through a variety of colleges in order – Moore College (ACT Sydney – Evangelical Calvinist), Trinity College (MCD Melbourne – Liberal, Anglo-Catholic), Ridley College (ACT Melbourne - Evangelical), Garden City College of Ministries (ACT Brisbane – Pentecostal), and Australian Catholic University (Brisbane - Catholic). Lecturers and Examiners, for instance, have included Jesuits (UFT), Evan Burge and John Gaden (Trinity), Graham Cole and Colin Kruse (Ridley), the former Archbishop of Sydney – Peter Jensen (Moore), and Professor James Torrance of Aberdeen University in Scotland. These people and more have challenged me over a period of thirty years, but throughout that process my own theological standpoint has not radically changed, but it certainly has been refined.

In my days as a lay leader working with Teen Challenge in Kings Cross I was called upon to preach in a number of different denomination churches throughout N.S.W. country areas and Sydney Metropolitan area. I began studying my Th.L., because I felt that if I was going to preach I should deepen my understanding of the Scriptures and Theology. I also wanted to be sure that the gospel I preached was truly the Gospel. I remember, in the early days, asking the Teen Challenge Rehabilitation Centre Director to define for me the "Gospel". He looked at me in silence and then turned about and walked away without giving an answer. I have no idea why he did that. But it was some years before *I knew that I knew* the true meaning of the Gospel we preach. This occurred during a Masters course-work subject on Paul and the Law in Galatians. I remember thoroughly enjoying the final examination of that subject because of what I had learnt in that course. I gained an extremely high score in the exam, which the examiner commented on, and found that indeed I had been preaching the Gospel – the good news of Jesus Christ for all those years. The results of that work can be read in the first chapter of my book *Holiness without the Law*.

I would like to share a further thought with those who struggle with academic study. Recently I was called a TOF by two medical professionals. The first time I had no idea what the person was talking about. I had in the past read books about a detective who was called *The Toff*. However, TOF means Tetralogy of Fallot. I was born with a number of holes in my heart, which was rectified by a major operation (called Tetralogy of Fallot) at John Hopkins Hospital in Baltimore, when I was about nine years of age. After the operation the surgeons told my parents that I would not put on very much weight, and *I would not excel at study*. During Holy Week 2011 I graduated with a Ph.D. from the Australian Catholic University on the theme *The effect of the emerging paradigm of diversity on the church and its leadership*. Because of the breadth of the theme I had to excel in five or six different academic disciplines, when you usually only cover one or two. Am I good at study? Absolutely not! I read a page and by the time I turn the page I have forgotten most of what I had just read. I have to summarise and summarise nearly everything I investigate. In addition, I have found one very helpful spiritual discipline that Paul notes in 1 Corinthians 2:16 – "You have the mind of Christ". Do you struggle with academic study and expression then just ask Jesus if you can borrow His mind. When I have asked, I have always found the answer to be yes! This is not cheating. For in all things Jesus Christ is everything. He is our strength, wisdom, sanctification and righteousness (1 Corinthians 1:30). So study to show yourself approved of God.

## MINISTRY EXPERIENCE

Ministry experience involves more than simply involving *developing leaders* in a church or community groups for some practical experience. It involves setting up a learning process so that the *developing leaders* can learn about ministry and themselves, whilst in the midst of actually doing ministry.

To do this we:

combine

# Ministry Task Projects

with

# Ministry (Learning) Covenants

## MINISTRY TASK PROJECTS

*Developing leaders* are encouraged to gain a variety of ministry experience through ministry tasks that reflect the real demands made upon ministers and pastors in some of the following areas:

- Pastoral Care
- Missions
- Preaching
- Administration
- Evangelism
- Teaching
- Community Liaison
- Meetings and Organization
- Planning - Development of Mission, Visions and Strategies
- Other……………………………………………………..

All *ministry* experience does not necessarily require a leadership position. However, the ministry experience should provide an opportunity for the expression of leadership qualities in some way or other. The following are examples of some ministry tasks that can be done:

- Children's Ministry
- Youth Ministry
- Leading or assisting with a small group/cell group
- Leading worship
- Being part of a worship team
- Preaching (approximately 4-5 sermons)
- Discipling a younger Christian

- Conducting or assisting with Baptism preparation classes
- Teaching Religious Education in schools
- Leading / organizing or assisting with a mission or outreach program
- Running or assisting with an Alpha course, etc
- Leading or assisting with a new Christians group
- Running or assisting with a church-based playgroup
- Running an outreach / activity program for seniors
- Leading / organizing or assisting with a church camp
- Leading / organizing or assisting with a youth group camp
- Participating in a S.U. camp or mission
- Involvement in Youth Alive schools program
- Other ………………………………………….

The mentoring process involves a combination of ministry opportunities or placements (in the case of students); ministry supervisors; mentors and ministry (learning) contract.

## MINISTRY TASK OPPORTUNITIES AND PLACEMENTS:

1. **Existing Ministry Positions:** Can be existing Ministry task projects and programs in which the *developing leader* is already involved. This is especially the case if the *developing leader* already holds a ministry or leadership role in his or her own church.

2. **New Ministry Tasks:** Or the *developing leader* can tackle a new ministry task project, as long as the ministry placement can be arranged and the task being attempted fits with his or her gifts and abilities.

3. **Ministry Recognition:** In cases where the *developing leader* is attempting a new ministry task or role, the *developing leader* needs to be recognised by the Church or community group involved, as officially doing that particular ministry or activity. This ensures that the *developing leader* doesn't have to navigate between unseen barriers to effectively carry out his or her ministry tasks. It also makes both the Church and the *developing leader* aware of the parameters of the *developing leader*'s role in the Church and ministry at that particular time.

4. **Ministry Task Plan:** Task areas need to be defined and specific. *Developing leaders* are there to grow through a learning process that involves them in a fairly defined ministry situation. Otherwise the learning process itself breaks down. Part of the

Ministry Placement Agreement includes a description of the ministry task the *developing leader* will be doing in the "Ministry (Vocational) Placement Plan."

5.  **Ambiguities:** Ambiguities in both the role of the *developing leader* and their ministry tasks need to be minimised where possible.

6.  **Accountability:** The *developing leader* is responsible to the Church Ministry Supervisor for the area of ministry task project in which they will be involved.

## MINISTRY SUPERVISOR

Supervised Ministry Experience enables a *developing leader* to learn ministry skills and abilities in a controlled environment. Those involved in ministry receive feedback concerning the effectiveness of their ministry from a variety of sources. Much of this is uncontrolled and often critical feedback delivered in such a form that gives the minister no opportunity to respond. It also rarely gives him or her an opportunity to grow and develop in the ministry area concerned. It is difficult to grow and develop whilst you are in a defensive mode.

The supervised ministry experience that we provide for *developing leaders* is aimed at providing a controlled environment within which *developing leaders* can learn ministry and have informative, challenging and supportive feedback in a controlled manner. To provide this sort of ministry experience requires the assistance of a firm, caring and supportive ministry supervisor.

The ministry supervisor is the person who has authority over and responsibility for the ministry work the *developing leader* is doing. The Ministry Supervisor plays an important role in the *developing leader's* development by giving the *developing leader* a model of ministry as well as direction as to how the *developing leader* is to carry out his or her ministry tasks. The Ministry Supervisor also keeps the *developing leader* accountable for the development of the particular ministry skills and inter-personal relational aspects of the *developing leader's* ministry experience.

## MINISTRY (LEARNING) COVENANTS

The *Ministry Learning Covenant* is an agreement between the *developing leader* and the mentor as to the particular reflective goals they will be working on during the mentoring period. This includes the means by which the development of such goals will be measured and assessed. This ensures that both the *developing leader* and the mentor know what they are meant to be working on during the mentoring sessions.

# CHAPTER ELEVEN

# MENTORING

## AIMS AND PURPOSES

In Ephesians 4:11-12 Paul notes, "And his (Jesus') gifts were that some should be apostles, some prophets, some evangelists, some pastors and teachers, to equip the saints for the work of ministry, for building up the body of Christ…" One the prime purposes for these gifts in the Church is to equip and enable the people of God to do ministry and to do it effectively. Paul proposes that the effectiveness of this ministry will be seen in the Church in the form of:

- a unity of faith;

- an experiential presence and knowledge of the Son of God;

- a maturity and stability in the Church;

- an openness and honesty in personal relationships; and

- a community permeated with the presence of the love of God, which is evident in the life of its members.[127]

**Supervised Experienced-based Learning** programme allows experienced Christian pastors and leaders not only to model effective ministry, but also to actively equip and enable *developing leaders* to improve their ability as pastors, missionaries and leaders. Supervised Experience-based Learning program aims to develop the following principles in a *developing leader's* ministry and personal life:

- **To Improve:** to help the *developing leaders* "improve" themselves and their ministry capabilities, not to "prove" themselves. If the *developing leaders* feel that they have to prove themselves in ministry development they will become defensive in their approach to this program;

- **Develop a New Habit:** to establish a new pattern in the *developing leader's* life of establishing growth and ministry goals on an annual basis;

- **A Process of Self-evaluation:** to establish a process of self-evaluation, linked with reflection, with either a mentor or consultative Committee, on those annual growth and ministry goals;

---

[127] See Ephesians 4:11-16.

- **Lifetime Activity:** To have established this self-evaluation process so well, that they will gladly do it for the rest of their lives.

Through the **Supervised Experienced-based Learning** program the *developing leaders* learns how to:

- establish ministry skills and personal goals;

- establish a reflection process with a mentor on the goals that have been set;

- establish a process of self-evaluation on how well those goals have been achieved;[128] and

- make decisions and monitor their outcomes.

This reflective process comes in the form of an advisory or helpful input that is collegial and constructive, not authoritarian or top-heavy. Callahan notes,

> The spirit of consultative evaluation is coaching, not correcting.
> ***Under threat, people wither. With encouragement, people achieve.***[129]

## GOOD MENTORING

Good mentoring has immense impact on all those involved in ministry and leadership. It is especially helpful in the early stages of our ministry experience and can establish patterns of ministry and growth that can continue to serve us throughout our life. Without such mentoring we can wander aimlessly through life facing setback after setback and never knowing why. A mentor can assist a person to find God's clear direction in their ministry life, as well as strengthening them in that ministry. The mentoring process is aimed at helping a person move from independence to interdependence, without leading them to dependence.[130]

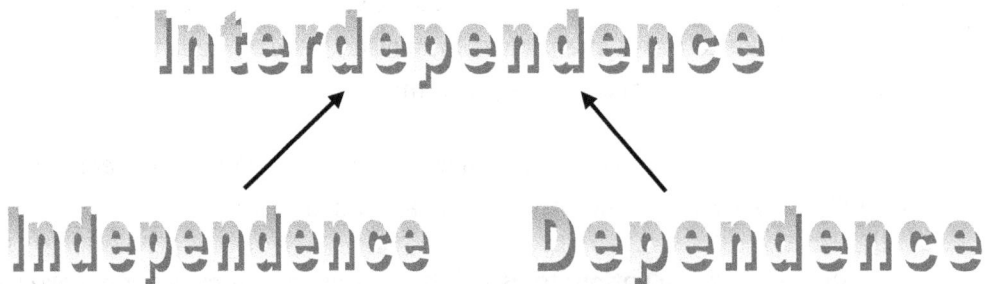

**Interdependence**

**Independence**          **Dependence**

---

[128] Callahan, 178. These principles are adapted from in Callahan's book *"Effective Church Leadership,"* where he outlines a process for a pastor, which involves self-evaluation with the use of consultative committee. See Appendix B for a brief outline of this process with a pastor and consultative committee.

[129] Callahan, 200.

[130] P.D. Stanley and J.D. Clinton, *Connecting* (Colorado Springs: Nappers, 1993), 35.

The difficulty, of course, is creating that sense of *interdependence* within a culture that on the one hand, promotes *independence* and, on the other hand, encourages deep levels of *dependency*, to the extent that people feel that the world owes them. As mentors we will find *developing leaders* come from both ends of the scale.

- The **independent** ones will find difficulty adjusting to the idea of having someone else involved in helping them set the agenda for their own personal lives and goals.

- The **dependent** ones will find difficulty with the idea that they have to take responsibility for their own growth and that the mentor will indeed be prodding them to own that responsibility.

The mentor has the difficult, but rewarding task of enabling that balance to occur in the *developing leader's* life. Stanley and Clinton note "Mentoring is a relational experience in which one person empowers another by sharing God-given resources."[131] It is a process that Paul himself notes when he writes, "My little children, with whom I am again in travail until Christ be formed in you!"[132]

## WHAT THE MENTOR BRINGS TO THE MENTORING PROCESS

The Mentor's ability to bring such a balance between independence and dependency, or at least to begin a process that will enable that balance to occur, depends not only on factors evident in the *developing leader's* life and attitude, but also in the Mentor's own life and attitude. What the Mentor brings to the mentoring process will have as much bearing upon the outcome as the aspects that the *developing leader* brings. What the Mentor brings to this process has been influenced by how he or she has been taught and instructed in the past. Many of us will have learnt in an environment that has been paternalistic in both its outworking and expectations. Such paternalistic methods have often resulted in the stereotyping of the *developing leader* to the extent that *developing leader's* individual uniqueness and differences are ignored or sometimes lost.

More often than not the learning process itself has served the agenda of the teaching body or mentor, rather than the individual needs of the *developing leaders* themselves. Such paternalistic methods no longer provide adequate ways for us as leaders, mentors and teachers to influence a new generation for Christ. I remember the interview I had with a prospective student whom the Bishop had asked us to receive for a parish placement in his final year of College. He had brought a friend with him to the interview. As I outlined the things he would be doing in the ministry life of our Parish the atmosphere grew tenser and

---

[131] Stanley and Clinton, 38.
[132] Galatians 4:19

tenser. It was only when I said to him that of course we expected him to bring his own unique skills and gifts as part of his ministry that then these two students opened up. They said that throughout their college experience no one had ever intimated that they might have their own unique skills and gifts, yet alone be encouraged to use them. That student had a great time with us in his placement and blessed us with the use of the unique gifts that God had given to him. When he was ordained and was heading off to his first curacy we encouraged him not to give up his love of rock climbing, as it was important for his overall health and ministry. Yet in his first curacy that enjoyment was pushed to the edge of his life and the church's agenda took over all his time. It wasn't long before he was out of ministry altogether.

## THE MENTOR AND THE MENTORING RELATIONSHIP

Mentors come in two forms. The first form is a mentoring model. This is a leader who is well-experienced and effective in ministry who become models of ministry for *developing leaders* to follow and in some cases imitate. These models are important because they show how things can be done! However, there are significant limitations with such models, often simply just the access a *developing leader* can have to such leaders. For many it means learning from a distance.

*Developing leaders* need a much more intimate and intense form of mentoring that can be provided by the second form of mentors. This type of mentor is one who is able to assist the *developing leader* reflect on his or her ministry call, its activity and outworking in the *developing leader's* life. This type of mentor is involved in ministry and leadership, and is stable and confident in his or her own life, calling and ministry. They do not need to have ministry experience in the same area as that of the *developing leaders*, but they do need to have the ability to help the *developing leader* reflect and grow through the mentoring process. They need to be able to ask the right type of questions and probing that will ensure that the *developing leader* is kept accountable to his or her reflective goals and activity. That is, they need to understand the importance of leadership praxis and how it assists the *developing leader* to grow and develop in leadership and ministry.

Mentors play an important part in the learning process and thus need to have certain characteristics, they need to be:

- **Experienced Leaders:** the mentor needs to be a person in ministry who can provide a positive demonstration of how to handle conflict, personality differences, and multiple demands on his or her time. During the mentoring time the mentor in many different ways will be sharing his or her concept and philosophy of ministry. It is important that the mentor does this wisely;

94

- **Open and Vulnerable:** the mentor needs to be able to share and demonstrate self-understanding, self-awareness, and self-acceptance. He or she needs to know who they are as persons, ministers and leaders;

- **Skilled:**   the mentor needs to be skilled in both doing ministry and reflecting on ministry processes;

- **Available:** it is important that the mentor takes seriously the process of learning going on in this project. He or she needs to have the right amount of time available to spend with the *developing leader*. This should be approximately 10-12 hours of mentoring time over a 10 to 12 monthly period;

- **Reflection:** the mentor needs to have qualities that lean towards helping the *developing leader* reflect on:

    - His or her ministry experience, in the light of the learning goals he or she sets;

    - Developing relational skills;

    - Theological and Biblical issues involved in their ministry.

- **Learning Covenant:** the mentor needs to be capable of helping the *developing leaders* put together a learning covenant that will provide the structure for the learning and mentoring process they will be involved in;

- **Limited Commitment:** the mentoring role does not infer an ongoing relationship with the *developing leader* after the course is finished.

It is natural that there will be differences between the Mentor and the *developing leader*. These will include, in most cases, the experience level in ministry, leadership, development of skills and the establishment of goals and their implementation.[133] They will also include differences in personal religious and theological understanding. R. Coll notes that the way these differences are addressed will affect the nature of mentoring and development that will occur. He notes three outcomes from these natural, yet important differences:

- **Poor mentoring:** rejects differences as unimportant and unacceptable and thus never entering into honest exchange;

- **Adequate Mentoring:** tries to ignore the differences and pretends that they do not affect ministry. It holds a sort of live-and-let-live attitude, acting as if all ideas, principles, and convictions are equally valid; as if it is only necessary to articulate our beliefs, never to have them challenged but only affirmed;

- **Excellent Mentoring:** differences are used regularly to enhance and enrich the learning experience for both the *developing leader* and mentor.[134]

---

[133] Collins, *Are All Christian Ministers?*, 22.
[134] Collins, *Are All Christian Ministers?*, 22-23.

The mentor supervises the reflective process the *developing leaders* goes through, not the ministry activity itself. The mentor is not there to tell the *developing leaders* how to do the ministry, but to encourage the *developing leader* to think through the issues related to ministry and leadership and bring understanding to the actions they take as leaders as well as the activity of ministry they carry out. To ensure that proper accountability is addressed in regards to the reflective process the mentor is not a best friend to the *developing leader*, even though their sessions will be carried out in a friendly manner.[135] The mentor is also not a counsellor. If, in the process of reflection a need for counselling arises, the mentor will suggest that the *developing leader* seek such counselling from someone else, not from the mentor. The mentoring process has its own agenda and goals to fulfil and both the mentor and *developing leader* need to remain accountable to that agenda and those goals, otherwise the mentoring process, with its leadership praxis, will fall short of the important development process it can achieve.

## DEVELOPING UNIQUE GIFTING

Peter Drucker, in his book, *"Managing in a Time of Great Change,"* notes the deep change in paradigm that has occurred in our culture. He proposes that this requires a reassessment of the development of learning in a person's life. He says, "All it requires is to focus on the strengths and talents of learners so that they excel in whatever it is they do well."[136] He makes the point that schools do not do it. They focus on a learner's weaknesses. The reason they do this is that no one can predict the long-term future of a child, so they feel the need to endow the child with basic skills. They have to be able to function.[137] We may or may not agree that all leaders should be able to read, write and do arithmetic. In order to function in our society. It helps for them to have a certain level of competency in those things.

However, each of those things is related to one type of intelligence, in which not all persons excel. In recent years many schools have become more aware of training leaders in more than one type of intelligence; noting also that no one type of intelligence is better than another; they simply have a different use and application. Charles Handy in his book *"Age of Unreason,"* outlines Howard Gardner's "Types of Intelligence," which identify different types of intelligence and thus, also different patterns of learning. These include:

- *Analytical intelligence;*
- *Pattern intelligence* – the ability to see patterns in things and to create patterns;

---

[135] Collins, *Are All Christian Ministers?*, 24.
[136] Drucker, *Managing in a Time of Great Change*, 229.
[137] Drucker, *Managing in a Time of Great Change*, 229.

- *Musical intelligence;*

- *Physical intelligence;*

- *Practical intelligence* – e.g. technicians;

- *Intra-personal intelligence* – in tune with feelings, their own and others; and

- *Inter-personal intelligence* – ability to get on with other people, to get things done with and through others. [138]

People will generally have one type of intelligence or a mix of different types of intelligence. Handy notes that it is important that every leader should leave school demonstrably successful in at least one of the above intelligences.[139] Though they may not necessarily excel in the basics, especially if those basics are analytically derived, they should at least excel in the area of the intelligence or intelligences they possess. Developing leaders in the area of their intelligence or intelligences is really building upon their strengths, not their weaknesses. It is important to note that not only do schools tend to focus upon the development of leader's weaknesses, but graduate and post-graduate teaching bodies, such as Theological or Bible Colleges, tend to do that too. They also reason that a person has to be able to function in ministry, so they make sure that they teach and equip their leaders in the basics.

In doing so, it is quite easy to establish a system that tends to focus on helping them improve their weaknesses, whilst not realizing that at the same time they are probably diminishing their strengths. Worse still is to focus on areas that previous leaders have been weak on, and try to instill them in new leaders who may or may not have those weaknesses. Drucker concludes:

> But one cannot build performance on weaknesses, even on corrected ones. One can build performance only on strengths.... Strengths do not create problems. And schools are problem-focused. [140]

It is not that we should ignore teaching leaders the basics, but that we should also be addressing their individual learning needs and enabling them to grow in the places where they are strong; that is, to grow in the areas where God has actually and uniquely gifted them.

John Maxwell makes a similar point when he proposes that it is a waste of time and effort to try to improve weaknesses instead of strengths. He notes that on a scale of 1 to 10 we can only really improve about 3 to 4 points. Thus if we have an ability that we would grade at "2 out of 10", any improvement of that ability would bring it up to a "5 or 6 out of 10".

---

[138] Handy, 20. 174.

[139] Handy, 20, 174.

[140] Drucker, *Managing in a Time of Great Change*, 229.

There is little point or purpose in improving such an ability. Whereas, if we have an ability that is a "5 out of 10", then working to improve that ability would mean it could become an "8 or 9 out of 10". That is well worth doing.

In the parable of the talents Jesus focuses upon the use of *opportunity* given to three different servants.[141] Each servant was given a different level of resource. Though the first two were given more than the third, the assessment of their success was based upon the use they made of their given resources not the level of them. The servant who had been given one talent was assessed on the lack of investment he made with what he had been given. He didn't use what he had. Two things robbed this servant of his destiny.

1. First, his perception of his master was different to that held by the other two servants. To him his master was a hard man, which hadn't seemed to bother the other two servants.

2. Second, he had allowed fear to rule his life and buried the resources that had been given to him. His perception and fear robbed him of the reward the other two servants received.

From the master's perspective, not to use the talent at all was worse than to have risked it and lost it. However, this perspective of the master was not obvious to the servant. Notice the subsequent description of the servant as one who was wicked and slothful. Does focusing on the weakness of a minister, servant or leader, rather than their strengths develop a process in their life that eventually leads to slothfulness and laziness? Certainly it leads to underachievement in the persons involved. However, this is not merely an underachievement in the area of their weaknesses, but more significantly in the area of their strengths.[142]

The importance of having some type of process that helps us key into the *developing leaders'* unique gift mix, capabilities and the application of their intelligences is further highlighted by the way in which people learn and the different way people take in information.

---

[141] Matthew 25:14-28.

[142] In order to help all our students and leaders identify and use their God given resources for the building of His Kingdom, we use the following mentoring programs:

1. *SAM* program (*Supervision – Accountability – Mentoring*), to help us focus upon the development of our pastors and leaders;

2. *Sebl* program (*Supervised Experience Based Learning*) to help us focus on the development and our college students. This provides at least one place in the leader's ongoing training and the student's education where we can address their unique and individual gifts, strengths and abilities and help them to grow in those abilities.

3. Gift Discovery Program - we also take the leader or student through a Gift Discovery Program called *Maximising People for Ministry*, that helps the leader and student understand the gifts, abilities and resources God has bestowed on him or her.

## The Way People Learn

The development of a leader's unique gifting also needs to take into account different learning styles, as well as, different intelligences learnt in different ways. We must, to a certain extent, address leader's individual learning styles. John Mallison notes the following styles of learning that different people use:

- Observation and asking questions;
- Listening and applying;
- Visual presentations;
- Reading; and
- Interacting in small groups.

He notes that adults primarily learn through experience-based learning because as people perform activities they find ways of doing things better. They tend to make conscious effort to process and learn from experiences.[143]

## The Way People Assimilate Information

Hersey, Blanchard and Johnson note that people's behavior is based upon certain psychological maps they form. These psychological maps relate not only to the information they take in, but also the means by which they assimilate that information. Though the information comes in via the senses of sight, hearing, smell, taste and touch, how they are assimilated is different. The selective awareness that creates these psychological maps is a result of a deluge of information that people just can't take in. These maps affect the way people *perceive* and *interpret* truth and reality. They note that:

> People use their psychological maps to make decisions, to get around in life. However, the map is not the territory. It is based upon perceptions of that territory. And these perceptions differ from person to person.[144]

They divide the different ways people assimilate information into four different groups, [145] which include:

- **Visuals:** are picture people. They are comfortable mapping their psychological worlds in pictures. During group sessions they tend to cluster to the rear of the room to keep all the data out in front of them.

---

[143] John Mallison, *Mentoring to Develop Disciples and Leaders* (Sydney: Open Books, 1998), 104-105; Mallison, 105.

[144] P. Hersey, K. Blanchard, D. Johnson, *Management of Organizational Behavior*, (NJ: Prentice Hall, 1996), 348.

[145] Hersey, Blanchard, and Johnson, 349.

- **Kinesthetics:** feelings people. They are most comfortable mapping their psychological worlds from internal and external feelings. During group sessions they tend to cluster up front, they want to feel the presentation.

- **Auditories:** sounds or "tonal" people. They tend to map their psychological world from sounds. During group sessions they tend to cluster to the side, depending on their best ear.

- **Digitals:** word people, a hybrid of the other three. They have to translate raw data into a specific language – through words or numbers or computer symbols – before they can map their psychological worlds. During group sessions they tend to move around, depending on what is being assimilated.

Although, in this mentoring process, we will not be focusing on all these aspects, it does enable us to begin to address the individual learning and growth needs in *developing leaders'* ministry lives. Growth needs that the *developing leaders* need to be as much aware of this as we are.

# Chapter Twelve

# Building Our Strengths

## Sane Estimate of Ourselves

Discovering and building on our strengths however are hampered by our perception of what those gifts could be. Paul writes,

> Don't cherish exaggerated ideas of yourself and your own importance, but try to have a sane estimate of your capabilities by the light of the faith that God has given to us all.[146]

A sane estimate of our capabilities means that we neither overestimate nor underestimate what God has given to us. In the parable noted above, the one talented servant underestimated the importance of the resource given to him. Many Christians, on the one hand, feel that it is vain or arrogant to claim any significant ability or skill and will rarely put themselves forward to do things, even though their heart and the Holy Spirit are calling them to do so. These people need to be encouraged to use the gifts and abilities God has given to them. Other Christians, on the other hand, have an overestimated and exaggerated perception of their gifts and abilities. Our difficulty with these types of Christians is twofold: first, they rarely listen to anything we say to dissuade them from the exaggerated opinion of their own gifts and abilities. Secondly, how do we know that God has not given them a vision of what they can be, that is in no way obvious now? It is also important to note that God has this intense penchant to use ordinary everyday people to achieve impossible feats. Paul writes,

> For the foolishness of God is wiser than men, and the weakness of God is stronger than men. For consider your call, brethren; not many of you were wise according to worldly standards, not many were powerful, not many were of noble birth; but God chose what is foolish in the world to shame the wise, God chose what is weak in the world to shame the strong, God chose what is low and despised in the world, even things that are not, to bring to nothing things that are, so that no human being might boast in the presence of God. (1 Corinthians 1:25-29).

## Biblical Perception of Strengths and Weaknesses

When we look at the Biblical testimony concerning the area of our weaknesses, we discover that our weaknesses do not daunt God anywhere nearly as much as they daunt us. In fact, God is more troubled by our unredeemed and unsanctified strengths, than any

---

[146] Romans 12:3 Phillips Bible.

weaknesses we might have. Paul understood the impact of his own weaknesses in his life, but learnt that God was able to turn those weaknesses into strengths. He wrote:

> Three times I besought the Lord about this, that it should leave me; but he said to me, "My grace is sufficient for you, for my power is made perfect in weakness." I will all the more gladly boast of my weaknesses, that the power of Christ may rest upon me.... for when I am weak, then I am strong" (2 Corinthians 12:8-10).

God through the sacrifice of His Son, Jesus Christ, upon the cross has supplemented our weaknesses with His own strength, so that when we turn those weaknesses over to Him He is able to do a unique work in us and through us, because of those weakness. Paul wrote:

> Blessed be the God and Father of our Lord Jesus Christ, the Father of mercies and God of all comfort, who comforts us in all our affliction, so that we may be able to comfort those who are in any affliction, with the comfort with which we ourselves are comforted by God (2 Corinthians 1:3-4).

Both Peter and Paul are in fact are quite concerned that we use the strengths that God has given to us and we develop and use the gifts that He has bestowed upon us. They write:

> As each has received a gift, employ it for one another, as good stewards of God's varied grace: whoever speaks, as one who utters oracles of God; whoever renders service, as one who renders it by the strength which God supplies; in order that in everything God may be glorified through Jesus Christ (1 Peter 4:10-11).

> For by the grace given to me I bid every one among you not to think of himself more highly than he ought to think, but to think with sober judgment, each according to the measure of faith which God has assigned him. For as in one body we have many members, and all the members do not have the same function, so we, though many, are one body in Christ, and individually members one of another. Having gifts that differ according to the grace given to us, let us use them (Romans 12:3-6).

> Now there are varieties of gifts, but the same Spirit; and there are varieties of service, but the same Lord; and there are varieties of working, but it is the same God who inspires them all in every one. To each is given the manifestation of the Spirit for the common good (1 Corinthians 12:3-7).

Part of our role is to help *developing leaders* to discover, test and use God given gifts, skills and abilities. We need to help them focus on what He called them to do and how to use the unique skills and abilities He has given to them. At the same time, we help them to understand themselves as people in ministry, to build upon their strengths and to minimize the impact of their weaknesses. The importance of this revolves around the fact that though we are redeemed and sanctified by the King of Kings, we are still "wounded healers".[147] As such, we minister out of an awareness of our unworthiness, our incompleteness and our weaknesses (2 Corinthians 12:7-10). It is important that we are aware of our own frailty when we minister to others, lest we carry our problems into their situation. The mentoring process also allows us to help *developing leaders* identify the activity of the Holy Spirit ministering through them to bring healing, restoration and new life to others.

## BUILDING STRENGTHS

The one talented servant, noted in the parable above, failed to see the latent power in the talent he had been given. He failed to use the strengths he had been given and subsequently lost everything because of it. When we focus on our weaknesses, instead of our strengths, we tend to lose the power of those strengths to overcome the difficulties we face. Kennon Callahan notes, "Substantial power is generated when we discover and claim our strengths: Power for the future is found in claiming our strengths, not in focusing on our weaknesses and shortcomings."[148] He notes that in order to use and develop our God-given gifts we need to:

- Identify our existing strengths;

- Own existing strengths;

- Develop existing strengths;

- Complement existing strengths.

### Identifying our existing strengths

- We have all been given strengths and abilities by God to be used for the building of His Kingdom. Identifying those strengths and abilities enables us to see how God wants to use us in the building of that Kingdom.

- Because we are focusing on God-given strengths and abilities it brings God into the centre of our vision and goal setting activities.

- It helps us to understand that no one person is competent in every area. God has given each of us different gifts and abilities. Callahan notes, "If God had wanted to create perfect pastors, likely, God would have done so. It is the sharing in diversity that creates mission and community."[149]

---

[147] See Henri Nouwen's *The Wounded Healer: Ministry in Contemporary Society.*
[148] Callahan, 178.
[149] Callahan, 178.

- We also need to identify and differentiate between primary and secondary strengths. Primary strengths are our core strengths that form the basis for our success and achievement. Secondary strengths are those that support the primary strength in the achievement of that success.

### Owning existing strengths

- As we saw with the one talented servant, if we do not own the strengths and abilities God has given to us, we will not use them for the building of His Kingdom.

- We not only need to own, but to use the strengths and abilities that God has given to us for the building of His Kingdom.

### Develop existing Strengths

- ***Becoming more effective in God's purposes*** - When we expand our strengths, gifts, graces, and talents, we become more effective in the mission and work God has called us to do.

- ***Diminishing strengths*** - When we become preoccupied with our weaknesses, we begin to lose our strengths as well. Strengths that are not used weaken and decay. Continued neglect of our strengths can produce atrophy and subsequently apathy to the call of God in our life and its outworking for the Kingdom of God. Rowthorn highlights this in her argument concerning the neglect of lay ministry and its effect when she writes, "The Church's laity are those who have been prevented from giving their gifts. When the voice cannot be heard, it becomes mute; when insights go unnoticed, sight is lost; when loving hands reach out to give a gift that is not received, the hands – and the whole body – become paralyzed."[150]

- ***The need to build our strengths*** - We need to be building our strengths through additional learning, experience and exercise. When we do not exercise our muscles then they become flabby. When we do not exercise our strengths then they too become flabby. Professional people continually train and tune up their skills. "But what differentiates the pro in any of these vocations is the capacity to discern what one is doing well, to recognize what one is doing poorly, and to initiate constructive action toward improvement." [151]

---

[150] Rowthorn, 22.
[151] Callahan, 176.

*Adding New Strengths:* [152]

- *Building on current strengths* - New strengths should build on present strengths in substantial and supplementary ways.

- *Resist the temptation to fill the gaps* - Most of us misunderstand this fundamental principle. Regrettably, we do a "fill the gaps" approach to developing our future. We focus on our weaknesses and rush around busily trying to fill all the gaps and overcome all those weaknesses. We imagine that all the gaps must be filled this year or next, and thus try to do too much too soon. We set ourselves impossible tasks, thus setting ourselves up for failure, and then becoming preoccupied with our newfound failures.

- *Strategic new strengths* - The art of long-range planning and goal setting in our lives is to decide those few strategic new strengths that it makes sense to add in the coming five to seven years.

- *Your best 20%* - The Pareto Principle notes that 20% of your priorities will produce 80% of your production, If you spend your time, energy, money, and personnel on the top 20% of your priorities.[153] Of ten objectives that you might work toward, two will be decisive in shaping your future. The other eight will be helpful and useful; the central two will be strategic and decisive. The art of strategic long-range planning is to focus on the 20% that will accomplish most of the results.

- *Guide to adding new strengths* - In adding new strengths, it is important that you decide on those few key strengths:

  1. That build on and supplement your present strengths, and

  2. That will be strategically decisive in advancing your future and destiny.

Part and parcel of the Christian life is an ongoing growth that produces fruitfulness in our lives. We need to focus on the development of our strengths so that we can continue to be one of God's laborers in the harvest.

---

[152] Kennon Callahan, *Twleve Keys to an Effective Church* (San Francisco: Harper, 1983), xviii.
[153] John Maxwell, *Developing the Leader within You* (Nashville: Thomas Nelson Publishers, 1993), 20.

# Chapter Thirteen

# The Mentoring Process

## Sharpening our self-awareness

The Johari Window provides a helpful model of how we learn by sharpening our self-awareness through the mentoring process. It is used by a variety of management gurus in relation to the development of people's skills and abilities. In this section I have adapted the version used by Hersey, Blanchard and Johnson in their book *Management of Organizational Behaviour*.

For our purposes the Johari window looks at aspects of our strengths and weaknesses that are known to us and others. In Figure 12-2 it divides the type of perception of these strengths and weaknesses into four quadrants: Public, Blind, Private and Unknown.

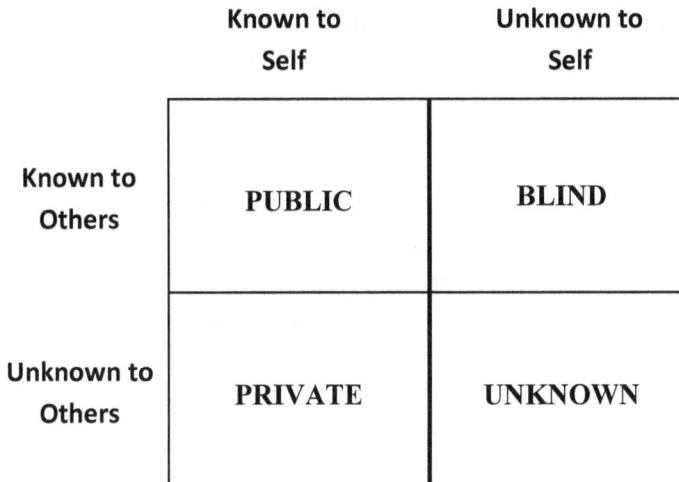

|  | Known to Self | Unknown to Self |
|---|---|---|
| **Known to Others** | PUBLIC | BLIND |
| **Unknown to Others** | PRIVATE | UNKNOWN |

**Diagram 12-2 The Johari Window.**[154]

1. **Public:** the open or public self refers to what I am aware of in myself (mannerisms, thoughts, feelings, beliefs, experiences, etc.), and which others are also aware of, either because it is obvious or because I have freely shared this information about myself with them.

2. **Blind:** the blind self refers to those aspects of myself to which I am oblivious, but which are obvious to others.

---

[154] Hersey, Blanchard, and Johnson, 304.

3. **Private:** the concealed or private self refers to information about myself that I withhold or try to hide from others. They are kept private because I may have:

   ▪ Come from a background that didn't encourage sharing self – stiff upper-lip;

   ▪ Been vulnerable in the past and had my trust betrayed, thus causing me to hold things in; and

   ▪ Have a low self-esteem and thus hide my true self behind a mask for fear of rejection.

   There are private aspects of our lives that are simply private; yet the sharing of other private aspects with a mentor help us discover the unknown potential within us.

4. **Unknown:** the unknown self refers to the realm of my hidden potential, the unconscious area of my life and perhaps also areas of repressed memories. [155]

## DEVELOPING OUR SELF - AWARENESS

*Diagram 12-2* above shows the interaction of different aspects of our personality, strengths and weakness which are known to us and others. In the following diagram – *Diagram 12-4 Effect Of Feedback & Disclosure on the Johari Window* - we see the movement within the window that occurs as a result of the mentoring process.

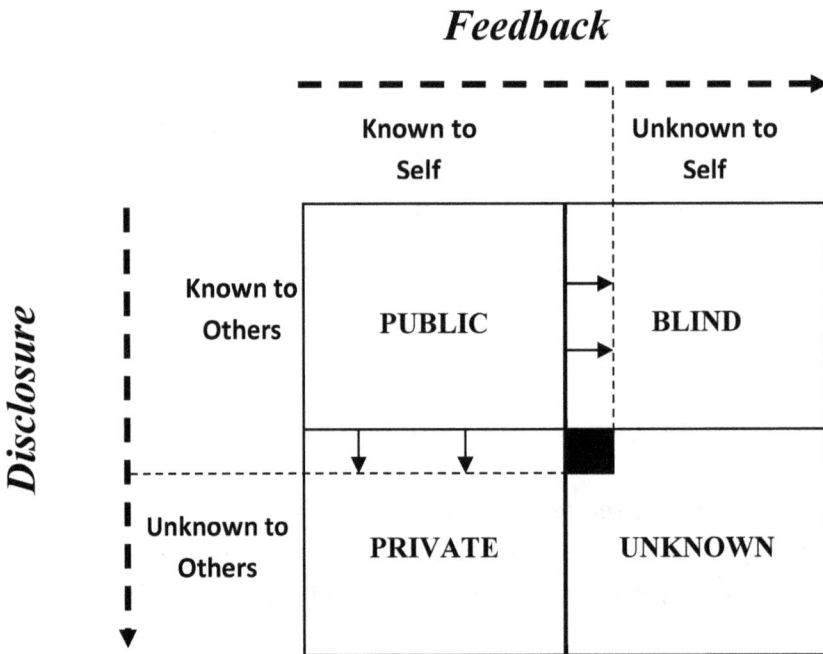

**Diagram 12-4 Effect Of Feedback & Disclosure on the Johari Window.[156]**

---

[155] Mallison, 72.
[156] Hersey, Blanchard, and Johnson, 308.

This shows the interaction in the mentoring process of the developing leader disclosing more of the private part of his or her life and reflective feedback from the Mentor. From this we see:

- A lot of our untapped potential lies in the "unknown" portion of our being.

- It is through the work of the Holy Spirit that God wants us to become more aware of ourselves and thus discover more of that "unknown" about ourselves. Paul writes,

  > But, as it is written, "What no eye has seen, nor ear heard, nor the heart of man conceived, what God has prepared for those who love him," God has revealed to us through the Spirit. For the Spirit searches everything, even the depths of God. For what person knows a man's thoughts except the spirit of the man, which is in him? So also no one comprehends the thoughts of God except the Spirit of God. Now we have received not the spirit of the world, but the Spirit which is from God, that we might understand the gifts bestowed on us by God *(1 Corinthians 2:9-12)*.

- We are thus able to utilise and develop parts of our life that we have not tapped in the past, primarily because we have been unaware of their existence;

- The small filled-in box in the top left-hand corner of the Unknown quadrant represents a part of the unknown about ourselves that we can discover through good use of supervised experienced-based learning;

- This occurs through small movements in a balance of receiving feedback from others, and further disclosing ourselves to someone in an atmosphere of trust and respect;

- It is small because we are vulnerable people and we should work carefully and slowly towards knowing more of ourselves and becoming more whole in our entire being.

## MODEL FOR LEARNING

The Supervised Experience-based learning program expects to help equip *developing leaders* to address and develop their strengths, whilst supplementing their weaknesses, in four ways:

1. To understand their own strengths and weaknesses in the light of which they will be developing a model for their own ministry and a clearer understanding of the theological basis of this ministry;

2. To nurture the ability to think theologically and biblically about the practical tasks of ministry;

3. To acquire the necessary skills for effective ministry; and

4. To help integrate the various components in their theological education with their life and ministry experience, namely, classroom learning, professional skills, personal attitudes and spiritual formation.[157]

The following learning model shows the stages involved in the process of learning, by reflection upon ministry experience, with the help of a mentor.[158]

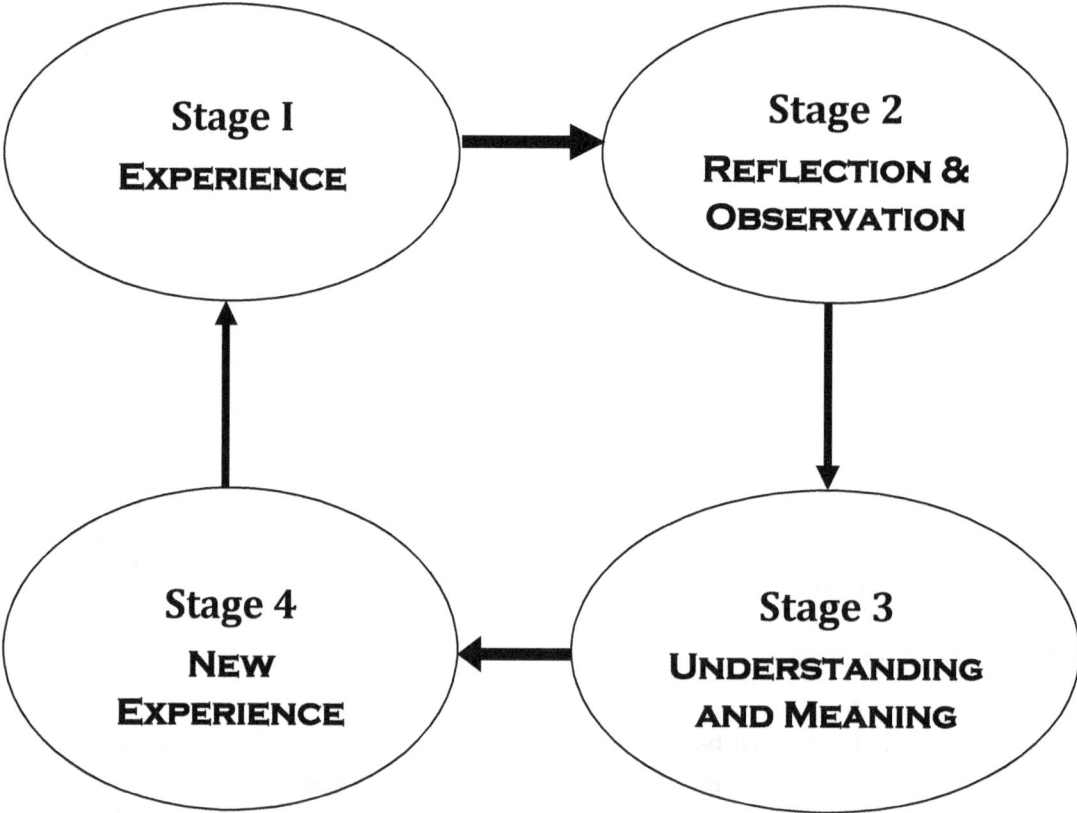

---

[157] Anglican Diocese of Melbourne, *Introduction to Supervised Field Education,* (Supervised Field Education), 4.
[158] Anglican Diocese of Melbourne, *Notes for Candidates,* (Supervised Field Education), 5.

**Stage 1: Experience** - this begins with what actually happened. It is the description of the incident, meeting, pastoral care situation, etc. with the use of reflective material such as verbatim, case studies, etc.

**Stage 2: Reflection and Observation** - this involves reflecting upon the experience and its impact. It means exploring some of the surrounding and underlying factors that influenced the experience – setting, time, mood, expectations.

**Stage 3: Understanding and meaning** - this involves the process of understanding the experience, and learning something of its meaning and importance in the light of the Biblical and theological teaching.

**Stage 4: New Experience** - In the light of this past experience, this involves preparing to move on to the next experience better equipped for ministry.

## THE MENTORING PROCESS

Essential elements in the mentoring model include:[159]

- **Presentation of Ministry Event or Experience** - the *developing leader* agrees to present an outline of an actual ministry event or experience. This is usually done by a verbatim or case study, but can also be presented by audio or video cassette, narrative account or by other means agreed to by the mentor;

- **Reflection on Ministry Experience** - the mentor helps the *developing leader* to reflect upon what happened. Mentoring is reflective discipline - a means by which the mentor can help the *developing leader* to be aware of possibilities, strengths, missed opportunities, blind-spots, etc. The aim is to help the *developing leader* strengthen his or her capacity of self-evaluation; and

- **Developing Ministry Skills** - personal development usually occurs in the mentoring process, but the main focus is on *developing ministry skills.* This is an educational model and needs to be distinguished from counselling or psychotherapy. If the *developing leader* shows a need for counselling or some other form of help, then the mentor will recommend they see someone who can help in that area of need.

---

[159] Anglican Diocese of Melbourne, *The Supervisory Process,* (Supervised Field Education), 1.

# CHAPTER FOURTEEN

# THE MENTORING SESSIONS

## THE MENTORING CONFERENCE

### Length and Time of Conferences

- **Total** of 10 to 12 hours of mentoring conference time spread out over the period of mentoring, usually ten to twelve months. This includes the evaluation process at the end of that time, but does not include the time preparing the learning covenant.

- **Length** of each conference should be about an hour, with one session in the middle of the time period of two hours.

### *Developing leader* Presentation at Conferences

- For each of these conferences the *developing leader* should present some form of written report (or tape or video presentation where applicable. E.g. tape or video of a sermon) on an aspect of his or her responsibilities.  These may be in the form of a verbatim, a case study, a report on a pastoral incident, a theological critique or some other written report as requested by the mentor, e.g. a manuscript of a sermon.

- Mentors may ask to receive a copy before the conference.

### The Conference Itself [160]

It is helpful to view the conference as having three main components:

- **Opening:**
  - Welcoming and catching up with one another;
  - Review agenda of conference, i.e. clarify what is expected to happen.

- **Main Focus:**
  - Presentation of material by the *developing leader;*
  - Response by the Mentor;

---

[160] Anglican Diocese of Melbourne, *Notes for Candidates,* 4.

- Discussion and exploration of ministry experience, strengths, areas needing attention; and ways of doing ministry more effectively.

- **Conclusion:**

  - Summarize any action needed to be taken by the *developing leader* before the next conference;

  - Work out details of material needed for the next conference;

  - Confirmation of time, date, and place of the next mentoring conference.

It is important to hold the mentoring conference as a separate meeting from other meetings at which the *developing leader* may be present, e.g. staff meetings. The goals of these two meetings are quite different. The task of the mentoring conference is to focus upon the educational needs of the *developing leader* and this task cannot be appropriately exercised in a meeting geared for a different purpose.[161]

## THE PROCESS OF MENTORING

In the reflection process, following the *developing leader's* presentation of a verbatim or case study (or similar), the Anglican Diocese of Melbourne' *The Supervisory Process notes* outline the following five basic types of mentoring response that are helpful:

- **Probing** - seeking further information about the situation, encouraging further discussion, querying;

- **Understanding** - making sure that the mentor has properly understood the meaning and importance of what the *developing leader* has presented. Some exploration of feelings may go on;

- **Evaluative** - indicating that the mentor has made some value judgment about the appropriateness, helpfulness or rightness of the *developing leader's* ministry or response;

- **Interpretive** - indicating that the mentor wishes to impart meaning to the *developing leader*, or adopt a teaching role; and

- **Supportive** - indicating the mentor's intention is to reassure the *developing leader*, reduce anxiety, and be generally helpful. [162]

---

[161] Anglican Diocese of Melbourne, *Notes for Candidates,* 4.
[162] Anglican Diocese of Melbourne, *The Supervisory Process,* 3.

## Problems about Learning

the Anglican Diocese of Melbourne' *The Supervisory Process notes* outline some typical problems that arise in the relationship between the mentor and *developing leader* are:

- **Authority of the Mentor** - some *developing leaders* find it hard to accept the authority of a mentor – suggestions are rejected and the *developing leader* finds it difficult to draw on the experience and wisdom of the mentor;

- **Dependence upon the mentor** - *developing leaders* can become so anxious that they are fearful of taking any initiative without consultation or advice. Often this is an indication that they are unable to trust their own experience, or that the mentor is too authoritarian;

- **Evasion of agreed procedures** - appointments are not kept, work is not produced on time, or *developing leaders* arrive late. Often, these behaviours indicate that all is not well with the relationship between mentor and *developing leader*, or that the learning covenant has been sabotaged. Sometimes the focus moves too often from the verbatim to the personal needs of the candidate (or mentor). At other times, problems can be intellectualized, i.e. an academic discussion rather than a focus on the issue at hand. [163]

## Games in Mentoring

In the mentoring process, opportunities for change and growth are always present. However, the challenge of change can be a painful and anxiety-provoking experience; thus some candidates attempt to reduce that anxiety by playing "games." The following are examples of the most common games played by *developing leaders* in pastoral education:[164]

*"I have three papers to write this week,"* i.e. I am too busy to worry about a verbatim;

*"You are the best mentor I have ever had,"* i.e. flattery will get you everywhere;

*"Treat me, don't beat me",* i.e. please counsel me;

*"Evaluation is not for friends",* i.e. we get along so well so don't ruin a good relationship by demanding work from me;

*"If you knew Tillich like I know Tillich",* i.e. my theological knowledge is more up-to-date than yours;

---

[163] Anglican Diocese of Melbourne, *The Supervisory Process*, 3.
[164] Anglican Diocese of Melbourne, *The Supervisory Process*, 4.

***"What do you know about it anyway"***, i.e. in some departments of life I'm more experienced than you;

***"I've got a little list"***, i.e. I'll keep you so busy with my list of questions that you won't have time to confront me;

***"Heading them off at the past"***, i.e. my work is really not up to the standard this week so there's not much point in wasting time considering it;

***"I did it as you told me"***, i.e. it's your fault it hasn't turned out right;

***"What you don't know won't hurt me"***, i.e. I'm only going to present those aspects that show me in a good light.

Note too that mentors can also play games!

When either the mentor or *developing leader* (or both) play "games" in the mentoring process then the two people involved enter into a non-work or work avoidance mental state. When either or both do that then they fail to achieve the purpose and goal for the mentoring conference itself, which is to work on the goals set down in the learning covenant. When such a non-work mental state exists then negative feelings rule and problem-solving becomes incomplete and inadequate. [165]

Games are only possible when two people desire to play them. The mentor can refuse to play, or confront the *developing leader* concerning the defensive mechanisms they are using. An exploration of why the *developing leader* needs to play such games and use defensive mechanisms can be a real growing point for both the *developing leader* and mentor.

## HOW *DEVELOPING LEADERS* CAN HELP THEIR MENTORS

Mentors expect certain things from their *developing leaders* that encourage them to maintain the relationship. John Mallison notes the following ways *developing leaders* can assist their mentors in the process of mentoring:

- **Teachable Spirit:** Mentors should never come across as know-it-alls and they certainly don't want that attitude in those they are seeking to help, though their *developing leaders* will often be ahead of them in various ways. They look for humble openness to learn. Most mentors will readily acknowledge that it is a learning experience for them also;

---

[165] Oscar Mink, Barbara Mink, and Keith Owen, *Groups at Work* (New Jersey: Educational Technology Publications, 1990), 18.

116

- **Ability to reflect:** your mentor will be helping you become more reflective by the questions he or she asks you. So be aware of not being defensive or over-reacting to such probing questions;

- **Performance:** mentors lose interest in *developing leaders* who don't take the relationship seriously – who repeatedly, without sound reasons, don't do the things they agreed to do. Mentors look for an eagerness to learn, courage to take risks, a growing maturity and readiness to take responsibility. Attitude and actions are important. Mentors enjoy seeing *developing leaders* growing personally and spiritually;

- **Growth in spirituality:** mentors don't look for unreal piety, but they are encouraged when the basic spiritual disciplines are taken seriously and progress becomes evident;

- **Responsibility:** dependency will be discouraged. Being responsible for one's own actions will be encouraged. *Developing leaders* should own their own attitudes and their behaviour and deal with these aspects appropriately. Mentors like to see *developing leaders* lead as leaders, being good team builders and knowing how to be answerable and accept that 'the buck stops' with them;

- **Reliability:** mentors are usually busy people so be on time for appointments. Seek to meet deadlines and pursue excellence in what you do;

- **Appreciation:** mentors need to be affirmed and encouraged too, but not flattered.[166]

---

[166] Mallison, 182.

# CHAPTER FIFTEEN

## THE MINISTRY (LEARNING) COVENANT

Supervised Experienced-based Learning uses a "Mentoring (Learning) Covenant" or agreement to develop and enhance the *developing leader's* ability to find God's direction for his or her life and ministry.

*"If you don't know where you are going,*
*you may end up somewhere else."*[167]

A learning covenant is established between the *developing leader* and his or her mentor. This covenant outlines the leaning goals that are being addressed, whilst the *developing leader* is involved in practical ministry.

Gary Pearson notes a number of ways in which a learning covenant helps the learning process:

- **God's Direction:** the learning covenant aims to help develop and enhance the *developing leaders'* ability to find God's direction for their life and ministry;

- **Ownership:** the learning covenant allows the *developing leaders* to take responsibility for their own learning and growth, which help to create;

- **Self-commitment:** they will be committed to make their goals become a reality because they have a major voice in setting those goals;

- **Self-motivation:** they will strive harder to reach their own goals;

- **Self-direction:** they can direct the working toward the fulfilment of their goals when they know the desired results and have developed a plan for reaching them;

- **Self-discipline:** they can use observations and feedback to make corrections;

- **Self-management:** they have more freedom to manage their time, energy, and other available resources;

- **Self-rewards:** they are not dependent on others to recognize meaningful results and increased competency;

- **Self-esteem:** they are building their own self-esteem throughout this process;

- **Trust:** the learning covenant helps to build trust between the developing leaders and the mentor – both know what they are there to do;

---

[167] David Campbell.

- **Uniqueness:** the learning covenant helps each developing leader to identify and develop his or her own unique gifts and skills. They are not there to be moulded by the ministry setting or to become a clone of the mentor;

- **Structure:** the learning covenant helps to provide the structure for the learning and ministry process;

- **Focus:** the learning covenant helps the *developing leader* to focus his or her time and energy on the ministry task and its learning component.[168]

## WRITING LEARNING GOALS

The first process in completing the Learning Agreement is establishment of certain goals. In the process of setting these goals, *developing leaders* and mentors are to keep in mind the four main areas of supervised experience-based learning:

1. The practice of ministry and the development of skills of ministry;

2. Personal growth;

3. Theological critique and reflection;

4. Spiritual formation and development. [169]

As *developing leader* and mentor consider the goals, it is helpful to keep in mind the possible ways for the achievement of these goals. It is important to be able to tell whether goals have been achieved. Such things as completion of a program, a number of tasks, or changes in the *developing leader's* way of ministering, are means of being able to discern whether goals have been achieved.[170] Gary Pearson describes the following SMART goal outline that gives us a basis for achieving those goals:[171]

**S** - **Specific** (an observable behavior if possible);

**M** - **Measurable** (how many, how long);

**A** - **Attainable** (with the resources available such as time, money, etc.);

**R** - **Relevant** (to the *developing leader's* vocational goal or personal growth, etc.);

**T** - **Trackable** (by what dates). [172]

---

[168] W.T. Pyle and M.A Sears, *Experiencing Ministry Supervision* (Nashville: Broadman & Holman, 1995), 51-53.
[169] Anglican Diocese of Melbourne, *Notes for Candidates,* 2.
[170] Anglican Diocese of Melbourne, *Notes for Candidates,* 3.
[171] Pyle and Sears, 60.
[172] Pyle and Sears, 60.

For each goal there must be some corresponding specific objective, which enables the intention of the goal to be checked in some measurable way. Thus it is important to ensure that just as the goals are realistic, so too the steps or specific objectives for their achievement are realistic. Some of the questions to be asked when finalizing objectives are:

1. Is it reasonable to expect the *developing leader* to achieve these objectives?

2. Do the *developing leader* and mentor have access to adequate resources to achieve these objectives?

3. Will these steps enable the *developing leader* to achieve these goals in the time allocated?[173]

A goal statement should answer three questions:

- What? - the end result you expect;

- When? - the target date for completion;

- Who? - the person responsible for doing what is to be done. [174]

## KINDS OF LEARNING GOALS

There are three specific areas that the *developing leader* and mentor need look at when formulating learning goals:

- **Cognitive goal:** a cognitive goal focuses on information you need to "know" - through the study of a formal course, a reading of a book or listening to tapes to learn more about the area of ministry the *developing leader* is doing;

- **Skills goal:** the skills goal is a professional goal that establishes "how to" objectives. It looks at what skills the *developing leader* may want to develop that will improve the *developing leader's* ability to minister to people in the area of the ministry task he or she is doing;

- **Personhood goal:** these goals involve "who you are" as a person. These look at how the *developing leader* might grow as a person in the midst of the ministry task that he or she is doing.[175]

---

[173] Anglican Diocese of Melbourne, *Notes for Candidates,* 2.
[174] Pyle and Sears, 60-61.

## Learning Covenant or Agreement will include:

- Cognitive, skills and personhood goals;

- Will follow the *SMART* goal outline in that each goal will be specific, measurable, attainable, relevant and trackable;

- Each goal will be noted on the Learning Covenant form;

- The Learning covenant has to be signed by the *developing leader*, the mentor and the mentoring programme coordinator before the program begins.

It is recognised that sometimes difficulties are encountered by *developing leaders* and mentors in the completion of the Learning Covenant or Agreement. Often *developing leaders* are not accustomed to determining their own learning goals and find difficulty in being specific about them. However, even these difficulties can provide excellent opportunities for mentors to encourage and guide *developing leaders* into new approaches to learning.[176]

## Learning Covenant or Agreement Form with Sample Completed Form:

The Learning Agreement form contains two sections:

**A/ Outline of Ministry Activity:** this notes the specific ministry work the developing leader will doing that will then be used in the mentoring process to be reflective on. In the case of *developing leaders* doing placement this ensures that the developing leader is doing significant ministry experience.

**B/ State Specific Learning Goals:** this notes the specific mentoring goals that are being addressed by the developing leader during the mentoring process. They include three types of goals:

1. **Cognitive Goals:**

2. **Skills Goals:**

3. **Personhood Goals:**

Under the heading of each of these goals there will be a space to complete:

1. **the strategy for achieving each goal or aim;**

2. **the measurement process that indicates that the goals and aims are being achieved.**

**Sample Form:** this shows how the forms can be completed and note the different goals and aims that can be addressed along with the means by which they can be measure for achievement.

---

[175] Pyle and Sears, 61.

[176] Anglican Diocese of Melbourne, *Notes for Candidates*, 3.

# Chapter Sixteen

# Sam / Sebl

# Ministry (Learning)
# Covenant

# SAM & SUPERVISED EXPERIENCE BASED LEARNING
## PROPOSED MINISTRY (LEARNING) COVENANT

*DEVELOPING LEADER'S* NAME: ......................................................................

ADDRESS: ...............................................................................................

............................................................................................................

TELEPHONE: ......................................................

# A/ OUTLINE OF MINISTRY ACTIVITY:

PROPOSED DATES...................................................................................

............................................................................................................

SUMMARY OF PROPOSED MINISTRY TASK PROJECT:

............................................................................................................

............................................................................................................

............................................................................................................

MENTOR'S NAME: ................................................................................

MENTOR'S ADDRESS: ...........................................................................

MENTOR'S PHONE: ..............................................................................

RELEVANT QUALIFICATIONS OF MENTOR: ............................................

............................................................................................................

WHICH TRAINING COURSE HAS MENTOR ATTENDED? .............................

............................................................................................................

PROPOSED MENTORING ARRANGEMENTS AND DATES: ............................

............................................................................................................

## B/ STATE SPECIFIC LEARNING GOALS:

## 1. COGNITIVE GOALS:

   a) …………………………………………………………………….

   b) …………………………………………………………………….

## 2. SKILLS GOALS:

   a) …………………………………………………………………….

   b) …………………………………………………………………….

### Strategy for achieving each goal:

   a) …………………………………………………………………….

   …………………………………………………………………….

   b) …………………………………………………………………….

   …………………………………………………………………….

### Measurement Process

   a) …………………………………………………………………….

   …………………………………………………………………….

   b) …………………………………………………………………….

   …………………………………………………………………….

# 3. PERSONHOOD GOALS:

a) ................................................................................

b) ................................................................................

## Strategy for achieving each goal:

a) ................................................................................

................................................................................

b) ................................................................................

................................................................................

## Measurement Process

a) ................................................................................

................................................................................

b) ................................................................................

................................................................................

NB. Upon acceptance of this proposal, it is the responsibility of the *developing leader* to:
- Make copies of the accepted proposal for all parties involved including the Mentor
- Return accepted proposal with the mentoring covenant evaluation report at the completion of the ministry experience to the co-ordinator of the SAM/*Sebl* and Ministry Placement program.

.............................................................     .............................................................
*Mentor*                                                        *Developing Leader*

**Date**   ........................................         **Date**   ........................................

---

## FOR MINISTRY DEVELOPMENT SUPERVISING USE ONLY:

Comments on the above proposal by the co-ordinator of the SEBL program

**Proposal Acceptance:** ....................................... **Date:** ...........................

(signature of *SAM/Sebl Program Co-ordinator*)

(After commenting on this proposal the co-ordinator will return this form to the *developing leader*)

SAM & SUPERVISED EXPERIENCE BASED LEARNING

# MINISTRY COVENANT EVALUATION REPORT

......................................................    ......................................................
            *Mentor*                                              *Developing Leader*

Date  .................................................    Date .................................................


......................................................    Date.................................................

*SAM/Sebl Program Co-ordinator*

# Chapter Seventeen

## Learning Covenant Sample

## B/ State Specific Learning Goals:

### 1. Cognitive Goals:

**a)** *MA subject on homiletics (preaching)*

**b)** *Reading on listening skills*

### 2. Skills Goals:

**a)** *Preaching*

**b)** *Listening – in organizational meetings*

### Strategy for achieving each goal:

**a)** *Preaching:*

1. *plan sermons;*

2. *practice delivery.*

**b)** *Listening – in organizational meeting:*

1. *being more attentive when people are speaking;*

2. *reflect back to them what I think they are saying;*

3. *acknowledge when I have not heard;*

4. *ask questions that indicate understanding.*

### Measurement Process

**a)** *Sermons:*

1. *Sermons are more coherent;*

2. *More confident in delivery;*

3. *Nervous mannerisms diminished.*

**b)** *Listening – in organizational meeting:*

1. *people acknowledge my hearing what they are saying;*

2. *people receptive to suggestions and proposals;*

3. *ideas are clarified and adopted.*

### 3. PERSONHOOD GOALS:

**a)** *overcoming anxiety in group situations*

**b)** *developing planning skills*

## Strategy for achieving each goal:

**a)** *develop a more focused attitude*

**b)** *Take time each day to plan next day's activities;*
*Implement plan;*
*Take time to evaluate achievement of each day's activities;*
*Revise plans when circumstances overwhelm me.*

## Measurement Process

**a)** *more confident to speak in group situations;*

*more relaxed and attentive to others in group situations.*

**b)** *More ready to spend time planning before starting new projects;*

*Reviewing plans regularly and changing and amending plans when necessary.*

NB. Upon acceptance of this proposal, it is the responsibility of the *developing leader* to:
- Make copies of the accepted proposal for all parties involved including the Mentor
- Return accepted proposal with the mentoring covenant evaluation report at the completion of the ministry experience to the co-ordinator of the SAM/*Sebl* and Ministry Placement program.

..................................................    ......................................................

*Mentor*                                  *Developing Leader*

**Date**  ........................................    **Date**  .................................................

---

## FOR MINISTRY DEVELOPMENT SUPERVISING USE ONLY:

Comments on the above proposal by the co-ordinator of the SEBL program

**Proposal Acceptance:** ................................. **Date:** ...........................
(signature of ***SAM/Sebl Program Co-ordinator***)

(After commenting on this proposal the co-ordinator will return this form to the *developing leader*)

# Section Four

# Maximising People for Ministry

## Gift Discovery Course

**Andrew Peters – Roy  Everett**

# Chapter Eighteen

## Welcome

We hope that your participation in this course will help you find further understanding of, and direction for, the purpose God has for your life.

This Gift Discovery Course has three very important purposes:

### The First: **Your destiny and purpose in life**

It aims to help you discover, identify and use your God-given gifts and abilities for the building up of the Kingdom of God and His Church.

### The Second: **The Church's Human Resources**

It aims to help your Church know what its human resources are so that it can effectively plan and implement the vision that God has given to your Church.

### The Third: **Building the Kingdom of God**

It aims to release you to serve God's purpose for the development and growth of His kingdom, that all may come to know and receive Jesus Christ as their Lord and Master.

# Chapter Nineteen

# Orientation

## THE CHURCH'S HEART

The heart of any church is made up of its people. We build and strengthen that heart when we minister to one another in the Lord and develop each other's potential. When we sow into each other's potential, then our local church begins to grow and build itself together in love.[177] A healthy body will grow and produce fruit. You do not have to tell children to grow. Just feed them and see. In the same way, you do not have to tell a healthy church to grow. When we sow into the potential of others and the health of our local church, we enable our Church to move spontaneously out towards the lost and forlorn world, camped on our borders. Not only that, but such movement will have a vibrancy about it that will impact the world for Jesus.

**Question:** How do people help us grow in potential?

.......................................................................................................................................

.......................................................................................................................................

.......................................................................................................................................

## GOD MADE US FOR A PURPOSE

God operates in a variety of ways, but He significantly operates through the local church. He wants to operate through your local church. Within the local church God operates through people like you and me. He has a call on your life and a part for you to play. God didn't make you, and then decide that He better find something for you to do. God had a purpose and He made you for that purpose. No one else can fill the role that God has planned for you in the same way that you can. You will find fulfilment and happiness when you reach for and attain your "reason for being."

**Question:** What do you like best about yourself?

.......................................................................................................................................

.......................................................................................................................................

.......................................................................................................................................

---

[177] Ephesians 4:12-16.

## YOUR REASON FOR BEING

To fulfil your "reason for being", it is important that you understand God's purpose for your life.  God's purpose is not always obvious, and often unfolds over time. Your gifts and abilities are important to the fulfilment of that purpose. Many Christians dissect themselves, and discount any gifts or abilities they possessed in their pre-Christian days, because they were a part of their unredeemed past. However, God gave you those skills and abilities because you need them to complete His work. Paul notes, "For we are his workmanship, created in Christ Jesus for good works, which God prepared beforehand, that we should walk in them."[178] What God never intended was that we walk apart from Him. He always intended us to relate to Him and walk with Him. He calls us to work towards the purpose He had for us from the beginning of the world - a purpose, which Paul notes, is an integral part of His overall purpose for the Church.[179]

**Question:** If you could make a wish that was guaranteed to come to pass, what would it be?

.......................................................................................................................................................

.......................................................................................................................................................

.......................................................................................................................................................

.......................................................................................................................................................

.......................................................................................................................................................

## ALIGNING YOUR DESTINY

This Gift Discovery Course aims to help you align with your God-given destiny and purpose. This may be merely a confirmation of what you already know, or a new revelation of what God has placed in your life and what He wants to do through you. It aims to help you discern those gifts and abilities that He placed in your life, while you were being conceived and born into this world,[180] as well as those He has given to you subsequent to your conversion and spiritual new birth into the Kingdom of His Son.[181] It enables you to become more focused on what you do best, and how that can be made profitable for the Kingdom of God and His Church.

---

[178] Ephesians 2:10.
[179] Ephesians 3:9-12.
[180] Psalm 139:13 – These gifts tend to take on much greater depth and impact once we have been converted.
[181] John 3:3,6; Colossians 1:12.

**Question:** Can you think of one thing that is out of kilter in your life? What could be done about it?

...............................................................................................................................................

...............................................................................................................................................

...............................................................................................................................................

## LETTING YOUR CHURCH KNOW

This Gift Discovery Course is also aimed at helping your local church. Your local church needs to know and understand the gifts and abilities of its people, so that it might be more confident in stepping out into the direction and purpose God has for it. So often the work of the church is left undone or is done poorly because those who are gifted to do the work are not brought into the right places. You might wonder why the church has never asked you to do the things that you really desire to do, or to participate in the area of ministry that is really on your heart. Do they know the desires of your heart? More importantly, do they know you have the gifts and abilities to achieve those desires? The information that is gained through this course not only allows you to understand the nature of the gifts and abilities God has given to you, but also helps the church to understand them. This information will always be treated in a confidential way, and will only be used for purposes that assist you in finding God's part for you in His church.

**Question:** Does your Church know your heartbeat? How could you help it to hear you better?

...............................................................................................................................................

...............................................................................................................................................

...............................................................................................................................................

## OUTLINE OF THE COURSE

The course has three components that will usually be achieved over three seminars of approximately two to two and a half hours per seminar:

1.  **Identifying your Gifts and Abilities**

    This section helps you to identify and understand the gifts, abilities and personality God has given to you. It also addresses the areas of accomplishment in your life.

## 2. Understanding your Purpose

This section helps you to understand the purpose and destiny that God has for your life. We take you through a number of indicators, that we find in the Bible and Christian Ministry that will help you identify God's activity in your life, and how He has been indicating His purpose and destiny for you.

## 3. Maximizing your Ministry

We have a responsibility to develop and use our gifts to build the Kingdom of God and His Church. This section helps you to understand the nature of servant-leadership and the things God wants you to do now, that will begin to realise your destiny. It is aimed at discovering the opportunities currently at hand that will maximize your effectiveness in ministry.

# Chapter Twenty

# Identifying Your Gifts

God has given to you a number of gifts and abilities. The ultimate purpose of these gifts and abilities is to help build the Kingdom of God. Jesus said, "But seek first his kingdom and his righteousness, and all these things shall be yours as well."[182] We will be doing three things to help you identify and recognize the gifts and abilities God has given to you.

1. **Gifts Questionnaire** - the "Gifts Questionnaire" has been developed to highlight the various aspects of a number of gifts that are identified in the Bible and in Christian Ministry. The aim of the questionnaire is to confirm and sometimes reveal resident gifts that people have and use.

2. **Gifts Definitions** - we will be working through the definitions of these gifts and discussing their application. You will have a chance to identify the various gifts that you might have, before we reveal the results of the Gifts Questionnaire.

3. **Best Fit** - we will look at the results of the Gifts Questionnaire. Where they differ from what you have identified for yourself, we will give you an opportunity to decide which gifts fit you best.

## 1.1 THE GIFTS QUESTIONNAIRE

The Gifts Questionnaire aims to show a number of aspects of the various gifts and abilities you might have that are active in what you do. Please identify to what extent each question applies to you. Write the appropriate number in the box on your answer sheet beside the corresponding question number. Your answers will range on a scale of "3 - 0".

| 3 | If you agree with the statement. |
|---|---|
| 2 | If the statement describes you most of the time. |
| 1 | If the statement describes you some of the time. |
| 0 | If the statement does not describe you at all. |

Turn to the Gift Discovery Workbook at the end of this section. Record your choice for each question in the **1.1 *Gifts Questionnaire Answer Sheet***. Take your time and answer the questions as they apply to you. The answers must honestly reflect the way that you are now, not the way you would like to be.

---

[182] Matthew 6:33.

# Gifts Questionnaire

| | | | |
|---|---|---|---|
| 1 | I have the ability to organize physical and/or human means to accomplish a goal or task. | 16 | Through a persistence of faith I have seen impossible situations change. |
| 2 | People tend to share their problems with me. | 17 | The Holy Spirit has given me insight into a person's need when praying for their healing. |
| 3 | I like working with physical materials. | 18 | The Holy Spirit has accomplished supernatural works through me. |
| 4 | I express my creativity through dance, song, music, song writing, painting, drawing, writing, etc. | 19 | The Holy Spirit has inspired me to give a prophecy that has encouraged the church or group. |
| 5 | I reassure people who feel uncertain or insecure. | 20 | The Holy Spirit gives me messages in tongues to build up people in church or a group setting. |
| 6 | I love to give to others. | 21 | The Holy Spirit has given me the interpretation of a message spoken in tongues. |
| 7 | I give my time and abilities to those who have a need. | 22 | I have a great sense of where God wants to take His Church. |
| 8 | I enjoy making others feel welcome and comfortable. | 23 | God often shows me what He is about to do |
| 9 | I can see beyond what is apparent in a situation. | 24 | Signs of healings and miracles follow my preaching of the gospel. |
| 10 | I have a clear vision of what needs to be done. | 25 | I guide, nurture and spiritually feed God's people. |
| 11 | The suffering in the world moves me to action. | 26 | Others have commented on how my teaching has helped them understand God's will and purpose. |
| 12 | I clearly impart my knowledge to others. | 27 | I share the gospel with others in a manner to which they can relate. |
| 13 | The Holy Spirit has revealed details of a specific situation to me, either by vision or word. | 28 | NA |
| 14 | The Holy Spirit has revealed to me the best action to take in a specific circumstance. | 29 | I am able to clarify what needs to be done to achieve certain tasks. |
| 15 | I have been able to redirect an individual or group, when influences other than God, have been driving its activity. | 30 | I seem to be able to motivate people to apply God-orientated answers to their lives. |

# Gifts Questionnaire

| 31 | I am skillful at creating things from materials. | 47 | I have given a prophecy and the church or group has been edified or encouraged. |
|----|--------------------------------------------------|----|---------------------------------------------------------------------------------|
| 32 | I use my artistic abilities to convey a message. | 48 | I have a strong sense of the Holy Spirit prompting me to give a message in tongues in church or a group setting. |
| 33 | I urge others to accomplish more. | 49 | I have interpreted a tongues message and the church or group has been edified. |
| 34 | I feel frustrated when I am unable to give to a certain project or need. | 50 | I am committed to helping struggling churches grow and become spiritually strong |
| 35 | I assist others in practical ways where I can. | 51 | I often see beyond the immediate into the future outcome of God's purposes |
| 36 | I enjoy sharing what I have with others. | 52 | When I preach the Word of God believers are encouraged to share their faith. |
| 37 | I am able to approach people in such a manner that they deal with the real issues in their life. | 53 | I have a deep concern for the spiritual welfare of God's people. |
| 38 | I have the ability to get people to do things they did not want to do, and love doing it. | 54 | I have a substantial knowledge of the scriptures and can explain them clearly, grounding others in the truth. |
| 39 | My compassion for those who suffer leads me to provide support. | 55 | People accept Christ when I share the gospel with them. |
| 40 | Others find it easy to learn from me. | 56 | NA. |
| 41 | The Holy Spirit has revealed the truth about an individual or situation to me that was hidden from natural understanding. | 57 | I have the ability to establish and/or change processes and procedures. |
| 42 | I have been given, by revelation, appropriate solutions to a problem. | 58 | I am able to help people progress towards wholeness. |
| 43 | The Holy Spirit enables me to distinguish the spiritual influence behind certain situations. | 59 | I am adept at using a variety of tools to produce a creative design. |
| 44 | I know that what God has promised for a specific situation, He will do. | 60 | I enjoy being part of the arts - performing, visual, stage productions, audio visual, puppetry, etc. |
| 45 | I understand the variety of supernatural ways that God brings healing into people's lives. | 61 | I lift up those who are downhearted. |
| 46 | The Holy Spirit has performed the impossible when I have prayed. | 62 | I gather resources such as clothes, food, or finances, to help others. |

# Gifts Questionnaire

| 63 | I step in and assist people where there is an immediate need. | 79 | God has used me to reveal His purpose and direction for the Church |
|---|---|---|---|
| 64 | My friendship extends to the stranger and foreigner. | 80 | People come to repentance and commitment to Jesus through my preaching the gospel. |
| 65 | I tend to intervene in a situation when I sense things are not right. | 81 | I enjoy equipping and supporting people, as they begin to participate in ministry. |
| 66 | I have the ability to influence people to achieve a common goal. | 82 | I enjoy using various resources to study the Word of God so I can equip others for service. |
| 67 | Injustice and human suffering moves me to provide support. | 83 | I am able to witness easily to my neighbours, colleagues and acquaintances about my faith in Jesus Christ. |
| 68 | I desire to share my knowledge with others so they can benefit. | 84 | NA. |
| 69 | I have known about certain circumstances through revelation by the Holy Spirit. | 85 | I have a need to bring order to chaos. |
| 70 | The Holy Spirit gives me a solution to a tense situation that calms anxiety. | 86 | I consider myself a confidential person, whom people tend to trust with their problems. |
| 71 | I have an inner witness to the spiritual influences active in certain circumstances. | 87 | I can use my practical skills to make objects of quality. |
| 72 | When the Holy Spirit gives me a Word of promise, I know obstacles will not prevent its accomplishment. | 88 | I have great imagination and creativity that is expressed through the arts. |
| 73 | The Holy Spirit has instantly healed people when I have prayed for them. | 89 | I tend to stick up for others and intercede on their behalf. |
| 74 | The Holy Spirit has worked through me to do supernatural signs and wonders. | 90 | I have the ability to get and give for the benefit of others. |
| 75 | Individual people have been encouraged by the prophetic word I have given. | 91 | I see tasks that need to be done and do them. |
| 76 | After I have given a tongues message, followed by someone interpreting, the church or group has been encouraged. | 92 | Guests are always welcome at my home. |
| 77 | People have been encouraged by the interpretation of a tongues message I have given. | 93 | I can sense if a person is going through difficulties. |
| 78 | I find God consistently doing signs and wonders as a part of my ministry. | 94 | I endeavour to develop people and help them reach their full potential. |

# Gifts Questionnaire

| | | | |
|---|---|---|---|
| 95 | I tend to find myself weeping with those who are in pain and agony. | 108 | I have seen people's lives transformed as they respond to my message. |
| 96 | I enjoy knowing that others have understood what I have explained. | 109 | I spend many hours helping and encouraging people become established in their faith. |
| 97 | I have seen people healed through my giving a word of knowledge. | 110 | People find it easy to grasp my teaching from God's Word and to apply it to their lives. |
| 98 | The Holy Spirit gives me a passage of Scripture to share that brings a solution to a problem. | 111 | I lead people to Christ on a one-to-one basis. |
| 99 | When someone claims to speak for God, I know when the words are humanly inspired. | 112 | NA |
| 100 | I have the ability to visualize what God wants to do, and to carry out the processes needed to achieve it. | 113 | I plan and organize the most efficient way of performing a task. |
| 101 | People have shown a definite spiritual growth after I have prayed for their healing. | 114 | I enjoy listening to a person so I can understand what they are really trying to say. |
| 102 | I have obeyed the Holy Spirit's leading which has seen a miraculous answer to a situation. | 115 | I can visualize objects that can be achieved from materials. |
| 103 | The prophetic word that I have given has encouraged a deeper worship of God. | 116 | I communicate a message to others through artistic activities. |
| 104 | I have given a tongues message in church or a group setting, and have afterwards given the interpretation. | 117 | I exhort others to continue their good work. |
| 105 | When I interpret a tongues message, it is given in a clear manner so people can understand. | 118 | I receive great joy when I provide for the physical needs of others from my abundance. |
| 106 | Jesus has given me a special commission to build and establish His Church. | 119 | I am willing to carry out a variety of tasks and do them well. |
| 107 | I find myself confirming through revelation the Church's present and future directions | 120 | I always attempt to make people feel relaxed and accepted. |

# Gifts Questionnaire

| | | | |
|---|---|---|---|
| 121 | I am able to gauge the atmosphere of a meeting or group of people. | 137 | I care for and nourish those who are struggling in their Christian walk. |
| 122 | I have the ability to make things happen. | 138 | I have a great desire to see people grow in their faith through my expounding of God's Word. |
| 123 | I am watchful to help in practical ways those who are suffering. | 139 | I seek opportunities to share the gospel with people I meet. |
| 124 | I present information in a clear and precise manner so others can learn. | 140 | NA. |
| 125 | When I am praying with a person the Holy Spirit reveals specific knowledge that brings release to them. | 141 | I am able to ensure that tasks are completed in a timely fashion. |
| 126 | The Holy Spirit has given me revelation that has provided guidance and direction in a situation. | 142 | I ask questions and make comments in order to help a person identify the nature of their problems. |
| 127 | I can recognize the spirit behind a prophetic or tongues message, or an interpretation. | 143 | I can design ways in which physical materials can be transformed into quality objects. |
| 128 | I have experienced God's supernatural provision because I believed his specific word of promise. | 144 | I develop visual or media aids to tell a story. |
| 129 | God has used me in a variety of ways to bring supernatural healing to people. | 145 | I seek ways in which I can motivate people to reach their full potential. |
| 130 | I have seen the Holy Spirit change impossible events when I have prayed. | 146 | I am a generous person who gives liberally to others. |
| 131 | Others have confirmed that the prophecy I gave was from God. | 147 | I prefer to be doing something practical rather than sitting around talking. |
| 132 | After giving a tongues message, I have prayed to interpret the message and have been given the interpretation. | 148 | I have a generous and gracious attitude that generally makes others feel at ease. |
| 133 | The interpretation of a tongues message that I have given has encouraged a deeper worship of God. | 149 | I feel some hesitation in confronting people with issues that I sense, but eventually tend to do it. |
| 134 | I have sought to re-establish and build up existing churches. | 150 | I have clear understanding and vision of where a group I direct needs to go. |
| 135 | I have a deep passion to preach the truth of God's Word | 151 | I empathize with, and comfort people who are in need. |
| 136 | It is important to me that new Christians are properly nurtured. | 152 | I enjoy studying so I can present my knowledge to others. |

# Gifts Questionnaire

| | | | |
|---|---|---|---|
| 153 | I have experienced Holy Spirit-given information in regard to a person or situation. | 168 | NA |
| 154 | The Holy Spirit has given me perception enabling me to give directional advice in specific situations. | 169 | I am able to discern the importance of a task despite its urgency. |
| 155 | I am able to identify when a demonic spirit influences a person's problem or trouble. | 170 | I am an active listener so I can help people become whole. |
| 156 | I have experienced an unshakeable confidence that God will do what He said He would do. | 171 | I spend time perfecting my creations, ensuring that they are of a high quality. |
| 157 | People have given a testimony of being healed when I have prayed for them. | 172 | I effectively use media or an art form to convey a message. |
| 158 | I have had an overwhelming compassion for a situation that has resulted in supernatural intervention. | 173 | I intentionally let people know they are appreciated. |
| 159 | I have been prompted by the Holy Spirit to give a prophecy in church or a group setting. | 174 | Financial management plays an important role in my ability to give. |
| 160 | I have been led to give a tongues message in a home group or small group. | 175 | I like assisting behind the scenes. |
| 161 | Others have confirmed that an interpretation of a tongues message I gave was from God. | 176 | I enjoy getting to know other people. |
| 162 | I have been instrumental in restoring lost truth to the Church. | 177 | I tend to go to the heart of the matter with a person or situation, which often results in change. |
| 163 | The messages I have brought from God have encouraged the Church to step out into His purposes and will | 178 | I have the ability to create a conducive environment within which the vision can flourish. |
| 164 | I have a conviction to get the message of the gospel out to non-believers. | 179 | I find opportunities to comfort those going through difficult times. |
| 165 | I nurture the Body of Christ so it becomes full of loving, growing, healthy Christians. | 180 | I search out new ideas and pass them on to others in ways they can understand. |
| 166 | Through careful study of the Word of God, I present its truth to others so they can grow spiritually. | 181 | I have been used by the Holy Spirit to accurately identify a situation in a person's life, which was subsequently resolved. |
| 167 | I find it easy to direct the conversation towards a person's relationship with Jesus. | 182 | I have received from the Holy Spirit direction on how God's principles need to be applied in a particular situation. |

# Gifts Questionnaire

| 183 | Through the Holy Spirit, I know the source behind the words, situations or actions of an individual or group. | 190 | I have overseen the planting and establishment of new churches or ministries. |
|---|---|---|---|
| 184 | In certain circumstances, I have known that God will do the impossible. | 191 | I have a desire to see God's people walk in the truth of His Word and fulfil His will |
| 185 | When I pray for the sick, they experience a definite improvement, sometimes immediately. | 192 | My preaching is overwhelmingly driven by a desire to preach the gospel. |
| 186 | I have had an incredible sense of God's love for people that has seen a miraculous provision for their needs. | 193 | I enjoy the ongoing relationship needed to develop and nurture people. |
| 187 | A revelation of God's mind, through a prophecy I have given, has brought a new level of repentance, commitment or action in the church or group setting. | 194 | When I study the Word of God, I have revelation to its meaning, so I can more effectively explain it. |
| 188 | Messages that I have given in tongues have encouraged a deeper worship of God. | 195 | I enjoy mixing with non-Christians and building relationships with them. |
| 189 | I have been prompted by the Holy Spirit to give the interpretation of a message in tongues in church or a group setting. | 196 | NA |

# Action Required

Once you have completed your **1.1 Gifts Questionnaire Answer Sheet**, please:

- Total each row.

*Example:*

| Gifts Questionnaire Answer Sheet | | | | | | | | | | | | | Totals | |
|---|---|---|---|---|---|---|---|---|---|---|---|---|---|---|
| 1 | *2* | 29 | *1* | 57 | *0* | 85 | *1* | 113 | *2* | 141 | *0* | 169 | *0* | *6* | A |
| 2 | *3* | 30 | *2* | 58 | *3* | 86 | *3* | 114 | *3* | 142 | *2* | 170 | *3* | *19* | B |

- We will be transferring the results a little later in this session.

## 1.2 GOD-GIVEN GIFTS

God had a purpose and He created you for that purpose. He also equipped you with everything you would need to complete and fulfil that purpose. A large proportion of the gifts and abilities God has given to us need to be trained and refined. However, the basic ingredients of those gifts and abilities are sown into our lives in two different ways and at three different times.

1.  The first impartation of our gifts is given to us when we are conceived and then born into this world through our parents. Though these gifts are natural to us, they gain greater depth and intensity when we receive our new spiritual birth.

2.  The second impartation of gifts, especially the gifts of the Holy Spirit (1 Corinthians 12) and the governance or leadership gifts (Ephesians 4), are given to us after our new spiritual birth into the Kingdom of God (John 3). This may happen immediately or take place over a number of years.

3.  The third impartation can occur after we have used the gifts and abilities we do have to their fullest (Matthew 25:14-29).

Our particular gift-mix has been given to us so that we can fulfil our own unique God-given purpose and destiny. That uniqueness is important to the particular purpose God created us to achieve. It also challenges the boxes we tend to put people and ourselves in when we look at ministry. We often consider some to be more gifted than others. We feel that others are more gifted than us. No gift is superior to another. Each gift has its own part to play in God's overall plan. Peter notes, "As each has received a gift, employ it for one another, as good stewards of God's varied grace."[183] God's main concern is that we use the particular gifts or gift-mix He has given to us. A failure to use our gifts can lead to slothfulness and wickedness.[184] The Bible outlines a number of different gifts that God gives to His people. We have also included a few that have borne fruit in Christian ministry and fall into similar categories found in the biblical texts. These are categorized into four different groups:

1.  **Motivational gifts;**

2.  **Holy Spirit gifts;**

3.  **Governance or Leadership gifts;**

4.  **Other Christian gifts.**

---

[183] 1 Peter 4:10.
[184] Matthew 25:26.

## 1.2.1  Motivational Gifts

Motivational gifts are gifts that motivate, inspire or drive us to do the things we do. Their activity and effectiveness is intensified when we become Christians, but they are in evidence throughout our life. These are generally the gifts that lead us to a certain career and the ones that our friends comment on. They are the gifts that we exhibit naturally and, because of that, are sometimes difficult for us to see. These are God-given gifts that are part and parcel of His equipping us for our purpose and destiny. Like all gifts there is potential for their misuse and abuse, as well as their non-use. These gifts help us serve and honour God through our lives. Some of these gifts are mentioned by Paul in Romans 12:1-8, and Peter mentions hospitality in 1 Peter 4:9. The following is a list of some of the common motivational gifts:

ADMINISTRATION is the ability to understand objectives and goals and to efficiently organize/manage the implementation of the processes and plans necessary to fulfil those objectives.

COUNSELLING is the ability to assist people towards psychological, emotional and relational wholeness through a process of listening to their problems, identifying the issues at hand, qualifying their accuracy, and enabling application to their life.

CRAFTSMANSHIP is the ability to excel in the creation, development, and production of physical objects that will be useful to others, by the diligent application of one's practical knowledge, skills and attention to detail.

> *Ex 31:1-7  God gave Bezaleel and Aholiab extra help, over and above their natural ability to build the tabernacle.*

CREATIVE COMMUNICATION is the ability to use one's artistic originality to communicate to others in a variety of media and art forms. This includes music, dance, drama, video, puppetry, etc.

ENCOURAGEMENT is the ability through word, attitude or action to lift up, reassure, and urge others into action.

> *Acts 4:36  Barnabus is called the son of encouragement.*

GIVING is the ability to create and gather resources, and with cheerfulness give those resources for the benefit of others and/or the promotion of God's Kingdom.

> *2 Corinthians 8:1-7  Paul commends the generous attitude of the churches in Macedonia.*

**HELPS** is the desire and ability to aid and assist others in any area of practical need.

*Acts 9:36,39  Tabitha was a woman full of good works,*
*especially helping the widows.*

**HOSPITALITY** is the generous and gracious attitude to share your food, friendship, lodgings, and possessions with others, so that they feel cared for and welcomed.

*Acts 16:14-15  Lydia opened her house to Paul.*

**INSIGHT** is the ability to see beyond what seems to be externally apparent, concerning a person or situation, and by speaking into the situation bring about positive change.

*Acts 8:18-23  Peter was able to see into the wrong attitude of*
*Simon of Samaria.*

**LEADERSHIP** is the ability to have a clear vision, understand how it can be achieved, and influence and develop others to accomplish it.

*Genesis 39-45  Joseph was a leader in Potiphar's house,*
*in prison, and in Egypt.*

**MERCY** is the ability to feel empathy and compassion towards those who are suffering and to give effective support and comfort.

*Luke 10:33-35  The Good Samaritan was merciful to the*
*one who fell among thieves.*

**TEACHING** is the ability to understand principles and concepts and clearly impart that knowledge and skill to others, so they can apply what they have learnt.

*Acts 18:24-26  Aquila and Priscilla taught Apollos.*

## 1.2.2 Gifts of the Holy Spirit

In one sense all the gifts we have as Christians could be considered gifts of the Holy Spirit. Certainly Paul considers even the motivational gifts as having been given to us by grace (Romans 12:6). However, the gifts mentioned in 1 Corinthians 12 need to be considered gifts of the Holy Spirit on two counts:

1) Paul's reference to them as spiritual gifts, and

2) the spiritual or directly supernatural nature of their use.

The Holy Spirit gives these gifts to us, at His own discretion, so that we can have supernatural assistance in caring for and ministering to the needs of others. These gifts may be given to assist in a certain situation, to meet a particular need, or they can be a means by which God uses us in a consistent way. These gifts are divided into three different categories, according to their nature and their use.

### *Revelation or Insight Gifts:*

WORD OF KNOWLEDGE is the revealing by the Holy Spirit, of information or knowledge that cannot be naturally known, which is relevant to a situation or issue in a person's life.

WORD OF WISDOM is the revealing of perception and understanding by the Holy Spirit, of the real issues involved in a situation or a person's life, which provides God's guidance and direction.

DISCERNING OF SPIRITS is the ability given by the Holy Spirit to distinguish between divine, human, or demonic influence behind words, actions or situations.

### *Demonstration or Power Gifts:*

FAITH is the special conviction given by the Holy Spirit that the Lord will bring to pass what He has specifically promised for a given situation, and the unwavering determination to see that promise fulfilled.

GIFTS OF HEALINGS is the working of the Holy Spirit, through a person, in a variety of supernatural ways, to bring spiritual, emotional, mental and physical healing.

WORKING OF MIRACLES is the supernatural work of the Holy Spirit, through a person, that brings about that which is normally impossible through natural means or efforts.

### *Inspiration or Speaking Gifts:*

PROPHECY is the ability given by the Holy Spirit to bring a message that reveals the heart and mind of God for His people, which then exhorts, encourages, builds up and comforts the Body of Christ.

TONGUES is the ability to deliver a message from the Holy Spirit, spoken in an unlearned language (tongues), for the encouragement and building up of people in a church or group setting. (This is distinct from tongues for personal use.)

INTERPRETATION OF TONGUES is the ability given by the Holy Spirit to interpret the message given in tongues.

## 1.2.3 Other Christian Gifts

**EVANGELISM** is the ability to present the gospel convincingly, on a one-to-one basis or in small groups, so that others accept Christ wholeheartedly.

## 1.2.4 Governance or Leadership Gifts

The governance or leadership gifts of apostle, prophet, evangelist, pastor/shepherd and teacher have a specific purpose and role in the Church. This is to equip and enable the people of God to do the work of ministry. This includes empowering them to build up the church and help it mature. They are revelatory gifts, which come with God-given authority and power, and have great impact upon the Church. They are easily misused, abused and redirected from their God-given purpose. When these gifts are operating properly in the Church, the people of God move into effective ministry. This results in: a unity of faith; an experiential presence and knowledge of the Son of God in the Church; a maturity and stability in the Body of Christ; an openness and honesty in personal relationships; and a community permeated with the presence of the love of God, which is evident in the life of its members (Ephesians 4:11-16).

**APOSTLE:** The Apostle is one specially commissioned by Jesus Christ to carry out God-given visionary leadership. This results in the raising up of new churches and ministries; the restoration of truth and sound doctrine to the Church; and the re-establishment, correction and building up of existing churches. In the early church, signs and wonders, along with an experience of the Risen Christ, seem to be an innate part of this gift.[185]

> Acts 2:42 "And they continued steadfastly in the apostles' doctrine and fellowship."

> Ephesians 2:20 "having been built on the foundation of the apostles and prophets, Jesus Christ being the chief cornerstone."

**PROPHET:** The Prophet is one specially anointed by God to bring understanding and knowledge of God's purpose to His Church and individuals. The Prophet provides both encouragement and direction to the Church and individuals to step out and fulfil God's will.

**EVANGELIST:** The Evangelist, through the effective preaching of the gospel, challenges non-believers, leads them to salvation in Jesus, and encourages believers in their faith. Healings, miracles, and the supernatural working of God often follow this ministry.

---

[185] 2 Corinthians 12:12.

**Pastor/Shepherd:** The Shepherd is one who cares for, guides, nurtures and spiritually feeds the people of God. This gift operates out of a deep concern for their welfare and growth.

**Teacher:** The Teacher is one divinely gifted in studying and expounding the Word of God. Through insight and revelation, the Teacher has the ability to present the truth in an understandable, uncomplicated manner that grounds and builds people in their relationship with the Lord.

## 1.3. Gift Discovery – Best Fit

We are now going to look at the gifts and abilities that God has given to you. This is a three-fold process that includes the results of the questionnaire that completed earlier, along with an opportunity for you to identify particular gifts that you might have that we defined in items 1.2.1 to 1.2.4. Once we have that we will be asking to choose which gifts best fit you.

## *Action Required – Personally Identified Gifts*

- Turn to the Gift Discovery Workbook at the end of this section - *1.3 Gift Discovery – Bests Fit.*

- In the **"Personally Identified Gifts"** column note the level of each of the gifts that you believe are evident or not evident in your life and ministry according to the following table:

| | |
|---|---|
| **16-21** | If you believe that the gift is strongly evident in your life and ministry. |
| **11-15** | If you believe the gift is evident in your life and ministry most of the time. |
| **6-10** | If you believe the gift is sometimes evident in your life and ministry. |
| **0-5** | If you believe you do not have the gift at all or it has occurred very randomly in your life and ministry. |

- *See example next page.*

- Example:

| | GIFT | PERSONALLY IDENTIFIED GIFTS | SCORES ON QUESTIONNAIRE | GIFT OWNERSHIP "BEST FIT" |
|---|---|---|---|---|
| A | Administration | 17 | | |
| B | Counselling | 15 | | |
| C | Craftsmanship | 8 | | |
| D | Creative Communication | 20 | | |

## Action Required - Questionnaire Results

Now that you have an understanding of the gifts, and have decided which gifts you believe are evident in your life and ministry, let us look at the results of the Gifts Questionnaire.

- In the *1.3 Gift Discovery - Best Fit* table of the Gift Discovery Workbook transfer the results of your *1.1 Gifts Questionnaire Answer Sheet* to the column headed **"Scores on Questionnaire."** See example:

| | GIFT | PERSONALLY IDENTIFIED GIFTS | SCORES ON QUESTIONNAIRE | GIFT OWNERSHIP "BEST FIT" |
|---|---|---|---|---|
| A | ADMINISTRATION | 17 | *19* | |
| B | COUNSELLING | 15 | *5* | |
| C | CRAFTSMANSHIP | 8 | *2* | |
| D | CREATIVE COMMUNICATION | 20 | *20* | |

The scores indicate the following:

| | |
|---|---|
| 16-21 | You probably exhibit this gift regularly. |
| 11-15 | You may exhibit this gift some of the time but it needs developing. |
| 6-10 | You may exhibit the gift some of the time but it is not developed. |
| 0-5 | You do not have the gift or if you do it has been suppressed. |

## 1.4 GIFT OWNERSHIP - BEST FIT

We are now going to compare the results of the Questionnaire and what you believe about your gifts. You may in fact agree or disagree with the results of the Gifts Questionnaire. In this section we give you the opportunity to decide what you believe best fits you. If you disagree with the results of the Gifts Questionnaire, on certain gifts, then you are welcome to note in the "Gift Ownership – Best Fit" column the nature of the gift that best fits you.

If you do disagree with some of the results you may wish to discuss the results with your Gift Discovery Course presenter or seek confirmation from a trusted friend or minister/pastor. And by all means, pray for God's confirmation. It may take a little time, but you need to be sure, so that you can take ownership of the gifts that God has given to you.

## *Action Required - Best Fit*

- In the *1.3 Gift Discovery - Best Fit* table of the Gift Discovery Workbook compare the results of the Questionnaire with what you believe about your gifts. List in each box of the **"Gift Ownership, Best Fit"** column, what you think best fits you. It may be the results of the Questionnaire, or what you identified yourself, or a combination of the two. See the following example.

   **Example:**

| | GIFT | PERSONALLY IDENTIFIED GIFTS | SCORES ON QUESTIONNAIRE | GIFT OWNERSHIP "BEST FIT" |
|---|---|---|---|---|
| A | ADMINISTRATION | 17 | 19 | 19 |
| B | COUNSELLING | 15 | 5 | 15 |
| C | CRAFTSMANSHIP | 8 | 2 | 6 |
| D | CREATIVE COMMUNICATION | 20 | 20 | 20 |

- When completed, circle the main gifts that you believe God has given to you, usually those that range between 15-21. If you have marked yourself really hard your scores might be lower, so you need to select the top 25% of your scores and circle them.

## 1.5 Learning Styles

Hersey, Blanchard and Johnson, in *Management of Organizational Behavior*, note that people tend to perceive their psychological worlds through the sensing systems they most prefer – the ones with which they are most comfortable. By that they mean that people tend to lean towards one of three modes of perception:

- What they see
- What they feel, or
- What they hear.[186]

**Visuals or Picture People:** Those who learn by what they see are called visuals. They are more comfortable learning through the means of pictures. They tend to want to see the big picture and like plenty of space. Visual people tend to cluster to the rear of the room to keep all the data out in front of them. They respond to teaching that uses diagrams, flow charts, and other graphics, particularly when learning complex information.

**Feelings:** Some people are feelings people or "kinesthetics". They are most comfortable learning through the means of internal and external feelings. They prefer people to be closer when communicating. Feelings people tend to cluster up front, close to the speaker; they want to feel they are part of the presentation. Feelings people tend to learn more readily in a relaxed atmosphere.

**Auditories:** Some people are sounds people ("auditories" or "tonals"). They learn through the means of hearing or sounds. They don't always "look people in the eye" because they're "tuning an ear." During a conversation or presentation, they may look elsewhere because they are listening and trying to take in data. Their intention is not to be rude or inattentive; they are trying to understand. Auditory people cluster to the side and, depending on their best ear, sit to the left or right side of the room.

**Digitals:** Word people, or "digitals," are a hybrid of the other three. They tend to learn through translating raw data into a specific language – through words or numbers or computer symbols. They like written information presented to them in a logical fashion. Digitals will tend to place themselves where they think they should be, in relation to the speaker, in order to filter data to the level of abstraction with which they are comfortable.[187]

## *Action Required*

Which Learning Style do you lean to?

- Record this in the "Learning Style" box *1.3 Gift Discovery - Best Fit* table of the Gift Discovery Workbook.

---

[186] P. Hersey, K. Blanchard, D. Johnson, *Management of Organizational Behavior*, NJ: Prentice Hall, 1996, 348.

[187] Hersey, Blanchard, Johnson, *Management of Organizational Behavior*, 349-.350.

## 1.6 My Unique History

In this section, we will be looking at the richness of your education, training, experience, personal skills and abilities, leisure-time activities, as well as a brief synopsis of your life's journey. These characteristics are important because they have helped develop you into who you are. No one else has walked the same earthly path that you have experienced. You bring a uniqueness and diversity to the Church. It is therefore important for you to take some time to dig, deeply if necessary, into your unique history and honestly answer the questions that follow.

As you complete each section, please summarize your details in the Gifts Discovery Workbook.

## Action Required

The following items are information that we need to know about you, to assist in identifying your gifts and abilities, and finding your niche in the ministry life of your church.

*Please have these filled in before our next session*.

- Turn to the Gift Discovery Workbook.

    o Please fill in your *Personal Details:*

- Turn to the Gift Discovery Workbook.

    o Please complete your:

    *1.6.1 Formal Education*

    *1.6.2  Non-Formal Training*

    *1.6.3  Self-taught Skills*

    *1.6.4 Current Work and Ministry Experience*

    *1.6.5 Work and Volunteer Experience (or Hobbies)*

    Many times a person's significant work and volunteer experience is not used in the ministry work of the Church, because the Church, on the one hand, is not aware of that experience, or on the other hand, the person is not aware that the Church is looking for someone with their experience.

# Action Required

Please tick the boxes that indicate that you have had significant and competent work or volunteer experience in that field.

| ✓ | ARTS & ENTERTAINMENT | ✓ | INFORMATION & MEDIA | ✓ | BUSINESS, FINANCE, LEGAL |
|---|---|---|---|---|---|
| | Stage Management | | Research | | Data Entry |
| | Stage Hand | | Library | | Word Processing |
| | Script Writer | | Computer Hardware | | Filing |
| | Theatre | | Computer Software | | Receptionist |
| | Set design/construction | | Systems Analysis | | Office Manager |
| | Mime | | Network Admin | | Mail Room |
| | Puppetry | | Web Designer | | Excel |
| | Music composition | | Graphics | | Access |
| | Music performance | | Journalism | | Power Point |
| | Music Arranging | | Writing | | Accounting |
| | Singing | | Book Illustrating | | Bookkeeping |
| | Choir Director | | Cartooning | | Financial Management |
| | Art/painting | | Literature/poetry | | Investment |
| | Crafts | | Media | | Administration |
| | Dance | | Publishing | | Legal Practice |
| | Drama | | Animation | | Advocacy |
| | Acting | | Photography | | Other |
| | Lighting | | Cooking | | **MARKETING** |
| | Audio Production | | Nutrition | | Advertising |
| | Video Production | | Waiter/Waitress | | Public Relations |
| | Video/film | | Other | | Tourism |
| | Television | | | | Marketing |
| | DVD Duplication | | | | Other |

| ✓ | CONSTRUCTION | ✓ | HEALTH & SOCIAL CARE | ✓ | RE-SOURCING |
|---|---|---|---|---|---|
| | Architect | | Aged Care | | Fund Raising |
| | Engineer | | Child Care | | Personnel Manage |
| | Interior Designer | | Social Work | | Negotiating |
| | Drafting | | Community Work | | Job Finding |
| | Masonry | | Youth Work | | Career counselling |
| | Plasterer | | Alcohol & Drug Rehab | | Club Management |
| | Building Maintenance | | Counselling | | **AGRONOMY** |
| | Building Contractor | | Natural Medicine | | Gardening |
| | Carpenter | | Nursing | | Flower Arranging |
| | Electrician | | Aerobics | | Landscaping |
| | Plumber | | Exercise / Fitness | | Lawn Mowing |
| | Heating | | Hairdressing | | Indoor Plants |
| | Air Conditioning | | Beauty therapy | | **RECREATION** |
| | Painter | | Other | | Boating/sailing |
| | **RETAIL & SERVICES** | | **EDUCATION & TRAINING** | | Fishing |
| | Customer Service | | Linguistics | | Lifeguard |
| | Bookstore | | TESOL | | Swimming |
| | Shop assistant | | Teaching | | Camping |
| | Retail business owner | | Tutoring | | Golf |
| | Property rental/sale | | Training | | Tennis |
| | Telecommunications | | Deaf Signing | | **TRANSPORT** |
| | Clothing | | Reading Aloud | | Bus Driver |
| | Fashion & Modelling | | **MAINTENANCE** | | Truck Driver |
| | | | Industrial Cleaning | | Pilot |
| | | | Domestic Cleaning | | Other |
| | | | Diesel mechanic | | |
| | | | Auto mechanic | | |
| | | | Security | | |

# Action Required

- Turn to the Gift Discovery Workbook.

- Choose up to eight (8) of your best areas of experience that you have noted above and transfer them to: *1.6.5 Work and Volunteer Experience (or Hobbies)*

## 1.6.6 Personal Skills

Please tick the following personal skills areas in which you feel particularly competent.

| ✓ | SKILL | ✓ | SKILL |
|---|---|---|---|
| | Ability to facilitate change | | Negotiating |
| | Budgeting and handling finances | | Mentoring & Evaluating Performance |
| | Building and leading teams | | Personal management and development |
| | Computer and internet literacy | | Researching |
| | Continuous improvement process | | Planning to reach your personal goals |
| | Cross cultural interaction | | Service to others |
| | Evaluating performance | | Solving problems |
| | Handling cultural diversity | | Strategic planning |
| | Interpersonal skills | | Strong interpersonal skills |
| | Making effective presentations | | Working with numbers/mathematics |
| | Marketing | | Writing |
| | Conflict Resolution | | Other…………………………………… |
| | Other…………………………… | | Other…………………………………… |

# Action Required

- Turn to the Gift Discovery Workbook.

- Please choose the four (4) personal skills in which you feel the most competent and copy them to: *1.6.6   Personal Skills*

### 1.6.7 Autobiography

Often our life's journey will reveal much about the way God has been directing us and may indicate where He is presently leading.

Take the time to consider the major events in your life, especially since you were saved. Go back over your life and highlight some of the important things that have happened to you. Look particularly at those areas where you have been using your gifts, maybe unknowingly. Also look for trends, to see if there is any recurring theme in your life.

## Action Required

- Turn to the Gift Discovery Workbook.

- Please include your autobiography as brief dot points under:
  ### 1.6.7 Autobiography

# Chapter Twenty-one

# Understanding Your Purpose

When we lack the knowledge of the Creator's purpose in bringing us into this world, we live far below that purpose. But when we know our destiny, we can rise to it and be all that we were created to be.[188]

You are not an accident going somewhere to happen. God made you for a purpose and has been at work in your life to bring you into that purpose. God didn't make you and then wondered what He should do with you. God didn't make you, and then leave you alone to fend for yourself, using your own devices to etch out a future for yourself, ignorant of His design. God had a purpose and He made you specifically for that purpose. He placed within you a unique mixture of gifts, abilities and personality so you could take up that purpose and fulfil your destiny. Your destiny is the fulfilment and completion of what God made you for in the first place, your reason for being here.

Destiny is not only something we take up and fulfil. Destiny bears fruit and results that we leave behind to benefit this world and the direction it needs to take in God. When we refer to destiny we are not speaking of a fatalistic approach to life, over which we have no control. Destiny is not automatic. It is not something that is going to happen anyway. It will not happen without our consent and ownership. Our purpose and destiny is something we take up and do, not something that is done to us. Casey Treat defines destiny as:

> *A course or path in life that includes both the God-given destination you are seeking at life's end and your own faith-filled journey toward that destination.[189]*

Destiny is taking a hold of and reaching our full potential. It is becoming all that we can be, and all God intended us to be. Destiny is a journey not simply an end. Destiny's fulfilment is the culmination of a progressive number of small fulfilments along the way. For all of us the final destination is heaven, but not before we have completed the race that is set before us and achieved the purpose God had for placing us here.[190]

Often we shy away from knowing our destiny for fear that God's purpose for us will be less than what we want it to be or more than we think we can handle. Many of us have been brought up with an understanding that the will of God will be something that we do not like and for which we have no natural gifts and abilities. Yet, even the rebellious Israelites, as they

---

[188] Casey Treat, *Fulfilling Your God-given Destiny*, Thomas Nelson Publishers, Nashville, 1995, 22.
[189] Casey Treat, *Fulfilling Your God-given Destiny*, 1.
[190] Hebrews 12:1-2.

were being carted off to captivity in Babylon, were promised a good future by God. Jeremiah notes:

> For I *know* the plans I have for you, says the LORD, plans for welfare
> and not for evil, to give you a future and a hope (Jeremiah 29:11).

God gives us the desires of our hearts, an enjoyment of life, and a sense of fulfilment when we are in the centre of His purpose and fulfilling our destiny. Many may not yet know that purpose and destiny, but as they move towards seeking God and understanding His ways, they discover a journey that puts them on the cutting edge of what God is doing.

## 2.1 THE APOSTLE PAUL

The apostle Paul was a man of destiny and purpose, aware of God's call upon his life. That purpose was confirmed throughout his life, even in the most difficult of circumstances. He was on the way to Rome to stand trial before Caesar as a Roman citizen, because of his preaching the gospel. During the journey, a massive storm hit the ship he was sailing on and it was about to be destroyed. Paul spoke to the Roman soldiers and crew who were on board saying:

" I now bid you take heart; for there will be no loss of life among you, but only of the ship. For this very night there stood by me an angel of the God to whom I belong and whom I worship, and he said, 'Do not be afraid, Paul; you must stand before Caesar; and lo, God has granted you all those who sail with you.' So take heart, men, for I have faith in God that it will be exactly as I have been told."[191]

Paul told them the ship was about to sink, but none of them would perish, because he had a destiny. He had an appointment in Rome for God and God was going to deliver him, along with them, to keep that appointment. That appointment was the culmination of a life of purpose given to bringing the good news to the Gentiles. Paul's purpose was to preach the gospel; his destiny was to take that gospel to the Gentiles, which culminated in his standing before Caesar of the Gentiles to deliver that gospel.

Our purpose and destiny are intertwined so closely together that it is often hard to tell them apart. Yet each contributes to our completing God's original reason for making us the way He

---

[191] Acts 27:22-25.

did. After Paul's (Saul of Tarsus) experience with Jesus on the Damascus road, whereby he was blinded, God spoke to a disciple named Ananias. God instructed Ananias to pray for Paul's healing. He also gave Ananias these words concerning Paul's purpose and destiny, "But the Lord said to him, 'Go, for he is a chosen instrument of mine to carry my name before the Gentiles and kings and the sons of Israel; for I will show him how much he must suffer for the sake of my name.' "[192] The preaching of the gospel motivated everything that Paul did from that time on. The interaction of Paul's purpose and destiny flow throughout the Book of Acts, through everything he did. On his missionary tours he would first enter the synagogues and take the gospel to the Jews. As a result, he inevitably ended up preaching to the Gentiles.[193] Paul would begin preaching to the Jews, but ended up preaching to the Gentiles; and finally before the kings and rulers of the Gentiles.[194] Paul goes to Rome to testify before Caesar because of conflict that arose with the Jews concerning his preaching of the gospel. As Paul carried out his purpose he fulfilled his destiny.

## 2.2 JOSEPH

Joseph's purpose was to serve; his destiny was to lead the greatest superpower nation of his day. Joseph knew, because of his dreams, that his destiny was to lead and to rule. In every circumstance he faced, from slavery in Potiphar's house to captivity in prison, Joseph served, and all that he did prospered.[195] The result of his serving brought him into leadership in every circumstance. In the final step to his destiny, Joseph served Pharaoh's dream, and led the greatest superpower nation of his time. The result of Joseph's fulfilling his purpose and destiny was the maturing and growth of a nation equipped to take the land that God had promised to their forefather Abraham.[196] Israel grew and multiplied during its time in Egypt.

## 2.3 GOD'S ACTIVITY

God's activity in the life of Paul and Joseph began long before they took up their purpose and fulfilled their destinies. Yet it is the things they learnt along the way that gave a unique edge to what they did. The richness of the Church's theology and understanding flowed from the pen of Paul as He recorded the meaning of the Christ event for us all. Without him we would have no understanding of spiritual gifts; no concept of the immeasurable grace of God and our partaking of that grace through Jesus by faith; we would have limited understanding of life after death; and much more. It was Paul's early Rabbinic learning and development, before his conversion, that gave him the unique perspective upon the Christ event that

---

[192]  Acts 9:15-16.
[193]  Acts 13:46; 18:6; 19:8-10.
[194]  Acts 18:12-17; 24:1-2ff; 25:1ff; 13ff.
[195]  Genesis 39:1-6; 19-23.
[196]  Genesis 46:1-4; Exodus 1:7-10.

enabled the Church to survive heretical and philosophical storms for over two thousand years. It was not only the churches he established, but the words he left behind, when he finally went to be with the Lord, that have enriched us so much.

Each of us is unique and has a different calling and reason for being. Each one of us has been given a different gift and ability mix. Each one of us has had different training and experiences. Each one of us has a different destiny. Some are called to be homemakers, others are called to preaching; pastoral care; missions; business; construction work; politics; administration; performing arts; leadership; and so on. As each one of us fulfils our purpose as part of the Church, God's overall purpose for the Church will be accomplished.

## 2.4  GOD IS NOT HIDING

God is not hiding His purpose from you. He wants you to understand. He wants you to know what He made you for and how He wants you to complete the race that is set before you. Sometimes it is made clear from birth, as in the case of John the Baptist. Other times it is when the need arises and the time is right that God reveals His purpose and destiny to you, as in the case of Gideon. However, and whenever, God reveals His purpose for you, it is important to note that He is still at work in your life, preparing you for the fulfilment of that destiny.

The aim of this course is not to determine you, or even to tell you what you must do. It is to help you identify and understand the call God has made upon your life, His purpose and destiny for you. In the questions that will follow, we will be using indicators that enable you to sense and understand what the purpose and will of God might be for you. We call them indicators because by themselves, they only indicate rather than determine what you should be. As in the Gift Discovery process you experienced in Part 1, you choose what you believe is His purpose for you, for it is your responsibility to own and fulfil that destiny.

Each indicator is a way in which God has spoken to others about His purpose for them, and it may also have been a way God has spoken to you. Please do not be concerned if you do not have responses to all the indicators. You may not need them. Not every one gets thrown off his donkey like Paul did.[197] Then not all of us need to be, for we readily hear the voice of God speaking to us and directing our way. There are those who need earthquakes to happen to hear God, and then others who are sensitive to that *still small voice* of the Spirit speaking into their lives.[198]

---

[197] Acts 9:1-6.
[198] 1 Kings 19:12 – Elijah journey to the mountain.

**Please Note:** *The answers that you will write down in the next few pages will be for your benefit only. At the end we ask you to make a summary in general terms and to then write that summary in the Workbook.*

# INDICATORS OF YOUR PURPOSE

## PROPHETIC WORD

God often speaks to people and gives them direction through the prophetic word. Paul's call to preach to the Gentiles came through the prophetic word given via Ananias, that we read earlier. Experience has taught us that the prophetic word needs to be followed or preceded by our own inner conviction and subsequent experience. The fulfilment of the prophetic word for Paul came about even when He wasn't trying to preach to the Gentiles. For instance, even when Paul purposed to preach to the Jewish community, he inevitably ended up preaching to the Gentiles. Andrew Peters notes that his call to be an Evangelist occurred in three stages, which included both the prophetic word and the inner conviction. He heard God's call to him whilst reading his Bible and having God enliven the word "Evangelist" to him. The next week at Teen Challenge in Kings Cross, one of the Directors prophesied over him about preaching and evangelism. The following week saw him led out onto the streets of Kings Cross, by the Holy Spirit, to preach the gospel.

If you have received direction through the prophetic word, please note it here. If you have received more than one word, then note them in the space provided.

-------------------------------------------------------------------------------------

-------------------------------------------------------------------------------------

-------------------------------------------------------------------------------------

-------------------------------------------------------------------------------------

-------------------------------------------------------------------------------------

-------------------------------------------------------------------------------------

-------------------------------------------------------------------------------------

-------------------------------------------------------------------------------------

-------------------------------------------------------------------------------------

-------------------------------------------------------------------------------------

## VISIONS AND DREAMS

God speaks to people through dreams and visions. God spoke to Joseph in a dream and told him the baby that Mary, his fiancée, carried in her womb was of the Holy Spirit and he was to marry her. His destiny was to nurture the early years and development of the Messiah, the Son of God. We have many dreams, but some are significant because they come with a sense of God has spoken. Martin Luther King expressed such a conviction when he proclaim "I have a dream!" His movement to fulfil that dream, to break down racism in his country, so changed American history and culture that it can never go back to what it was before. It also cost him his life.

Has God spoken to you through dreams, or given you a vision of what could be? Please note it here.

--------------------------------------------------------------------------------

--------------------------------------------------------------------------------

--------------------------------------------------------------------------------

--------------------------------------------------------------------------------

--------------------------------------------------------------------------------

--------------------------------------------------------------------------------

--------------------------------------------------------------------------------

--------------------------------------------------------------------------------

--------------------------------------------------------------------------------

--------------------------------------------------------------------------------

## OTHER PEOPLE

Other people often see us better than we see ourselves. God places people in our lives who give us wise counsel and direction. This can often be a two-edged sword, for many have experienced people who wished to determine them, rather than to help them discover God's plan and purpose for their life. However, those who give *wise* counsel, also seem to have the ability to leave the decision up to us. They have learned the hard way about the dangers of trying to determine people.

Have you had wise people speak into your life, giving you a sense of direction or opening up meaning about yourself ? Please note what they have said here.

-------------------------------------------------------------------------------

-------------------------------------------------------------------------------

-------------------------------------------------------------------------------

-------------------------------------------------------------------------------

-------------------------------------------------------------------------------

-------------------------------------------------------------------------------

## DESIRE OF YOUR HEART

We cannot underestimate the Heart. It is the centre of God's operation in our lives. He tells us to bring our hearts to Him and not just our garments. He tells us to guard our heart, for from it flows the springs of life.[199] He also promises to give us the desires of our hearts when we delight in Him.[200] Often God's purpose for us comes through a God-given desire of our hearts. We often mistake that desire to be our own selfish purpose, rather than God's purpose. If we have given ourselves to God through Jesus Christ and are determined to serve God in whatever way He wants, then those desires of our hearts may well be His purpose for us. Some people have had a heartfelt desire to be a doctor for as long as they can remember. Some have had the courage to step out and do it. They trained and equipped themselves and fulfilled that desire.

Do you have any heartfelt desires that relate to ministry or service, either in or outside the Church?

-------------------------------------------------------------------------------

-------------------------------------------------------------------------------

-------------------------------------------------------------------------------

-------------------------------------------------------------------------------

-------------------------------------------------------------------------------

-------------------------------------------------------------------------------

[199] Proverbs 4:23.
[200] Psalms 37:4; 145:19.

## CONTENTEDNESS WITHIN

Sometimes God's purpose for us is indicated by the things that we love to do. There are things that we feel most contented doing, and if it was possible we would just love to do them all the time. When these things are linked to the ministry we do they give us a sense of fulfilment and purpose with God.

Are there things related to ministry that you just love doing? Are there things that give you contentment and fulfilment when you do them? Please note them here.

------------------------------------------------------------------------------------

------------------------------------------------------------------------------------

------------------------------------------------------------------------------------

------------------------------------------------------------------------------------

------------------------------------------------------------------------------------

------------------------------------------------------------------------------------

## WHAT WE VALUE

**Aubrey Malphurs** in his book Ministry Nuts & Bolts refers to a Core Values Audit that notes a variety of Christian ministries and attitudes (he notes 46) and asks us to indicate which ones we value the most.[201] A sample of these includes, godly leadership, well-mobilized laity, effectiveness, home missions, cultural relevance, inspiring worship, etc.

The **Franklin Covey** course notes a similar process, which they call "Governing Values – My Highest Priority." They ask you to identify the things that matter most to you and ask you to identify governing values that you would wish to develop over a lifetime.[202] A sample of their governing values include:- authenticity, excellence, generosity, prosperity, loyalty, family, etc.

Both of these programs are well worth doing in themselves.

What we want you to do here is to think through what you value the most, without our suggesting too many options. What you value the most will give you some indication of God's purpose for your life. What you value the most may not be something that you will wish to do, but it may give some indication of what you might like to sow your life or your finances into.

---

[201]   Aubrey Malphurs, *Ministry Nuts & Bolts*, Kregel Publications, Grand Rapids, 1997.
[202]   Franklin Covey, *What Matters Most, Participant Workbook*, Franklin Covey, Salt Lake City, Utah, 1998.

Please list the eight things you value the most.

1 _____     5 _____

2 _____     6 _____

3 _____     7 _____

4 _____     8 _____


## WHAT YOU DO BEST

John Maxwell notes the Pareto Principle, which simply means:- 20% of your priorities will give you 80% of your production or results.[203] What you do best is what produces most of the results in your life, work and ministry. Not only that, but what you do best might indicate the purpose God has for your life.

Please note here the things you do best.

-------------------------------------------------------------

-------------------------------------------------------------

-------------------------------------------------------------

-------------------------------------------------------------

-------------------------------------------------------------

-------------------------------------------------------------

-------------------------------------------------------------

-------------------------------------------------------------

-------------------------------------------------------------

-------------------------------------------------------------

[203] John Maxwell, *Developing the Leader within You*, Thomas Nelson Publishers, Nashville, 1993, 20-21.

## Compassionate Concerns

Many people go through deeply traumatic experiences, often over long periods of time. They find that the compassionate love of God brings them through and renews their life so that they feel called to help others going through the same sort of experiences. These are people who have come through drug addiction, terminal illness, financial adversity, sexual immorality, depression, persecution, ministry hardship and the like. During this time they have come to know the comfort of God, which has deeply impacted their lives, as Paul notes:

> Blessed be the God and Father of our Lord Jesus Christ, the Father of mercies and God of all comfort, who comforts us in all our affliction, so that we may be able to comfort those who are in any affliction, with the comfort with which we ourselves are comforted by God. For as we share abundantly in Christ's sufferings, so through Christ we share abundantly in comfort too. [204]

Do you feel a special affinity with and desire to help people who have gone through similar experiences to you or to those closely related to you?

------------------------------------------------------------------------

------------------------------------------------------------------------

------------------------------------------------------------------------

------------------------------------------------------------------------

------------------------------------------------------------------------

------------------------------------------------------------------------

------------------------------------------------------------------------

------------------------------------------------------------------------

## Task or People

People tend to be either more task orientated or relationship orientated. Some people are really good at doing tasks, whilst others are really good with people. Many people are able to move between the two: task-orientated in some situations, and people orientated in others. God honours both and has a purpose for task-orientated people as well as for those who are relationship orientated.

------------------------------------------------

[204] 2 Corinthians 1:1-7.

Are you a more task or relationship orientated person? Give an example.

----------------------------------------

----------------------------------------

----------------------------------------

----------------------------------------

----------------------------------------

----------------------------------------

## WHAT WOULD YOU LIKE TO CHANGE

Some of the greatest men and women of God have come to the forefront because they just felt something had to be changed, and they were the ones who had to make it happen. In *I'm not Mad at God,* David Wilkerson[205] notes that those who see the need have a responsibility to work to see that need met. He writes, "A man who walks with God can never erase the sight of human need from his heart. He must act or forever shut his eyes. He cannot see and then be at ease. Vision carries with it a great obligation."[206] David Wilkerson is not talking about us meeting every need, but the one we see. It is the need that gets us steamed, the one we feel something really needs to be done about. That need comes with a responsibility.

Is there something you really feel needs to be changed, in the world or in the Church? What could you do about it?

----------------------------------------

----------------------------------------

----------------------------------------

----------------------------------------

----------------------------------------

----------------------------------------

----------------------------------------

[205] David Wilkerson was the founder of Teen Challenge in the United States of America. Teen Challenge is a Christian outreach organization that has been effective in reaching and bringing drug addicts to the Lord and seeing them set free from their addictions. Teen Challenge has been established in Australia since the late sixties and early seventies.

[206] David Wilkerson, *I'm not Mad at God*, Bethany Fellowship, Minneapolis, 1967, 48.

## Have you been Passionate in the Past

In his letter, Paul strongly encourages his disciple, Timothy, to stir up the gift that is within him, which had been given through the laying on of hands. He said, "Hence I remind you to rekindle the gift of God that is within you through the laying on of my hands..."[207] Through the rough and tough of ministry life and experience we often get knocked about by what people have said, or by the disappointments we have experienced. This can often diminish the enthusiasm and passion we have to do work for God. Passion is the fire and heart we need to achieve the purpose that God has for us. It becomes the energy driving force that helps us to rise up and achieve what God has called us to do. When it diminishes or is suppressed, we also tend to draw back from those tasks or ministry activities. We also tend to rationalise our lack of enthusiasm and interest in things that have excited us and driven us to achieve great things for God and His kingdom in the past. Like Timothy we need to rekindle the gift that lies within us.

Have you had enthusiasm and excitement about ministry activity or service that no longer moves you at all? Please list those activities and why you lost your enthusiasm.

-------------------------------------------------------------------------------------------------------

-------------------------------------------------------------------------------------------------------

-------------------------------------------------------------------------------------------------------

-------------------------------------------------------------------------------------------------------

-------------------------------------------------------------------------------------------------------

-------------------------------------------------------------------------------------------------------

-------------------------------------------------------------------------------------------------------

-------------------------------------------------------------------------------------------------------

## God speaks in other ways

God speaks to people in a variety of ways that helps them to understand who they are and what He expects of them. He does this through sermons and through the reading of the Bible and Christian books. God has also spoken to people through an encounter with an angel or through His own appearance. For example, an angel of the Lord appeared to Gideon and

---

[207] 2 Timothy 1:6.

declared, "The LORD is with you, you mighty man of valour."[208] When the angel spoke that day God called Gideon by his rightful name, "O mighty man of valour," and Gideon knew that was his name. With that declaration God highlighted Gideon's purpose and destiny. God's purpose is often declared by the calling of our name, or by the redefinition of our names, as God did with Abraham and Sarah.[209] Many people have for various reasons changed their names, when coming to a new country or making a new beginning.

Has God spoken to you in any other way? Has God redefined your purpose by calling you by another name? Have you changed your name in the past?

---

---

---

---

---

---

## THAT STILL SMALL VOICE

After his victory against the prophets of Baal and the restoration of faith to the nation of Israel, Elijah fled to the mountains for fear of reprisal from Jezebel.[210] There God revealed Himself to Elijah and spoke to him about how God communicates to us His purpose and will.

> And he said, "Go forth, and stand upon the mount before the LORD." And behold, the LORD passed by, and a great and strong wind rent the mountains, and broke in pieces the rocks before the LORD, but the LORD was not in the wind; and after the wind an earthquake, but the LORD was not in the earthquake; and after the earthquake a fire, but the LORD was not in the fire; and after the fire a still small voice.[211]

God speaks to us in many ways, but one of the most important ways is through the still small voice of the Holy Spirit. God does not shout at us, nor does he shove or push us, but speaks through the stillness of His voice into our lives, so that we may know His purpose and will.

---

[208] Judges 6:12.
[209] Genesis 17:5,15.
[210] 1 Kings 19:3.
[211] 1 Kings 19:11-12.

What things has God spoken to you about, in regards to your ministry and service, through the still small voice of the Holy Spirit?

-------------------------------------------------------------------------------

-------------------------------------------------------------------------------

-------------------------------------------------------------------------------

-------------------------------------------------------------------------------

-------------------------------------------------------------------------------

## ACTION REQUIRED

God is not hiding His purpose for your life. The following questions aim to assist you to identify where God has spoken into your life, in the area of His purpose and destiny for your life. That may still not be clear, but you may see some clues to that purpose in what you have written. Please answer the following questions in a general sense:

### 2.1 MY CALLING

#### 2.1.1 Arena of Your Purpose/Destiny: ...................................................................

This is just the general area of calling such as administration, helps, missions, pastoral ministry, evangelism, etc.

#### 2.1.2 Geography of Purpose/Destiny: ...............................................................

This is only relevant if you feel God has called you to a particular place, such as your local church, inner city work, Africa, outback, Gold Coast, etc.

#### 2.1.3 Particular People Group: ..........................................................................

This is only relevant if you feel called to a particular group of people, such as strangers, visitors or new people, multicultural group, children, youth, aged care, etc.

#### 2.1.4 Particular Need: ......................................................................................

This is only relevant if you feel called to help alleviate a particular need, such as the impact of poverty, abused children and wives, drug addicts, lonely people, rich people, etc.

Once you have completed answering the above questions please transfer those answers to the Gift Discovery Workbook, under the heading: *2.1 My Calling.*

# Chapter Twenty-Two

# Servanthood

## 3.1 ENGAGING SERVANTHOOD

In the previous section we worked through the arenas or areas of ministry or service that God has called us to do. For some of us that arena may not be entirely clear at this point, but as you continue to seek God it will become clearer to you. What we aim to do now is to bring the picture of God's purpose and destiny for us into the here and now. What does God want you to do in the next twelve months? For some, it will mean continuing in the same area of ministry or service, but with greater enthusiasm and purpose. For others, it will mean some changes need to occur so that you can move towards what God wants for your life. For others, it will be a time of refining or training the gifts and skills God has given to you. This may include both formal and informal training in ministry.

*For all of us however, it will be a time of serving.*

## 3.1.1 *Serving Your Purpose and Destiny*

You cannot divorce servanthood from the fulfilment of God's purpose and destiny for your life. Serving is the means by which we own, engage and fulfil our God-given purpose and destiny. Serving was the means by which Jesus fulfilled His purpose and destiny as Saviour and Redeemer of all people. We know that, and Jesus makes it clear that He wants us to serve too. For many of us, we still have some serious reservations about serving and servanthood. Most of us interpret the word 'serving' to mean menial chores and tasks. We believe that servants do all the things that nobody else likes to do or are too busy to do. Certainly, there is an element of menial service in this concept of servanthood. Jesus at the Last Supper washed His disciples' feet. It was seen as a menial task. This was reflected by Peter's reaction, when he refused to have his feet washed by his "Lord." Jesus then rubs it in and notes that if their Lord and Teacher did this for them, then they should do this for one another.[212] Such an element of menial service also arises from the background of the usage of the Greek word, *diakonia* or *diakonos*, which was the main word used in the New Testament for serving. It meant to serve, to render service or to wait upon, "to wait at table."[213] It was the word that Jesus used when He referred to His own serving, when He said to His disciples:

---

[212] John 13:1-15.
[213] K. Giles, *Patterns of Ministry Among the First Christians*, Collins Dove, Melbourne, 1989, 50.

*"You know that the rulers of the Gentiles lord it over them, and their great men exercise authority over them. It shall not be so among you; but whoever would be great among you must be your servant, and whoever would be first among you must be your slave; even as the Son of man came not to be served but to serve, and to give his life as a ransom for many."*[214]

**Question:** Note an instance where someone has blessed you and assisted you by doing a menial task for you.

..........................................................................................................................................

..........................................................................................................................................

..........................................................................................................................................

..........................................................................................................................................

..........................................................................................................................................

Though Jesus, at the last Supper, performed an act of menial service for His disciples, menial service was not the primary thing that Jesus was referring to when He made this statement. Jesus served by fulfilling the purpose that God had for His life. That purpose was to give His life as a ransom for many. How much easier it would have been for Him to serve at tables than to go to the Cross? How much easier would it have been for Him to set up a carpenter's shop in Nazareth, or a franchise in Capernaum, than to return to Jerusalem where certain death awaited? Jesus served God's purpose, and it cost Him His life. But in serving that purpose He fulfilled His destiny and brought salvation and redemption to a lost and forlorn world. When Jesus asked His disciples to serve, what was He really asking them to do? When He asked them to be slaves to one another, what was He really calling them to achieve? He was not primarily calling them to do menial chores for one another. If Jesus was not referring to menial chores, then what did He really mean?

1.  Firstly, He was calling them to serve one another's God-given purpose. Remember the issue arose over who was going to get the right and left-hand positions when He came into His kingdom.[215] When we serve one another's purpose, then we will bring about the fulfilment of our own purpose. Paul notes this in Philippians when he says, "Let each of you look not only to his own interests, but also to the interests of others."[216] Charles Finney was one of the greatest evangelists of the 19th Century. His effectiveness in preaching the gospel was significantly enhanced by Fr Nash serving him in prayer.[217]

---

214 Matthew 20:25-28.
215 Matthew 20:20-24.
216 Philippians 2:4.
217 Basil Miller, *Charles Finney*, Dimension Books, Minnesota, 1941, 47 Fr Nash would go into a town three days ahead of Finney and pray constantly for revival to occur in that town.

**Question:** Note an instance where you assisted someone else in their project and found that you received a blessing as well.

..................................................................................................................................

..................................................................................................................................

..................................................................................................................................

..................................................................................................................................

..................................................................................................................................

..................................................................................................................................

2.  Secondly, He calls us to serve by fulfilling God's purpose for our lives. When we set out to accomplish God's purpose, then we fulfil our destiny in Him. Jesus focused His serving upon giving His life as a ransom for many, which was God's purpose in sending His Son into the world. Our serving must also be focused in God's purpose and destiny for our lives. It is the reason why He made us the way He did. Stevens & Collins note that, "Simply put, Christian leaders serve God and God's interests in the world first."[218] When we serve God's purpose, we help Him to achieve what He intended to achieve and make us a blessing in the lives of others.

    **Question:** Note something that you have done that was focused upon God's purposes.

..................................................................................................................................

..................................................................................................................................

..................................................................................................................................

..................................................................................................................................

..................................................................................................................................

..................................................................................................................................

..................................................................................................................................

---

[218] R. Paul Stevens & Phil Collins, *The Equipping Pastor*, Alban Institute, New York, 1993, 110.

## 3.1.2 Focused Serving

To serve the purposes of God and His will for our lives, our serving needs to be focused. Certainly there are people with a gift of helps, and they like to serve wherever they can be of help and in whatever capacity. But even they need to be focused in their helping. Too many eager and willing people have been handed job after job in the church until they collapse under the weight or burn out in the service of God. Eugene Peterson in *The Gift* highlights the need for us to focus on the actual work God wants done and simply not to be seen to look busy.[219] Busyness arises out of continually allowing other people to set the agenda for us, instead of us getting hold of God's agenda and fulfilling His purpose.[220] We have a responsibility to get a hold of God and to know His purpose and will. Paul says, "Do not be conformed to this world but be transformed by the renewal of your mind, *that you may prove what is the will of God, what is good and acceptable and perfect.*"[221]

It is our responsibility to seek out and find the purpose of God for us and to take whatever avenue we can find to fulfil it. Though the Church is called to encourage us in stepping out into God's purpose and destiny for us, we are responsible for its fulfilment.

> **Question:** Rather than being busy for God, what happens in our lives when we begin to do the things that God wants done? If possible, please give an example.

...............................................................................................................................

...............................................................................................................................

...............................................................................................................................

...............................................................................................................................

...............................................................................................................................

...............................................................................................................................

...............................................................................................................................

...............................................................................................................................

...............................................................................................................................

...............................................................................................................................

---

[219] Eugene H. Peterson, *The Gift*, Marshall Pickering, 1995, 17.
[220] Peterson, *The Gift*, 18.
[221] Romans 12:2.

## 3.2 YOUR AVAILABILITY

How much time can you realistically commit to using your gifts for the kingdom of God?

We all live busy lives, but to be effective, we need to prioritise our commitments and then organize our time appropriately. The following is a typical list of our priorities as Christians in order of importance:

1. Personal time developing my relationship with God.

2. Personal time developing myself – mentally, emotionally, physically.

3. Personal time with my husband or wife.

4. Personal time with my children.

5. Work and career requirements.

6. Christian service related activities.

7. Leisure time activities.

This list is obviously flexible because at any one point in our lives an item of lesser priority may temporarily and for a short time become of greater importance. But we need to take care that the urgent need does not become the norm and overshadow the eternally important things in our lives.

And obviously, not all categories may apply - for example, if you are unmarried or do not have children. However, you may have parents who need your attention.

These are our typical priorities. They do not indicate the amount of time required for each activity nor the free time that we have available.

The time we have available for our Christian service related activities should be prayerfully considered so that we can make a real commitment to the time we can spend in these activities.

## *Action Required*

- Turn to the Gift Discovery Workbook.

- Please enter your availability under: *3.2 My Availability*.

## 3.3 What's the Next Step – Finding Opportunity

Casey Treat posed the question during a Hillsong conference, What's the next step? You want a church of 10,000 people. Whilst you keep focusing on the 10,000 you will never achieve it. The question is: what is the next step? If you have a church of 200 people, what do you have to do to move it to 400 people? Also what will your church need to be doing to minister to a church of 400 people? If you have a church of 2,000 people, what do you have to do to move it to 4,000 people? Even more important what will your church need to be doing to minister to 4,000 people? It is when a church understands what the next step is in the progress towards its destiny that it can take that step into the future.

We also need to look at the next step into our future. We may have a vision of what God wants us to be and the destiny He has for us. Unless we know what the next step towards that destiny might be, we will never achieve it. We need to step out and use the gifts and abilities God has given to us in the situation at hand, the opportunity that is available now. When we use our gifts, we will grow and develop. Demos Shakarian wrote, "I believe God has a particular gift for each of His servants, some special ability we're to use for His Kingdom. I believe if we find that gift – and use it – we'll be the happiest people on earth. And if we miss it, no matter how many excellent things we do, we'll be utterly miserable."[222]

Opportunities for ministry and service occur inside and outside your local church. We all need to be active in the ministry and fellowship life of our local church. At the same time there are enormous opportunities within our local community and beyond for ministry and service. Now that you have identified the nature of the gifts and abilities God has given to you, you need to find the opportunity to use them. The following exercise asks you to look carefully at the opportunities currently available in your local church, as well as opportunities beyond your church, for you to be actively engaged.

There are also times when God will ask us to pioneer a new work in our local church or beyond. If there are no self-evident opportunities available for you in the area of your gifting or purpose, then you might need to discuss with your minister/ministers what you could do to start such a ministry in your local church or community.

---

[222] Demos Shakarian, *The Happiest People on Earth*, Hodder and Stoughton, London, 1996, 110-111.

### 3.3.1 Working Out Your Opportunities

## *Action Required*

Turn back to section *2.1 MY CALLING* and copy the answers you had for the general area of your purpose and destiny to the table below.

2.1.1    Arena of Your Purpose/Destiny ..................................................................

2.1.2    Geography of Purpose/Destiny ..................................................................

2.1.3    Particular People Group ..................................................................

2.1.4    Particular Need ..................................................................

What opportunities are available within your local church or community that indicate the next step God has for you to fulfil your destiny?

*Please complete this table with the best options you have right now. These options will change over time.*

| Your Local Church | Beyond Your Local Church |
|---|---|
|  |  |
|  |  |
|  |  |
|  |  |

| What steps do you need to take to engage that opportunity? |
|---|
| 1/ |
| 2/ |
| 3/ |
| 4/ |

Transfer your choice of "Your Local Church" & "Beyond Your Local Church" Opportunities to Gift Discovery Workbook under: *3.3.1 My Choice of Opportunities.*

## God gifts us for ministry and anoints us for effectiveness

God does not call us to ministry and then leave us bereft of assistance. Jesus tells us that we can do nothing effectively for the Kingdom of God and His Church without Him [John15:4]. Just as the branches of a vine tree are dependent upon the vine for sustenance and life, so are we dependent upon Him for our life and ministry (John 15:1-6). Jesus calls us to be effective or fruitful in the purpose God has for our lives and the destiny that lies before us. God empowers us through the Holy Spirit so that we can achieve all that God want us to achieve and more (Acts 1:8). Along with empowerment for ministry God calls us to develop character (Romans 5:1-5). Walking with the Father through Jesus Christ, and in the power of the Holy Spirit means an ongoing growth and development of the following aspects of our lives:

- Our attitudes
- Our character
- Our relationships
- Our unhealed hurts
- Our level of discouragement & cynicism
- Our mindsets and perceptions
- Our ministry skills and abilities
- Our level of training

As you begin to re-focus on God's call in your life and the things He wants you to do, you need to allow Him to continue to grow and develop you. In this time of paradigm change and great change you need to develop a heart for learning, no matter how old or experienced you might be. Ongoing training and development of your gifts and abilities is essential to you being effective and fruitful in the things that God wants you to do. Taking time out to learn will focus you more clearly on the real things God wants you to achieve and helps to eliminate those things that are periphery to His purpose.

## *Action Required*

Turn to the Gift Discovery Workbook and answer the question:

### 3.4.1 Further Development & Training

## 3.5 GROUND TAKEN[223]

### 3.5.1 Personal Ground

During this course you have taken new ground towards the completion and fulfilment for God's purpose for your life and your destiny:

**Question:** What have you learnt about yourself during This course? Write them down here.

.................................................................................................................................

.................................................................................................................................

.................................................................................................................................

.................................................................................................................................

**Question:** Did some things surprise you? Make a note of them here.

.................................................................................................................................

.................................................................................................................................

.................................................................................................................................

.................................................................................................................................

**Question:** What things confirmed what you already knew about yourself? Make a note of them here.

.................................................................................................................................

.................................................................................................................................

.................................................................................................................................

.................................................................................................................................

It is interesting and exciting to discover new things about ourselves, but it is also satisfying to have an external source confirm what we already knew. This confirmation gives us new incentive to continue on and develop further, refining and polishing so that we can shine and reflect the glory of our King.

---

[223] Note: The material included in section 3.5 was compiled by Lynette Peters.

### 3.5.2 God's Purpose and Vision

To use our gifts according to God's purpose we need to be submitted to His purpose rather than our own. We need to know the direction He is leading the Church and how He is building it.

**Question:** What is the Vision of your Church? Note here the aspect of your Church's vision that inspires you the most

...........................................................................................................................................

...........................................................................................................................................

...........................................................................................................................................

...........................................................................................................................................

...........................................................................................................................................

**Question:** Do you see an area where you can contribute to the fulfilment of that Vision, using your gifts and abilities? Note it here.

...........................................................................................................................................

...........................................................................................................................................

...........................................................................................................................................

...........................................................................................................................................

...........................................................................................................................................

If you are not already contributing in some way to that Vision, it is time to take what you have learned and discuss it with a leader in your Church. Let them know that you are willing to be fully part of your Church's Vision and together you (you, your leaders, your Church and the Holy Spirit) can form an awesome and impacting partnership for God's glory and the building of His Kingdom.

# Chapter Twenty-Three

# GIFT DISCOVERY COURSE

# WORKBOOK

ANDREW PETERS   -   ROY EVERETT

## Personal Details:

| | | | |
|---|---|---|---|
| **Name** | | | |
| **Address** | | | |
| | | | |
| | | **Postcode:** | |
| **Telephone** | **(B)** | **(H)** | |
| **Fax** | | **Mobile:** | |
| **E-mail** | | | |
| **Date of Birth** | | | |
| **First Language** | | | |
| **Other Languages** | | | |
| **Spouse** | | | |
| **Child** | | **Birthday** | |
| **Child** | | **Birthday** | |
| **Child** | | **Birthday** | |
| **Child** | | **Birthday** | |
| **Child** | | **Birthday** | |
| **Date Saved** | | | |
| **Date Baptised** | | | |

| | | | | | | | | | | | | | Totals | |
|---|---|---|---|---|---|---|---|---|---|---|---|---|---|---|

## 1.1 Gifts Questionnaire Answer Sheet

| | | | | | | | | | | | | Totals | |
|---|---|---|---|---|---|---|---|---|---|---|---|---|---|
| 1 | | 29 | | 57 | | 85 | | 113 | | 141 | | 169 | | | A |
| 2 | | 30 | | 58 | | 86 | | 114 | | 142 | | 170 | | | B |
| 3 | | 31 | | 59 | | 87 | | 115 | | 143 | | 171 | | | C |
| 4 | | 32 | | 60 | | 88 | | 116 | | 144 | | 172 | | | D |
| 5 | | 33 | | 61 | | 89 | | 117 | | 145 | | 173 | | | E |
| 6 | | 34 | | 62 | | 90 | | 118 | | 146 | | 174 | | | F |
| 7 | | 35 | | 63 | | 91 | | 119 | | 147 | | 175 | | | G |
| 8 | | 36 | | 64 | | 92 | | 120 | | 148 | | 176 | | | H |
| 9 | | 37 | | 65 | | 93 | | 121 | | 149 | | 177 | | | I |
| 10 | | 38 | | 66 | | 94 | | 122 | | 150 | | 178 | | | J |
| 11 | | 39 | | 67 | | 95 | | 123 | | 151 | | 179 | | | K |
| 12 | | 40 | | 68 | | 96 | | 124 | | 152 | | 180 | | | L |
| 13 | | 41 | | 69 | | 97 | | 125 | | 153 | | 181 | | | M |
| 14 | | 42 | | 70 | | 98 | | 126 | | 154 | | 182 | | | N |
| 15 | | 43 | | 71 | | 99 | | 127 | | 155 | | 183 | | | O |
| 16 | | 44 | | 72 | | 100 | | 128 | | 156 | | 184 | | | P |
| 17 | | 45 | | 73 | | 101 | | 129 | | 157 | | 185 | | | Q |
| 18 | | 46 | | 74 | | 102 | | 130 | | 158 | | 186 | | | R |
| 19 | | 47 | | 75 | | 103 | | 131 | | 159 | | 187 | | | S |
| 20 | | 48 | | 76 | | 104 | | 132 | | 160 | | 188 | | | T |
| 21 | | 49 | | 77 | | 105 | | 133 | | 161 | | 189 | | | U |
| 22 | | 50 | | 78 | | 106 | | 134 | | 162 | | 190 | | | V |
| 23 | | 51 | | 79 | | 107 | | 135 | | 163 | | 191 | | | W |
| 24 | | 52 | | 80 | | 108 | | 136 | | 164 | | 192 | | | X |
| 25 | | 53 | | 81 | | 109 | | 137 | | 165 | | 193 | | | Y |
| 26 | | 54 | | 82 | | 110 | | 138 | | 166 | | 194 | | | Z |
| 27 | | 55 | | 83 | | 111 | | 139 | | 167 | | 195 | | | AA |
| 28 | | 56 | | 84 | | 112 | | 140 | | 168 | | 196 | | | AB |

**Instructions:**

Enter: 3 in the box if you agree with the statement.   Enter: 2 in the box if you agree most of the time.

Enter: 1 in the box if you agree some of the time.   Enter: 0 in the box if you disagree with the statement

## 1.3 Gift Discovery - Best Fit

| | Gift | Personally Identified Gifts | Scores on Questionnaire | Gift Ownership "Best Fit" |
|---|---|---|---|---|
| A | Administration | | | |
| B | Counselling | | | |
| C | Craftsmanship | | | |
| D | Creative | | | |
| E | Encouragement | | | |
| F | Giving | | | |
| G | Helps | | | |
| H | Hospitality | | | |
| I | Insight | | | |
| J | Leadership | | | |
| K | Mercy | | | |
| L | Teaching | | | |
| M | Word of knowledge | | | |
| N | Word of wisdom | | | |
| O | Discerning of spirits | | | |
| P | Faith | | | |
| Q | Gifts of healings | | | |
| R | Working of miracles | | | |
| S | Prophecy | | | |
| T | Tongues | | | |
| U | Interpretation of | | | |
| V | Apostle | | | |
| W | Prophet | | | |
| X | Evangelist | | | |
| Y | Pastor/Shepherd | | | |
| Z | Teacher | | | |
| AA | Evangelism | | | |
| Learning Style | | | | |

### 1.6.1 Formal Education

Please tick boxes that indicate your formal education levels.

SECONDARY SCHOOL: Grade 10 ☐ Grade 12 ☐

TERTIARY COLLEGE (TAFE LEVEL): Certificate ☐ Dip/Adv. Diploma ☐

Field Of Study: ………………………………………………………………

UNIVERSITY LEVEL: Bachelor ☐ Post-Grad Cert/Dip ☐

Masters ☐ Doctorate ☐

Field Of Study: ………………………………………………………………

### 1.6.2 Non-Formal Training

Please list any training courses you have completed.

#### WORK-BASED TRAINING COURSES:

☐ ………………………………………… ☐ …………………………………………

☐ ………………………………………… ☐ …………………………………………

#### CHURCH OR VOLUNTEER BASED TRAINING COURSES:

☐ ………………………………………… ☐ …………………………………………

☐ ………………………………………… ☐ …………………………………………

### 1.6.3 Self-taught Skills

Please list any significant self-taught skills and abilities you have acquired

#### SELF TAUGHT SKILLS & ABILITIES:

☐ ………………………………………… ☐ …………………………………………

☐ ………………………………………… ☐ …………………………………………

## 1.6.4 Current Work and Ministry Experience

1.  **Work Position:**   Managerial ☐   Employee ☐   Self-employed ☐

    Role or Title:................................................................

    Nature of Work:............................................................

    Full-time ☐   Part-time ☐   Casual ☐

2.  **Work Position:**   Managerial ☐ Employee ☐   Self-employed ☐

    Role or Title:................................................................

    Nature of Work:............................................................

    Full-time ☐   Part-time ☐   Casual ☐

3.  **Ministry Position:**   Leadership ☐   Employee ☐   Volunteer ☐

    Role or Title:................................................................

    Nature of Work:............................................................

    Full-time ☐   Part-time ☐   Casual ☐

4.  **Ministry Position:**   Leadership ☐   Employee ☐   Volunteer ☐

    Role or Title:................................................................

    Nature of Work:............................................................

    Full-time ☐   Part-time ☐   Casual ☐

## 1.6.5   Work and Volunteer Experience (or Hobbies)

☐  ........................................   ☐  ........................................

☐  ........................................   ☐  ........................................

☐  ........................................   ☐  ........................................

☐  ........................................   ☐  ........................................

### 1.6.6 Personal Skills

☐ ..............................................  ☐ ..............................................

☐ ..............................................  ☐ ..............................................

### 1.6.7 Autobiography

_____

_____

_____

_____

_____

_____

_____

_____

_____

_____

_____

_____

_____

_____

_____

## 2.1    My Calling

2.1.1    Arena of Your Purpose/Destiny ...................................................................

2.1.2    Geography of Purpose/Destiny ...................................................................

2.1.3    Particular People Group ...................................................................

2.1.4    Particular Need ...................................................................

## 3.2  My Availability

Please indicate the day/days and the time/times you can be available and commit to Christian service activities. Eg Sunday morning once a month, Saturday 4 hours flexible, Tuesday evenings 6-10 pm.

| Day | Available Time |
|---|---|
| Sunday | |
| Monday | |
| Tuesday | |
| Wednesday | |
| Thursday | |
| Friday | |
| Saturday | |

## 3.3.1  My Choice of Opportunities

I would like to be involved in the following areas:

1/ In my Local Church: ...................................................................

...................................................................

2/ Beyond my Local Church: ...................................................................

...................................................................

### 3.4.1  Further Development and Training

I would like to receive further ministry equipping, training and development through my Church's Ministry and Leadership development programs.

☐   Yes, please.                    ☐   Not at this time, thank you.

## ACKNOWLEDGEMENT

I, (name)   ................................................................   acknowledge   and   agree   that   the information I have provided, in this Gift Discovery Workbook, can be made available to the Senior Leaders of my church: ..............................................................................................
for appropriate use in developing my ministry and its opportunities.


Signed       ...........................................................       Date    ......................................

# APPENDIX

# APPENDIX 1

## EVALUATION OF ORDAINED LEADERS

### EFFECTIVENESS VERSES EFFICIENCY

Peter Drucker notes that "Effectiveness is the foundation of success – efficiency is a minimum condition for survival after success has been achieved. Efficiency is concerned with doing things right. Effectiveness is doing the right things."[224] John Maxwell in expounding the Pareto Principle notes that "Success is the progressive realization of a predetermined goal."[225] The Pareto principle itself notes that 20 percent of our priorities will give us 80 percent of our production. It means that effectiveness is directly related to what we give our time to, not what time we give. In a day of changing paradigms the Church's issue with evaluation of ordained leaders must focus on their ability to bring new success by identifying those "right things," and not just to be efficient in doing things right. It is our lack of effectiveness that stimulates the current push for clergy evaluation, but it is our propensity for efficiency that will impede the effectiveness of that evaluation. This is because efficiency is the foundation for survival, whereas effectiveness is the foundation for success.[226]

That is, efficiency enables us to maintain the successes of the past, but does nothing to enhance the future. Effectiveness, on the other hand, comes when we identify what things we can do in the present that will produce fruit for the future.[227] Learning to become effective however can only occur in a system that encourages and stimulates that to happen. The reason that the church has a propensity for efficiency is that efficiency requires no change to the system itself. Because it maintains past successes, it requires no commitment to or investment in the future in regards to time, money and support. But once the evaluation focuses upon making ordained leaders more effective, then it confronts those factors in the church's life, both local and Diocesan, which hinder that effectiveness. If ordained leaders are to work smarter, rather than harder,[228] then clergy effectiveness, and its evaluation, can no longer be seen in isolation to the situation in which they work.

---

[224] Hersey, Blanchard, & Johnson, *Management of Organizational Behavior,* 144.

[225] Maxwell, *Developing the Leader Within You,* (Thomas Nelson Publishers, Nashville, 1993), 21.

[226] Maxwell, *Developing the Leader Within You,* 21-22

[227] Drucker, Peter *"Managing in a Time of Great Change,"* (Butterworth-Heinmann, Oxford, 1995),. vii, 36. Peter Drucker notes that "one cannot make decisions for the future. Decisions are commitments to actions. And actions are always present, and in the present only." (p. vii). And again he says, "Successful innovations exploit changes that have already happened. They exploit the time lag between the change itself and its perception and acceptance".

[228] Handy, Charles *The Age of Unreason,* 113.

The nature of ministry and leadership is changing rapidly in a day of changing paradigms, and clergy evaluation can either contribute to or distract from the ordained leader's ability to move with those changes and grow. Jill Hudson warns us that underlying currents can severely impact the validity and effectiveness of clergy evaluation. These relate directly to its motivation and purpose. The reason that formal evaluation is often resisted and is seen to be both scary and threatening is because "We generally associate "evaluation" with "judgement," and no one likes to be judged."[229] But worse than that she notes that, "Pastors often fear that evaluations will reveal painful critiques of their leadership, or – even worse – be used to orchestrate their departure."[230] The problem at the heart of this of course is that those fears "too often are founded in reality."[231]

We must understand however, that clergy evaluation neither serves the purpose of justifying the removal of a pastor nor his or her retention. To use it for such purposes is to practice some form of psychological terrorism. Jill Hudson goes on to say,

> Pastors, congregational leaders, and members are all earthen vessels. We can be excellent carriers, we can be full, we can be empty. But we need care in handling. Vessels can be turned over, chipped, and broken and the valuable resource inside lost. Evaluations should further equip us to carry the Gospel into the world. They should never be used to punish.[232]

Even in such cases where correction and re-direction is needed, and may instigate some form of discipline of the ordained leader, Hersey, Blanchard and Johnson note, "The problem solving nature of *constructive discipline* differentiates it from punitive discipline. As such, constructive discipline is designed to be a learning process that provides an opportunity for positive growth." However, it is important to note that the effectiveness of constructive discipline is seen in whether it produces positive growth.

## EVALUATION AS JUDGMENT

Because of its very nature, "evaluation" has not only the propensity to be seen as "judgement" but to actually become "judgement." To "evaluate" means to "determine or estimate the value of something or to assess its value".[233] Once we invoke a process that determines or assesses the value of an ordained person's ministry then we lay that person open to judgement of that ministry. Evaluation and judgement are certainly not the same thing, but one can certainly lead to the other as "to judge" carries the connotations of, "to

---

[229] Hudson, Jill M. "Evaluating Ministry, Principles and Processes for Clergy and Congregations," (Alban Institute Publication, New York, 1992) 1.

[230] Hudson, *Evaluating Ministry, Principles and Processes for Clergy and Congregations,* 2.

[231] Hudson, *Evaluating Ministry, Principles and Processes for Clergy and Congregations,* 2.

[232] Hudson, *Evaluating Ministry, Principles and Processes for Clergy and Congregations,* 8.

[233] Microsoft, *"Microsoft Bookshelf Basics Edition – Dictionary,"* (Microsoft Corporation 1996) The Australian Oxford Dictionary (Herron Publications, West End Qld 1988), 154.

hear and determine authoritatively … to decide the merits of; to find fault with, to censure, condemn; to decide; to award; to estimate; to form an opinion on; to conclude; to consider (to be).[234] Since the potential to move from evaluation to judgement is so immense it is important to consider the desired results of our efforts. Kennon Callahan notes the results of an evaluation process that he calls "top-down," which originates from the top of the denomination and calls for some form of committee to evaluate the pastor. He proposes that this form of evaluation process creates in the pastor certain results:

1. Passive-aggressive behavior;

2. Low-grade hostility;

3. Subliminal resentment; and

4. Eruptive forms of anger.[235]

He goes on to say, "Other than these four results, a top-down process does not accomplish a single thing. (On reflection, the top-down process does also produce reactive, passive, organizational, institutional pastors.)"[236] What is does not produce is effective pastors. Callahan's difficulties are with the type of evaluation process being carried out, not the idea of evaluation itself.  He proposes that a more effective form of evaluation involves the ordained leader carrying out a self-evaluation that is a realistic assessment of one's own current competencies, which is then linked to a consultative committee that forms an advisory and helpful input, that is both collegial and constructive. Callahan concludes by saying, "The spirit of consultative evaluation is coaching, not correcting. Under threat, people wither. With encouragement, people achieve". [237]

The Apostle Paul provides some important insights at this juncture. In his dealing with the Corinthian Church. Paul had to defend both his calling and the administration of his apostleship.[238] Though he defends his apostleship throughout the two letters, he does not give the Corinthians any grounds to think that they have a right, let alone a duty, to evaluate or judge his ministry. "But with me it is a very small thing that I should be judged by you or by any human court. I do not even judge myself. I am not aware of anything against myself, but I am not thereby acquitted. It is the Lord who judges me."[239] For Paul his ministry was instigated by Christ, established by Christ, enabled by Christ and it is Christ

---

[234] Microsoft, "Microsoft Bookshelf Basics Edition – Dictionary.

[235] Callahan, Effective Church Leadership, 180, 185.

[236] Callahan, Effective Church Leadership, 185.

[237] Callahan, Effective Church Leadership, 178, 185. 200. He says, "Key principle: The evaluation process of an organization develops the nature of leadership in the organization. To change the nature of leadership, one must change the evaluation process".

[238] 2 Corinthians 10:7ff (RSV). The intensity of this dispute grows through the two letters and eventually goads Paul into statements about his apostleship that he feels inappropriate, but called for.

[239] 1 Corinthians 4:3-4 (RSV).

whom he served and to whom he was responsible to be trustworthy.[240] For Paul it is the source of his ministry that determines who has a right to judge that ministry and to whom he has to give account. Though the outworking of the ministry occurred within the context of the Body of Christ and the world,[241] the source and assessment of that ministry lied with God.[242]

However, Paul was not willing to escape assessment altogether. In his letter to the Galatians Paul notes his efforts to have his ministry assessed and valued.

> Then after fourteen years I went up again to Jerusalem with Barnabas, taking Titus along with me. I went up by revelation; and I laid before them (but privately before those who were of repute) the gospel which I preach among the Gentiles, lest somehow I should be running or had run in vain.[243]

Although Paul did this willingly he also did it warily, being careful as to who had access to that process and who didn't. "But because of false brethren secretly brought in… to them we did not yield submission even for a moment."[244] Paul takes this process very seriously and inferred that the process itself held some form of submission to the evaluation of his ministry by those who were of repute. He also notes that the process itself had dangers that could effectively bring his team, himself, and their ministry into bondage. If the wrong people had access to the evaluation process then the process itself could serve to bind and make ineffective the ministry from that point on, rather than enhancing it and enabling it to grow. Paul reports a successful evaluation process and recognises that the right hand of fellowship offered to him at the end of the process further strengthened and established the authenticity of their ministry.[245]

The judgement motifs in the Biblical text create a tension for us between the reality of the judgement of our ministries and the Church's part in that process. However, judgement itself is seen in a positive light, as Geoffrey Bromiley notes:

> judgement itself lays bare our hidden essence… exposing the hypocrisy of acting only for show, for hope of reward, or for fear, …and summoning us to true love of God on the basis and in the power of God's love for us.[246]

Judgement is a work of God and clearly belongs to Him. This is no less the case when we

---

[240] 1 Corinthians 4:1-2 (RSV). "This is how one should regard us, as servants of Christ and stewards of the mysteries of God. Moreover it is required of stewards that they be found trustworthy".

[241] 2 Corinthians 4:5 (RSV). *"for we preach not ourselves, but Jesus Christ as Lord, with ourselves as your servants for Jesus's sake".*

[242] 2 Corinthians 4:1 (RSV). *"Therefore, having this ministry by the mercy of God, we do not lose heart".*

[243] Galatians 2:1-2 (RSV).

[244] Galatians 2:4,5 (RSV).

[245] Galatians 2:4b, 6 7-10 (RSV).

[246] Bromiley, Geoffrey W. *"Theological Dictionary of the New Testament,"* (William Eerdmans Publishing Company, The Paternoster Press, Grand Rapids, Michigan, 1985), 473.

come to the assessment of the effectiveness of our ministry.[247] We are warned about pronouncing judgement upon one another,[248] often because of our lack of clarity and our propensity to make judgements upon the wrong basis.[249] Yet it is in the area of the pastor's administration of his or her ministry that we are most prolific in making judgements and seem to feel that we can do so with impunity. Jill Hudson notes, that "evaluation is a daily occurrence in the life of the Parish. It happens in the parking lot, over the telephone, in the manse".[250]

It would seem that it would be better to leave it alone and let God correct His ministers in his own way and in His own time. However, it is not as simple as that. The writer of the letter to the Hebrews exhorts us not only to remain faithful and believing, but also to encourage one another on an ongoing basis, so that none of us falls away because of sin.

> Take care, brethren, lest there be in any of you an evil, unbelieving heart, leading you to fall away from the living God. But exhort one another every day, as long as it is called "today," that none of you may be hardened by the deceitfulness of sin. For we share in Christ, if only we hold our first confidence firm to the end.[251]

We cannot thus allow those who are under our authority and care to conduct their lives and their ministries in a manner that leads to destruction, without some substantial attempt to redeem them. In the fulfillment of this role, the General Synod of the Church of England's book *Under Authority* notes that the Bishop is

> "also called, as the Shepherd, to care for and pastor the flock. This will include affirming and encouraging clergy, amongst others. And this is particularly vital for those struggling to meet the demands of their vocation."[252]

The question is how does evaluation help or hinder that process?

## Does Evaluation Assist or Hinder

In Jesus' parable of the talents, the five and two talent persons are the ones most likely to take to the right type evaluation process and use it effectively to further enhance their ministries.[253] They are like the "pro" that Kennon Callahan mentions when he says, "But what differentiates the pro in any of these vocations is the capacity to discern what one is doing well, to recognize what one is doing poorly, and to initiate constructive action toward improvement."[254] However, the one talented servant is of great concern. We see the immense loss of this person, whose fear of the severity of his master caused him to act in a slothful and wicked way, that cost him both his reward and his place in the kingdom.

---

[247] 1 Corinthians 4:5 (RSV).
[248] James 4:12 (RSV).
[249] John 7:24 (RSV).
[250] Hudson, *Evaluating Ministry, Principles and Processes for Clergy and Congregations,* 1.
[251] Hebrews 3:12-14 (RSV).
[252] General Synod of the Church of England, *"Under Authority,"* (Church House Publishing, London, 1996), 30.
[253] Matthew 25:24-30 (RSV).
[254] Callahan, *Effective Church Leadership,* 176.

His fear, which stems from a wrong perception of his master, has paralyzed him and created habits of slothfulness and laziness. He is overwhelmed by the task that lies before him and has no idea how to take the necessary risks needed to become effective and to multiply the talent that had been given to him.

Unless some intervention occurs his ministry will stagnate, those around him will deteriorate, and that which had begun with great hope will end up barren and finally lost. It is precisely at this point that the top-down evaluation process runs into major hurdles simply because we assume that the one talented person is not committed. Yet it is some of our most committed clergy, that are not only more susceptible to overstress and burnout, but also seem to develop ministry habits that are self-defeating and contribute to their ineffectiveness. Roy Oswald highlights this cycle (see diagram "1" ). The problem occurs at step VII.

> The end result is a drive to try even harder to make our ministry work which cycles us around again. Each cycle deepens our frustration and cynicism. The last stage of burnout are a despairing of the whole religious enterprise and a giving up on God, ourselves and the church.[255]

Unless we understand that the core problems are ones of misconception of both the nature of ministry and our roles in that ministry, the evaluation process will only serve to deepen the cycle not resolve it. Stevens and Collins note that, "Some people, thinking they are servant-leaders, are actually functioning as doormats, thinking they are doing God's will by doing everyone else's will."[256]

The difficulty with this group of ordained leaders is that the evaluation process will work only too well, especially if it is of the top-down variety. It will tend to reinforce the heavy laden of guilt already evident, and coax them to try even harder to improve than they have before. The problem is that unless the misconceptions are confronted and exposed, the cycle of ineffectiveness will not be broken. The top-down process also has a tendency at this point to focus on its perception of the ineptitude of the ordained leader, which serves to isolate its evaluation of the leader from the context in which he or she works. It becomes evaluation in a vacuum. "Ministry is and must be mutual. Therefore, no individual's performance in ministry can be reviewed with fairness apart from the whole. To look at the pastor's performance in isolation from that of the other key ministers in the congregation (e.g. the members) encourages defensive, win-lose behavior and feelings."[257] In the case of the one talented servant such a process would exaggerate the situation rather than to alleviate it.

---

[255] Oswald, Roy, *Clergy Burnout,* Ministers Life Resources, Inc The Alban Institute Inc, New York, 1982), 36.

[256] Stevens, R. Paul and Collins, Phil *"The Equipping Pastor,"* (An Alban Institute Publication, New York City, 1993), 110.

[257] Hudson, *Evaluating Ministry, Principles and Processes for Clergy and Congregations,* 3.

I.

**Call from God**
**Commitment to Serve**
**High Ideals**

VII.

**Rededication**
**To try even harder**

II.

**Too many to serve.**
**Surrounded by a**
**Sea of human need**

*Clergy*
*Burnout*
*Cycle*

VI.

**Guilt/shame**
for feeling guilt that "I
entered ministry to serve
people and now resent them

III.

**Physical exhaustion.**
**Abuse of body.**
**Strain on family, marriage**
**And other relationships**

V.

**Resentment**
**At Parishioners/clients**
**Sarcasm and biting humor**

IV.

**Helplessness/hopelessness.**
**Trapped feeling**
**quiet despair**

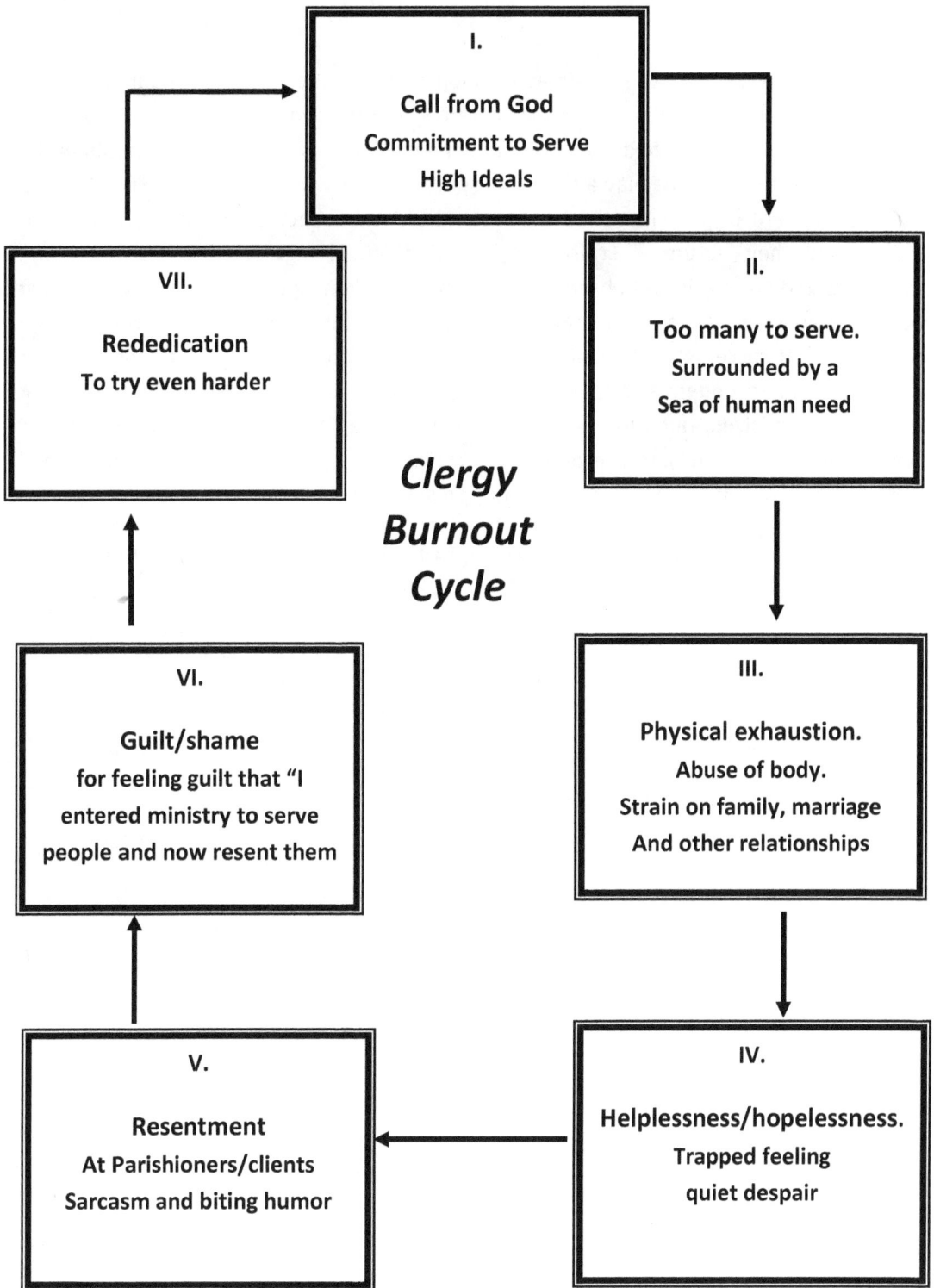

Diagram 1    -    Clergy Burnout [258]

---

[258] Oswald, Roy,  *"Clergy Burnout,"* 35.

Evaluation can serve to make an ordained person more effective once we understand what the process of effectiveness entails. Such terms as effectiveness and success are not divorced from the biblical texts when we understand that the "fruitfulness" motifs in the New Testament documents play a significant part in God's work in our lives. They form "a decisive standard of judgement" of human actions and reflect both the sources of our actions and their nature.[259] Fruitfulness is an essential ingredient in our lives and ministries, and any significant absence of it cannot be taken lightly.[260] Though some might want to draw some distinctions between the call of the Kingdom and its fruitfulness and the essence of success and effectiveness we cannot ignore their impact altogether. It is important also to understand that the goal is effectiveness, not just success. Not that success isn't involved, but success by itself doesn't mean that we are effective. Hersey, Blanchard and Johnson note the difference between mangers that are "successful" and mangers that are "effective."[261] One does not presume the other.

A manager or leader can be both successful and effective, or successful and ineffective:

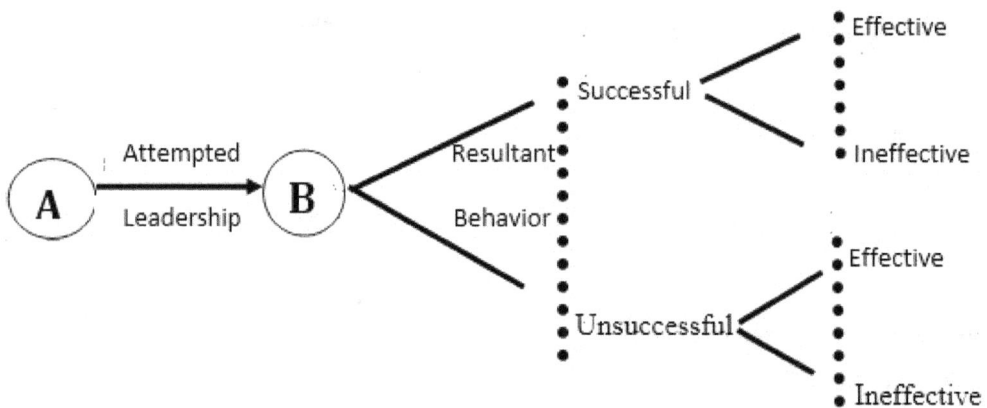

*Figure 6-2 Bass's Successful and Effective Leadership Continuums[262]*

---

[259] Bromiley, *Theological Dictionary of the New Testament,* 416.
The "fruitfulness" motifs are used: to show signs of repentance (Matthew 3:8); to indicate the authenticity of our lives and ministries (Matthew 7:17); in assessing the value of our lives and ministry (Luke 13:7); as evidence of the work of the cross in our lives (John 12:24; Romans 7:4); as a sign of the work of the Holy Spirit in our lives (Galatians 5:22); as a sign that we belong to the kingdom of light and reflect its values (Ephesians 5:9); to indicate a fundamental purpose of God in our lives, whereby He prunes us to bear even more fruit (John 15:1-10); and to focus our attention upon a harvest that is more than ready to be reaped (John 4:35-38).

[260] Galatians 6:9; Mark 11:13-14; 2 Timothy 4:2 (RSV). The tension thus lying between fruitfulness being a seasonal thing and God expecting us to bear fruit in season and out of season. This is seen in the tension that lies between Paul's exhortation that we will reap in due season and Jesus' destruction of the fig tree and Paul exhortation to Timothy the labour in season and out of season.

[261] Hersey, Blanchard, & Johnson, *Management of Organizational Behavior,* 147.

[262] Hersey, Blanchard, & Johnson, *Management of Organizational Behavior,* 147.

Effective managers tended to have more satisfied committed employees and high-performing departments.[263] Ineffective success is usually short-term and has occurred at an enormous cost, burning out the human resources and often heightening the restraining forces so that a repeat of the success is unlikely.[264] Effective success has usually occurred by building the human resources and reducing the restraining forces so that a repeat of the success is more than likely. However, without some formal way of reflecting upon our ministry and its results we may not even recognise the successes that have occurred and how we might repeat the process. "Evaluation can be considered an ongoing process that strengthens our ministry, giving us the opportunity to reflect periodically on how well we are fulfilling our commitments to Christ, the church and one another."[265] It is not so much a question as to whether we should or should not be evaluated, but what type of evaluation that will significantly help us to grow in fruitfulness, success and effectiveness.

## EVALUATION AND THE NATURE OF ORDAINED LEADERSHIP AND MINISTRY

The evaluation of an ordained leader has to take into account the succinct aspects of their work that is significantly different to that of a business manager or leader in other organizations. "The doctor or lawyer rarely tries to change the client's life goals. The minister has a far more complicated relationship with parishioners, making success or failure far harder to measure."[266] As well as this they are meant to be God-orientated servant-leaders. Stevens and Collins make the point, "Simply put, Christian leaders serve God and God's interests in the world first. Only secondarily do they serve people. The order is profoundly important. For a Christian leader, the need is not the call. The call originates in the initiative of God, not the cry of humanity."[267]

The "ordained" leader has been purposely and concretely identified as having been set apart for this "holy ministry."[268] As such any type of evaluation process has to have, as its core purpose, an aim to enhance this relationship with God within the ordained leader's life. For it is only as God-orientated servant-leaders that they can possibly benefit the Body of Christ and enable it to fulfil God's purposes. "And because the servant is dedicated to the Lord's interests, the deepest needs of the people will eventually be served.[269] It is important to note that effective ministry can only occur if this orientation is right. Stevens and Collins note that if the needs of the people are primary then the leaders will either exhaust themselves or become messianic. More than this the ministry will tend to draw attention to itself rather than God. Stevens and Collins define leadership as:

---

263 Hersey, Blanchard, & Johnson, *Management of Organizational Behavior,* 147.
264 Hersey, Blanchard, & Johnson, *Management of Organizational Behavior,* 152.
265 Hudson, *Evaluating Ministry, Principles and Processes for Clergy and Congregations,* 2.
266 Hudson, *Evaluating Ministry, Principles and Processes for Clergy and Congregations,* 13.
267 Stevens,. & Collins, *The Equipping Pastor,* 110.
268 Anglican Church of Australia, *"An Australian Prayer Book,"* (AIO Press, Sydney 1978), 608.
269 Stevens,. & Collins, *The Equipping Pastor,* 110-111.

Christian leadership is the God-given ability to influence others so that believers will trust and respond to the Head of the church for themselves, in order to accomplish the Lord's purposes for God's people in the world."[270]

If the purpose of this type of leadership is to draw attention to God and not itself, then the evaluation process itself must also enhance that purpose.

An extensive congregation based evaluation process, such as the McKinley Church and Foundation review of its co-pastors, reflects some of these difficulties. The McKinley church's "Personnel, Goals and Objectives Committee" canvases a multitude of people, including every member and participating adult of the congregation and the foundation, as well as individuals in the greater Champaign/Urban community.[271] Assessment questions cover five areas of ministry that include: Morning Worship, Personal Contact/Counselling, Teaching, Working with small groups, and Ministry beyond the congregation. They finish with questions asking "In your opinion, what are his strengths?" and "In what ways might he change to improve his performance?"[272] Though both Pastors report positive results and note areas where change has improved their effectiveness, to what extent though has their leadership and vision been "determined" by the process rather than "enhanced." Leaving aside the issue of the three-month period that the process entailed, what is of concern is that the whole church is now focused on how well are our pastors leading us.

If the pastors and their families were not living in a glass fishbowl[273] before this process, you can be sure that they are now. How much now is the pastor's priorities and time commitment determined by the results of this process rather than with serving "the Lord's interests." With such an extensive range of opinions, both positive and negative, who ends up leading whom? "Warren Bennis observed that "the single defining quality of leaders is their ability to create and realize a vision."[274] Widespread feedback might be important for a leader to know whether the vision and its strategies are working, but not to determine what that vision should be, nor even how he or she should implement it. This process also opens the pastors up to very type of danger that Paul went to great lengths to avoid. The nature and activity of "false brethren secretly brought in..." may be different today, but their existence is real. Such influences can selectively and determinably seek, not only to bind the pastor and his or her team, but to quieten the voice of God in the pastor to such an extent that he no longer sees the Lord's interests, but simply those of the people.

Such an undermining of the church's ministry would only occur progressively over time, but would be aided by this type of evaluation process. Its results could well be the same as that reflected by Isaiah when he wrote,

---

[270] Stevens,. & Collins, *The Equipping Pastor,* 117.

[271] Hudson, *Evaluating Ministry, Principles and Processes for Clergy and Congregations,* 19.

[272] Hudson, *Evaluating Ministry, Principles and Processes for Clergy and Congregations,* -32.

[273] Oswald, Roy, *"Clergy Self-care – Finding a balance for Effective Ministry,"* (Alban Institute Publication, New York City, 1991), 90.

[274] Hersey, Blanchard,. & Johnson, *Management of Organizational Behavior,* 92.

> For this is a rebellious people, false sons, sons who refuse to listen to the instruction of the LORD; who say to the seers, "You must not see visions"; and to the prophets, "You must not prophesy to us what is right; speak to us pleasant words, prophesy illusions, get out of the way, turn aside from the path, let us hear no more about the Holy One of Israel."[275]

The evaluation process must enhance the effectiveness of the ordained leader's ministry not determine its outworking. For what the Church needs in this time of changing paradigms are leaders who are strong and focused upon God's purposes in our midst and have enhanced their effectiveness in bringing the Lord's purposes into reality. "To underscore that the servant-leader is not a doormat, but a visionary leader, Greenleaf makes the point that servant-leadership is characterized by vision."[276]

Since it is the ordained leader that shapes and shares the vision, which gives point to the work of others,[277] feedback from the congregation is an essential ingredient in a balanced evaluation of his or her ministry. Nevertheless, a congregation based evaluation process that solely focuses upon the ministry of the ordained leader can only serve to bind and not release the effectiveness of that ministry. The difficulty we face is that an ordained leader's ministry cannot be evaluated outside of the context in which it occurs. Any attempt to do so serves to subtly undermine a proper understanding of ministry. "It is easy for us to forget that the work of the church does not rest on the clergy alone. When we isolate the pastor for evaluation we risk slipping into the mindset that the work of Christ in the world is only accomplished by those called to ordained, professional ministry."[278]

## EVALUATION AND THE MATRIX OF THE COMMUNITY

Whatever form the ordained leader's ministry might take it is best understood as ministry in community – distinctly the community of faith or congregations of a local church. Gauging the health of that community then becomes the best way to assess the effectiveness of that ministry. Kevin Giles notes that "the church should be defined as 'the Christian community.'"[279] However, it is not to be seen as a community established and defined once for all, but a community in transition.[280] This also means that its ministerial structures should also be in transition, in order to meet the ongoing needs of the community.[281] If God provides the leadership the community needs at each of its points in

---

[275] Isaiah 30:8-11 (NASB).

[276] Stevens, & Collins, *The Equipping Pastor,* 117.

[277] Handy, *The Age of Unreason*, 105.

[278] Hudson, *Evaluating Ministry, Principles and Processes for Clergy and Congregations,* 9.

[279] Giles, Kevin, *"What on Earth is the Church?"* (Dove, Harper Collins Publishers, Nth Blackburn, Victoria, 1995), 182.

[280] Giles, *What on Earth is the Church?* 182.

[281] Giles, *What on Earth is the Church?* 187 "This means the church is not defined by its ministerial structures; it is defined by its communal existence given by God in Christ, and by the presence of the Spirit who provides the leaders needed." Whether we can equate the threefold order of bishops, priests and deacons with that of the fivefold order of apostles, prophets, evangelists, pastors and teachers, is uncertain. However, the impact of each group's work in bringing health and welfare the community of the church, must be equated.

transition, then the communal nature of the church becomes the matrix within which the evaluation of that ministry should occur. The reason that this forms the matrix of that evaluation is because "leadership equals the function of the leader, the followers and the situation."[282] Any evaluation of leadership must take into account not only the qualities of the leaders, but also the nature of the followers and their situation. Stevens and Collins note that the "function of the pastor-leader in the living system of the church is to direct the whole body to the end that the parts of the church mesh with one another and exercise mutual care and help so that in the interaction the whole body grows."[283]

If the function of the pastor-leader is so intertwined with the development of the church, of which the pastor-leader himself is an integral part,[284] then the effectiveness of the pastor-leader can only be seen in the light of the effectiveness of the church in both its mutual care for each other and the growth of the body itself. Paul's understanding of the role of ministry in Ephesians 4:11-16 sees ministry operating within a community system, the body of Christ, and implies that the matrix of the evaluation of ordained leadership lies in the heart of the community's health and welfare. The leadership roles of apostle, prophet, evangelist, pastor and teacher are precisely aimed at developing the community, its nature and its life.[285] Since the ordained leader accepts a leadership role within the context of the development of this community and its life, then any assessment of the effectiveness of that ministry must be carried out in the light of that development. The difficulty is that a functional evaluation of the ordained leader may never fully understand why his church might, on the one hand, be strong, vital, stable and growing, or on the other hand, be stagnating, suffocating, and dying, if it is not also linked to some form of evaluation of the community itself and the way it functions.

Parsons and Leas provide a means of reviewing the interrelationship of the dimensions of a congregational system through their CSI (Congregational Systems Inventory).[286] They propose that seeing your congregation as a system assumes that there are many contributing factors or multiple causes to any given set of circumstances, rather than a simple cause.[287] They further note "that rather than churches diminishing tension, they should be looking towards *creating* healthy tensions between two excesses of chaos and

---

[282] Stevens. & Collins, *The Equipping Pastor,* 9.

[283] Stevens. & Collins, *The Equipping Pastor,* 9.

[284] Stevens. & Collins, *The Equipping Pastor,* 3, 5. "But the change will not even begin unless the pastor joins the church. The people must perceive that the pastor is really part of the system." "Leaders thrive and effectively lead precisely because they are like the system, like the people."

[285] Ephesians 4:11-16 (RSV). Its purpose is to improve the health and welfare of the body of Christ by: developing unity, understanding and maturity (v. 13); bringing a growing sense of discernment and interdependence (v. 14); establishing open communication systems and bringing growth to both the individual and the community as a whole (v. 15), based on an ongoing sustaining love (v. 16).

[286] Parsons, George and Leas, Speed *"Understanding Your Congregation as A System,"* (Alban Institute Publication 1993), 3.

[287] Parsons, & Leas, *Understanding Your Congregation as A System,* 17.

over-control in each of the seven continuums they have developed.[288] This healthy tension would enable the congregation to maintain variety, as well as staying flexible and open to renewal."[289] By enabling a congregation to seek a "balance in tension" they also enable the congregation to break loose from homeostatic forces that have locked it into self-defeating practices from the past and enable it to meet new demands in new ways.[290] The essence of the process they have developed places the ordained leader within the context of the situation he or she leads, and assesses them in the light of other factors also operating within the community.

Since the health of the congregation or church is a significant aspect of the appraisal of the ordained leader, then it includes moving away from simply an appraisal of the normal functional roles he or she fulfils. Rather, it looks more carefully at the interaction of the ordained person in relationship to producing effective leadership. It is not interested, for instance, so much in how interesting or long the sermon might be, but rather how effective is it in bringing ongoing growth in the lives of God's people. Similar to business appraisals of managers, such as Mobil Australia, it focuses not so much on the skills themselves, but on the effectiveness of their use.[291] The appraisal areas which include such things as measuring key competencies and practices; encouraging teamwork; giving recognition; developing and coaching others; managing diversity, etc. have a greater potential in stimulating growth in effectiveness than does assessment of traditional clergy roles.

## EVALUATION AND COLLEGIALITY

Charles Handy notes in a time of changing paradigms that the "wise organization realizes, too, that intelligent individuals can only be governed by consent and not by command, that obedience cannot be demanded and that a collegiate culture of colleagues and a shared understanding is the only way to make things happen."[292] This places an onus on church governing bodies, such as the Anglican diocesan hierarchy, to develop an evaluation process that goes to great lengths to establish a sense of collegiality in any evaluation process it might establish. That collegiality must exist both within the Diocesan and congregational components of the appraisal to ensure that the ordained leader is not set up to try and prove their worth. If the ordained leaders senses that in some way or other they have to prove themselves, then that significantly defeats the purpose of evaluation, "which is not to prove but to improve."[293] At the same time the appraisal should not be aimed at finding fault, but to discover and encourage the ordained leader to grow and

---

[288] Parsons, & Leas, *Understanding Your Congregation as A System*, 7, 23 These seven areas include Strategy, Authority, Process, Pastoral Leadership, Relatedness, Lay Leadership, and Learning.

[289] Parsons, & Leas, *Understanding Your Congregation as A System*, 23.

[290] Parsons, & Leas, *Understanding Your Congregation as A System*, 7.

[291] Mobil Australia *"Notes on Mobil Appraisal and Personal Development System.*

[292] Handy, The Age of Unreason, 113.

[293] Hudson, *Evaluating Ministry, Principles and Processes for Clergy and Congregations*, 2.

develop their existing strengths.

Peter Drucker makes the point, "But one cannot build performance on weaknesses, even on corrected ones. One can build performance only on strengths... Strengths do not create problems."[294] Kennon Callahan makes the point, "Substantial power is generated as a congregation discovers and claims its strengths: Power for the future is found in claiming our strengths, not in focusing on our weaknesses and shortcomings."[295] Again he notes "When it becomes preoccupied with its weaknesses, it begins to lose its strengths. Strengths that are not used weaken and decay."[296] What applies to the congregation here even more importantly applies to its leaders. Our evaluation processes so often focus on how to challenge the leader to improve his or her weaknesses, that we actually link that leader into self-defeating activities that will sap them of their strength and rob them of their effectiveness. This is where the decision between a desire for effectiveness must be made over and above that of efficiency, for what we need to do is to find ways to supplement a leader's weaknesses, whilst at the same time building upon their strengths. This is not only a change in mindset that must be made, but one that is essential if we a truly going to equip our ordained leaders as ministers of a new paradigm. "Little things and an attitude of mind – attention, encouragement and genuine care and freedom – add up to a culture of learning, in a learning organization in love with change."[297]

"Consultative evaluation helps persons to reclaim some sense of constructive power, some sense of growth, some sense of hope that their lives might count. Consultative evaluation is at the very heart of a new understanding of the nature of ministry."[298] A good evaluation process can only serve to assist in equipping ordained leaders to be more effective and versatile in their ministries. It not only highlights their strengths, but reveals factors operating within their own lives and the situation in which they minister, that either contribute to or diminish that effectiveness. The learning process involved is at its best when it combines both helpful feedback from those within the situation the leaders operate and open disclosure on the part of the leaders themselves.[299] This is best served by an evaluation process that evaluates both the leader and the situation in which he or she ministers together.

---

[294] Drucker, Peter F. "*The New Realities,*" (Manderin Paperbacks, London, 1990), 229.
[295] Callahan, Kennon "*Twelve Keys to an Effective Church*" (Harper, San Francisco, 1983), xvi.
[296] Callahan, *Twelve Keys to an Effective Church,* xvii.
[297] Handy, *The Age of Unreason,* 186.
[298] Callahan, *Effective Church leadership,* 201.
[299] Hersey, Blanchard, & Johnson, *Management of Organizational Behavior,* 308.

# Appendix 2

## Kennon Callahan – Pastoral Evaluation Model

Callahan proposes that the most effective form of evaluation involves the pastor or leader carrying out a self-evaluation that is a realistic assessment of one's own current competencies, which is then linked to a consultative committee (or mentor) that forms an advisory and helpful input, that is both collegial and constructive.[300] This process involves:

- ❖ **Ministry Objectives:** noting and looking at the results of the two to four key major ministry objectives for the past year. [301]

- ❖ **Reflection on the results:** assessing both the strengths and the weaknesses of the results, with a time of reflection upon each major objective. [302]

- ❖ **Competency or Personal Growth Objectives:** assessing personal growth and development, in regards to personal competency objectives for the year. [303]

- ❖ **Preparation for the Consultative Process:** identifying the three principal areas for consultation with the consultative committee or mentor.

- ❖ **New Objectives for the Coming Year:** selecting two to four key major ministry objectives, and one to two major competencies for the coming year. [304]

- ❖ **Consultative Committee:** The emphasis of the consultation part of the process is upon coaching rather than. correction, its spirit is one of mutuality and sharing, one that collegial and community, not top-down and authoritarian. [305]

- ❖ **Consultative Process:** The consultation session includes the pastor or leader sharing his or her self-evaluation; the consultative team sharing; the pastor and team developing areas of mutual agreement; and finally a consensus on the two to four key major projects, and the one to two specific competencies for the coming year. [306]

---

[300] Callahan, Kennon    *"Effective Church Leadership,"* 178.
[301] Callahan, Kennon    *"Effective Church Leadership,"* 190-191.
[302] Callahan, Kennon    *"Effective Church Leadership,"* 191.
[303] Callahan, Kennon    *"Effective Church Leadership,"* 192-193.
[304] Callahan, Kennon    *"Effective Church Leadership,"* 194-105.
[305] Callahan, Kennon    *"Effective Church Leadership,"* 196-197.
[306] Callahan, Kennon    *"Effective Church Leadership,"* 198-199.

# BIBLIOGRAPHY

**Anglican Church of Australia**, "An Australian Prayer Book," AIO Press, Sydney 1978

**Anglican Diocese of Melbourne**, *Introduction to Supervised Field Education,*(Supervised Field Education),

**Anglican Diocese of Melbourne**, *Notes for Candidates,* (Supervised Field Education),

**Anglican Diocese of Melbourne**, *The Supervisory Process,* (Supervised Field Education),

**The Australian Oxford Dictionary**, Herron Publications, West End Qld 1988) p. 154

**Bonhoeffer, Dietrich.** *Ethics*, ed. Eberhard Bethge, trans. Neville Horton Smith, London: Collins, 1964.

**Brown, Colin, ed.** *The New International Dictionary of New Testament Theology.* Vol. 3. Devon: The Paternoster Press, 1986.

**Bromiley, Geoffrey W.** *Theological Dictionary of the New Testament*, Grand Rapids, Michigan: William B. Eerdmans Publishing Company, The Paternoster Press, 1985.

**Bullinger, E. W.** *A Critical Lexicon and Concordance to the English and Greek New Testamen*. London: Samuel Bagster and Sons Limited, 1971.

**Callahan, Kennon.** *Effective Church Leadership*, San Francisco: Harper and Row, 1990.

**Callahan, Kennon.** *Twelve Keys to an Effective Church*, San Francisco: Harper, 1983.

**Clinebell, Howard.** *Basic Types of Pastoral Care and Counselling* London: SCM Press Ltd, 1984.

**Cloud, Henry.** *The Power of the Other*. Harper Business: New York, 2016.

**Coll**, R. *Supervision of Ministry Students,* Minnesota: The Liturgical Press, 1992.

**Collins**, G.R. *Christian Counselling*, Berkhamsted, Herts: Word Publishing, 1980.

**Collins, J.N.** *Are All Christian Ministers?* Newtown, N.S.W.: E.J. Dwyer, David Lovell, 1992.

**Cook, James, ed.** *The Church Speaks: Papers of the Commission on Theology Reformed Church in America 1959-1984`*. Vol. 15, The Historical Series of the Reformed Church in America. Grand Rapids, Michigan: Wm B. Eerdmans Publishing Co, 1985

**Covey, Franklin.** *What Matters Most, Participant Workbook*, Salt Lake City, Utah: Franklin Covey, 1998.

**Drucker, Peter.** *Managing in a Time of Great Change*, Oxford: Butterworth-Heinmann, 1995.

**Drucker, Peter.** *The Age of Discontinuity, Guidelines to Our Changing Society,* New Brunswick: Transaction Publishers, 1992; reprint, 2003.

**Drucker, Peter.** *The New Realities,* London: Manderin Paperbacks, 1990.

**Ferencz, Nicholas.** *American Orthodoxy and Parish Congregationalism.* New Jersey: Georgias Press, 2006.

**General Synod of the Church of England,** *Under Authority,* London: Church House Publishing, 1996.

**Giles, Kevin,** *What on Earth is the Church?* Dove, Nth Blackburn: Harper Collins Publishers, Victoria, 1995.

**Giles, Kevin.** *Patterns of Ministry Among the First Christians,* Melbourne: Collins Dove, 1989.

**Green, J.B., Scot McKnight, and I. Howard Marshall.** *Dictionary of Jesus and the Gospels.* Accessed: Intervarsity Press, 1997.

**Handy, Charles.** *The Age of Unreason,* London: Business Books Ltd, 1989.

**Hersey, Paul, Blanchard, Kenneth H. & Johnson, Dewey E.** *Management of Organizational Behavior,* Upper Saddle River, New Jersey: Prentice Hall, 1996.

**Hudson, Jill M.** *Evaluating Ministry, Principles and Processes for Clergy and Congregations,* New York: Alban Institute Publication, 1992.

**Jones, W.T.** *Kant to Wittgenstein and Sartre.* New York: Harcourt, Braxe & World, Inc, 1969.

**Koselleck, Reinhart.** *Critique and Crisis: Enlightenment and the Pathogenesis of Modern Society.* Cambridge, Massachusetts: The MIT Press, 1988.

**Kuhn, Thomas.** *The Structure of Scientific Revolutions.* Chicago: University of Chicago Press, 1970.

**Küng, Hans.** *Global Responsibility: In Search of a New World Ethic.* Translated by John Bowden. London: SCM Press, 1991.

**Limerick, David and Cunnington, Bert.** *Managing the New Organisation,* Chatswood, N.S.W.: Business & Professional Publishing, 1993.

**Macquarie, John,** *Three Issues in Ethics,* London: SCM Press Ltd, 1970.

**Mallison, John.** *Mentoring to Develop Disciples and Leaders,* Sydney: Openbooks, 1998.

**Malphurs, Aubrey.** *Ministry Nuts & Bolts,* Grand Rapids: Kregel Publications, Grand Rapids 1997.

**Maxwell, John.** *Developing the Leader Within You,* Nashville: Thomas Nelson Publishers, 1993.

**Maxwell**, **John**. *Developing the Leader within You*. Nashville: Thomas Nelson Publishers, 1993.

_____. *Becoming a Person of Influence*. Nashville: Thomas Nelson Publishers, 1997.

**Maxwell, John.** *The Winning Attitude*.

**Mead**, **Loren**. *The Once and Future Church*. New York: Alban Institute Publications, 1991.

_____. *Transforming Congregations for the Future*. New York: Alban Institute Publications, 1994.

**Metz, Johann Baptist.** "Unity and Diversity." In *Faith and Future*, edited by Johann Baptist Metz and Jürgen Moltmann. New York: Orbis Books, 1995.

**Mink**, **Oscar**, **Barbara Mink**, **and Keith Owen**. *Groups at Work*. New Jersey: Educational Technology Publications, 1990.

**Microsoft.** *Microsoft Bookshelf Basics Edition - Dictionary*, Microsoft Corporation 1996.

**Miller, Basil .** *Charles Finney,* Minnesota: Dimension Books, 1941.

**Mobil Australia.** *Notes on Mobil Appraisal and Personal Development System*.

**Nadler, David and others**, *Discontinuous Change,* San Francisco: Jossey-Bass Publishers, 1995.

**Neill, S. and H. Weber** (eds) *The Layman in Christian History*. London: SCM Press, 1963.

**Oswald, Roy**. *Clergy Burnout*, New York: Ministers Life Resources, Inc The Alban Institute Inc, 1982.

**Oswald, Roy.** *Clergy Self-care – Finding a balance for Effective Ministry*, New York City: Alban Institute Publication, 1991.

**Oswalt**, J.N. *The Book of Isaiah, Chapters 40-66,* Michigan: William B. Eerdmans Publishing Co., 1998.

**Papesh**, **Micahel**. *Clerical Culture: Contradiction and Transformation*. Collegeville, Minnesota: Liturgical Press, 2004.

**Parsons, George and Leas, Speed.** *Understanding Your Congregation as A System*, New York: Alban Institute Publication, 1993.

**Peters**, **Andrew**. *The Emerging Paradigm of Diversity: Its Effect on the Church and Its Leadership*. Mansfield, Qld: A.E & L.A. Peters Outreach Enterprises, 2013.

**Peterson, Eugene H**. *The Gift*, Marshall Pickering, 1995).

**Pyle, W.T. and Seals, M.A. eds.**, *Experiencing Ministry Supervision,* Nashville: Broadman and Holman, 1995.

**Rowthorn, A.** *The Liberation of the Laity,* Connecticut: Morehouse-Barlow, 1986.

**Schaeffer, Francis**. *The Church at the End of the Twentieth Century*. London: Hodder and Stoughton, 1995.

**Schaller, Lyle E**. *The Change Agent,*. Nashville: Abingdon Press, 1986.

**Shakarian, Demos**. *The Happiest People on Earth,* London: Hodder and Stoughton, 1996.

**Stanley, P.D. and Clinton, J.D.** *Connecting,* Colorado Springs: Nappers, 1993.

**Steinke, Peter.** *Healthy Congregations, a System Approach*. New York: Alban Institute, 1996.

**Stevens, R. Paul and Collins, Phil.** *The Equipping Pastor*, New York City: An Alban Institute Publication, 1993.

**Tillich, Paul**. *The Shaking of the Foundations*. Harmondsworth: Penguin, 1962.

**Treat, Casey**. *Fulfilling Your God-given Destiny,* Nashville: Thomas Nelson Publishers, 1995.

**Wenham, J.W.** *Elements of New Testament Greek,* Cambridge: Cambridge University Press, 1965.

**Wilkerson, David**. *I'm not Mad at God,* Minneapolis: Bethany Fellowship, IS 1967.

www.ingramcontent.com/pod-product-compliance
Lightning Source LLC
Chambersburg PA
CBHW081359270326
41930CB00015B/3349